Justice, Gender, and the Family

Justice, Gender, and the Family

JUSTICE, GENDER, AND THE FAMILY

Susan Moller Okin

Basic Books, Inc., Publishers

NEW YORK

For Bob, Laura, and Justin

Library of Congress Cataloging-in-Publication Data

Okin, Susan Moller.
   Justice, gender, and the family / Susan Moller Okin.
     p. cm.
   Bibliography: p.
   Includes index.
   ISBN 0-465-03702-X
   1. Sex discrimination against women—United States. 2. Women's
rights—United States. 3. Sex role—United States. I. Title.
HQ1426.085 1989
305.42'0973—dc20
                                          89-042519
                                             CIP

CONTENTS

PREFACE

The injustice that results from the division of labor between the sexes affects virtually all women in our society, though not in all the same ways. A pervasive social problem, it is inflicting increasingly serious damage on children as well as women, and it is also destroying the family's potential to be the crucial first school where children develop a sense of fairness. This book is about that injustice and its detrimental repercussions.

A number of concurrent factors spurred me into writing the book, and writing it the way I did. While academic feminism is alive and well, and some of it is thoroughly and usefully engaged with issues important to most women, some feminist theory—especially in recent years—has fallen into the academic trap of becoming too arcane to be understood even by most educated people. At the same time, in the political climate of the United States in the 1980s, the impetus toward greater equality for women has not only become stalled but is, in some respects, being reversed. I, like many others who came to feminism in the 1960s and 1970s, have worried about what our primary focus should be and which directions we should now be taking. At the same time, my own life experiences have impressed on me the importance of taking up again the task I embarked on in *Women in Western Political Thought*, published ten years ago. My direct experience of the difficulties of being a fully participating parent while being a member of the workplace as currently structured has reinforced the conclusion I reached then: considerable reforms are essential if women are to be treated justly and to have anywhere near their fair share of influence on politics and society. And my continuing work as a political theorist has made me increasingly aware that major contemporary theorists of justice are not doing much better at confronting the issues of justice and gender than did the theorists of the past, whose ideas I critiqued in my first book. All these factors inspired me not only to write about justice, gender, and the family but to put these ideas into a book that would be accessible to as broad a range of people as I could make it.

I am grateful to the Rockefeller Foundation, whose Changing Gender Roles Fellowship enabled me to devote the 1986–87 academic year to this project. What I began during that year could not have been completed without the support, encouragement, and valuable criticism of a number of friends and colleagues. Sissela Bok, Bob Fullinwider, David Johnston, Paschalis Kitromilides, Martha Minow, Carole Pateman, John Rawls, Amélie Rorty, Ian Shapiro, and Joan Tronto read and offered helpful advice on various chapters. Cass Sunstein, who read a related paper, made very useful suggestions on how to organize my arguments about the public and domestic spheres. Nancy Fraser, Amy Gutmann, Will Kymlicka, Jane Mansbridge, Molly Shanley, Iris Young, and Michael Walzer each read all or most of the manuscript, and their support and criticism have been most helpful. Discussions with Jeffrey Abramson have helped me to see more clearly some of the implications of my proposals. I am especially grateful to Bob Keohane and Nancy Rosenblum. They read and commented incisively on the entire manuscript—most of it more than once—and they offered constant friendship and true collegiality throughout the course of the project. Indeed, without Bob Keohane's help in developing the theoretical framework for chapter 7, I would probably still be buried under a mass of data. Leigh Peake was an excellent research assistant for chapter 7, Linda Carbone copyedited with sensitivity and intelligence, Michael Wilde saw the book safely through production, and Steven Fraser at Basic Books not only offered many very good suggestions but also exerted precisely the right amount of editorial pressure to help me complete the book on time.

With both the justice they practice and the deep love they give, my husband, Bob, and our children, Laura and Justin, mean more than words can express. To them, with love, I dedicate this book.

Justice, Gender, and the Family

1

Introduction:
Justice and Gender

We as a society pride ourselves on our democratic values. We don't believe people should be constrained by innate differences from being able to achieve desired positions of influence or to improve their well-being; equality of opportunity is our professed aim. The Preamble to our Constitution stresses the importance of justice, as well as the general welfare and the blessings of liberty. The Pledge of Allegiance asserts that our republic preserves "liberty and justice for all."

Yet substantial inequalities between the sexes still exist in our society. In economic terms, full-time working women (after some very recent improvement) earn on average 71 percent of the earnings of full-time working men. One-half of poor and three-fifths of chronically poor households with dependent children are maintained by a single female parent. The poverty rate for elderly women is nearly twice that for elderly men.[1] On the political front, two out of a hundred U.S. senators are women, one out of nine justices seems to be considered sufficient female representation on the Supreme Court, and the number of men chosen in each congressional election far exceeds the number of women elected in the entire history of the country. Underlying

3

and intertwined with all these inequalities is the unequal distribution of the unpaid labor of the family.

An equal sharing between the sexes of family responsibilities, especially child care, is "the great revolution that has not happened."[2] Women, including mothers of young children, are, of course, working outside the household far more than their mothers did. And the small proportion of women who reach high-level positions in politics, business, and the professions command a vastly disproportionate amount of space in the media, compared with the millions of women who work at low-paying, dead-end jobs, the millions who do part-time work with its lack of benefits, and the millions of others who stay home performing for no pay what is frequently not even acknowledged as work. Certainly, the fact that women are doing more paid work does not imply that they are more equal. It is often said that we are living in a postfeminist era. This claim, due in part to the distorted emphasis on women who have "made it," is false, no matter which of its meanings is intended. It is certainly not true that feminism has been vanquished, and equally untrue that it is no longer needed because its aims have been fulfilled. Until there is justice within the family, women will not be able to gain equality in politics, at work, or in any other sphere.

As I argue in detail in chapter 7, the typical current practices of family life, structured to a large extent by gender, are not just. Both the expectation and the experience of the division of labor by sex make women vulnerable. As I shall show, a cycle of power relations and decisions pervades both family and workplace, each reinforcing the inequalities between the sexes that already exist within the other. Not only women, but children of both sexes, too, are often made vulnerable by gender-structured marriage. One-quarter of children in the United States now live in families with only one parent—in almost 90 percent of cases, the mother. Contrary to common perceptions—in which the situation of never-married mothers looms largest—65 percent of single-parent families are a result of marital separation or divorce.[3] Recent research in a number of states has shown that, in the average case, the standard of living of divorced women and the children who live with them plummets after divorce, whereas the economic situation of divorced men tends to be better than when they were married.

A central source of injustice for women these days is that the law, most noticeably in the event of divorce, treats more or less as equals those whom custom, workplace discrimination, and the still conventional division of labor within the family have made very unequal. Central to this socially created inequality are two commonly made but inconsistent presumptions: that women are primarily responsible for the rearing of children; and that serious and committed members of the work force (regardless of class) do not have primary responsibility, or even shared responsibility, for the rearing of children. The old assumption of the workplace, still implicit, is that workers have wives at home. It is built not only into the structure and expectations of the workplace but into other crucial social institutions, such as schools, which make no attempt to take account, in their scheduled hours or vacations, of the fact that parents are likely to hold jobs.

Now, of course, many wage workers do not have wives at home. Often, they *are* wives and mothers, or single, separated, or divorced mothers of small children. But neither the family nor the workplace has taken much account of this fact. Employed wives still do by far the greatest proportion of unpaid family work, such as child care and housework. Women are far more likely to take time out of the workplace or to work part-time because of family responsibilities than are their husbands or male partners. And they are much more likely to move because of their husbands' employment needs or opportunities than their own. All these tendencies, which are due to a number of factors, including the sex segregation and discrimination of the workplace itself, tend to be cyclical in their effects: wives advance more slowly than their husbands at work and thus gain less seniority, and the discrepancy between their wages increases over time. Then, because both the power structure of the family and what is regarded as consensual "rational" family decision making reflect the fact that the husband usually earns more, it will become even less likely as time goes on that the unpaid work of the family will be shared between the spouses. Thus the cycle of inequality is perpetuated. Often hidden from view within a marriage, it is in the increasingly likely event of marital breakdown that the socially constructed inequality of married women is at its most visible.

This is what I mean when I say that gender-structured marriage *makes* women vulnerable. These are not matters of natural necessity, as some people would believe. Surely nothing in our natures dictates that men should not be equal participants in the rearing of their children. Nothing in the nature of work makes it impossible to adjust it to the fact that people are parents as well as workers. That these things have not happened is part of the historically, socially constructed differentiation between the sexes that feminists have come to call *gender*. We live in a society that has over the years regarded the innate characteristic of sex as one of the clearest legitimizers of different rights and restrictions, both formal and informal. While the legal sanctions that uphold

5

male dominance have begun to be eroded in the past century, and more rapidly in the last twenty years, the heavy weight of tradition, combined with the effects of socialization, still works powerfully to reinforce sex roles that are commonly regarded as of unequal prestige and worth. The sexual division of labor has not only been a fundamental part of the marriage contract, but so deeply influences us in our formative years that feminists of both sexes who try to reject it can find themselves struggling against it with varying degrees of ambivalence. Based on this linchpin, "gender"—by which I mean *the deeply entrenched institutionalization of sexual difference*—still permeates our society.

The Construction of Gender

Due to feminism and feminist theory, gender is coming to be recognized as a social factor of major importance. Indeed, the new meaning of the word reflects the fact that so much of what has traditionally been thought of as sexual difference is now considered by many to be largely socially produced.[4] Feminist scholars from many disciplines and with radically different points of view have contributed to the enterprise of making gender fully visible and comprehensible. At one end of the spectrum are those whose explanations of the subordination of women focus primarily on biological difference as causal in the construction of gender,[5] and at the other end are those who argue that biological difference may not even lie at the core of the social construction that is gender[6]; the views of the vast majority of feminists fall between these extremes. The rejection of biological determinism and the corresponding emphasis on gender as a social construction characterize most current feminist scholarship. Of particular relevance is work in psychology, where scholars have investigated the importance of female primary parenting in the formation of our gendered identities,[7] and in history and anthropology,[8] where emphasis has been placed on the historical and cultural variability of gender. Some feminists have been criticized for developing theories of gender that do not take sufficient account of differences *among* women, especially race, class, religion, and ethnicity.[9] While such critiques should always inform our research and improve our arguments, it would be a mistake to allow them to detract our attention from gender itself as a factor of significance. Many injustices are experienced by women *as women*, whatever the differences

6

among them and whatever other injustices they also suffer from. The past and present gendered nature of the family, and the ideology that surrounds it, affects virtually all women, whether or not they live or ever lived in traditional families. Recognizing this is not to deny or de-emphasize the fact that gender may affect different subgroups of women to a different extent and in different ways.

The potential significance of feminist discoveries and conclusions about gender for issues of social justice cannot be overemphasized. They undermine centuries of argument that started with the notion that not only the distinct differentiation of women and men but the domination of women by men, being natural, was therefore inevitable and not even to be considered in discussions of justice. As I shall make clear in later chapters, despite the fact that such notions cannot stand up to rational scrutiny, they not only still survive but flourish in influential places.

During the same two decades in which feminists have been intensely thinking, researching, analyzing, disagreeing about, and rethinking the subject of gender, our political and legal institutions have been increasingly faced with issues concerning the injustices of gender and their effects. These issues are being decided within a fundamentally patriarchal system, founded in a tradition in which "individuals" were assumed to be male heads of households. Not surprisingly, the system has demonstrated a limited capacity for determining what is just, in many cases involving gender. Sex discrimination, sexual harassment, abortion, pregnancy in the workplace, parental leave, child care, and surrogate mothering have all become major and well-publicized issues of public policy, engaging both courts and legislatures. Issues of family justice, in particular—from child custody and terms of divorce to physical and sexual abuse of wives and children—have become increasingly visible and pressing, and are commanding increasing attention from the police and court systems. There is clearly a major "justice crisis" in contemporary society arising from issues of gender.

Theories of Justice and the Neglect of Gender

During these same two decades, there has been a great resurgence of theories of social justice. Political theory, which had been sparse for a period before the late 1960s except as an important branch of intellectual history, has become a flourishing field, with social justice as its central concern. Yet, remarkably, major contemporary theorists of justice have almost without exception ignored the situation I have just described. They have displayed little interest in or knowledge of the findings of feminism. They have largely bypassed the fact that the society to which their theories are supposed to pertain is heavily and deeply affected by gender, and faces difficult issues of justice stemming from its gendered past and present assumptions. Since theories of justice are centrally concerned with whether, how, and why persons should be treated differently from one another, this neglect seems inexplicable. These theories are *about* which initial or acquired characteristics or positions in society legitimize differential treatment of persons by social institutions, laws, and customs. They are *about* how and whether and to what extent beginnings should affect outcomes. The division of humanity into two sexes seems to provide an obvious subject for such inquiries. But, as we shall see, this does not strike most contemporary theorists of justice, and their theories suffer in both coherence and relevance because of it. This book is about this remarkable case of neglect. It is also an attempt to rectify it, to point the way toward a more fully humanist theory of justice by confronting the question, "How just is gender?"

Why is it that when we turn to contemporary theories of justice, we do not find illuminating and positive contributions to this question? How can theories of justice that are ostensibly about people in general neglect women, gender, and all the inequalities between the sexes? One reason is that most theorists *assume*, though they do not discuss, the traditional, gender-structured family. Another is that they often employ gender-neutral language in a false, hollow way. Let us examine these two points.

THE HIDDEN GENDER-STRUCTURED FAMILY

In the past, political theorists often used to distinguish clearly between "private" domestic life and the "public" life of politics and the marketplace, claiming explicitly that the two spheres operated in accordance with different principles. They separated out the family from what they deemed the subject matter of politics, and they made closely related, explicit claims about the nature of women and the appropriateness of excluding them from civil and political life. Men, the subjects of the theories, were able to make the transition back and forth from domestic to public life with ease, largely because of the functions performed by women in the family.[10] When we turn to contemporary theories of justice, superficial appearances can easily lead to the impression that they are inclusive of women. In fact, they continue the same "separate spheres" tradition, by ignoring the family, its division of labor, and the related economic dependency and restricted opportunities of most women. The judgment that the family is "nonpolitical" is implicit in the fact that it is simply not discussed in most works of political theory today. In one way or another, as will become clear in the chapters that follow, almost all current theorists continue to assume that the "individual" who is the basic subject of their theories is the male head of a fairly traditional household. Thus the application of principles of justice to relations between the sexes, or within the household, is frequently, though tacitly, ruled out from the start. In the most influential of all twentieth-century theories of justice, that of John Rawls, family life is not only assumed, but is assumed to be just—and yet the prevalent gendered division of labor within the family is neglected, along with the associated distribution of power, responsibility, and privilege (see chapter 5).

Moreover, this stance is typical of contemporary theories of justice. They persist, despite the wealth of feminist challenges to their assumptions, in their refusal even to discuss the family and its gender structure, much less to recognize the family as a political institution of primary importance. Recent theories that pay even less attention to issues of family justice than Rawls's include Bruce Ackerman's *Social Justice in the Liberal State*, Ronald Dworkin's *Taking Rights Seriously*, William Galston's *Justice and the Human Good*, Alasdair MacIntyre's *After Virtue* and *Whose Justice? Whose Rationality?*, Robert Nozick's *Anarchy, State, and Utopia*, and Roberto Unger's *Knowledge and Politics* and *The Critical Legal Studies Movement*.[11] Philip Green's *Retrieving Democracy* is a welcome exception.[12] Michael Walzer's *Spheres of Justice*, too, is exceptional in this regard, but, as I shall show in chapters 3 and 6, the conclusion that can be inferred from his discussion of the family—that its gender structure is unjust—does not sit at all easily with his emphasis on the shared understandings of a culture as the foundation of justice.[13] For gender is one aspect of social life about which clearly, in the United States in the latter part of the twentieth century, there are no shared understandings.

What is the basis of my claim that the family, while neglected, is *assumed* by theorists of justice? One obvious indication is that they take mature, independent human beings as the subjects of their theories without any mention of how they got to be that way. We know, of course, that human beings develop and mature only as a result of a great deal of attention and hard work, by far the greater part of it done by women. But when theorists of justice talk about "work," they mean paid work performed in the marketplace. They must be assuming that women, in the gender-structured family, continue to do their unpaid work of nurturing and socializing the young and providing a haven of intimate relations—otherwise there would be no moral subjects for them to theorize about. But these activities apparently take place outside the scope of their theories. Typically, the family itself is not examined in the light of whatever standard of justice the theorist arrives at.[14]

The continued neglect of the family by theorists of justice flies in the face of a great deal of persuasive feminist argument, as I shall explain further in chapter 6. Scholars have clearly revealed the interconnections between the gender structure inside and outside the family and the extent to which the personal is political. They have shown that the assignment of primary parenting to women is crucial, both in forming the gendered identities of men and women and in influencing their respective choices and opportunities in life. Yet, so far, the simultaneous assumption and neglect of the family has allowed the impact of these arguments to go unnoticed in major theories of justice.

FALSE GENDER NEUTRALITY

Many academics in recent years have become aware of the objectionable nature of using the supposedly generic male forms of nouns and pronouns. As feminist scholars have demonstrated, these words have most often *not* been used, throughout history and the history of philosophy in particular, with the intent to include women. *Man, mankind,* and *he* are going out of style as universal representations, though they have by no means disappeared. But the gender-neutral alternatives that most contemporary theorists employ are often even more misleading than the blatantly sexist use of male terms of reference. For they serve to disguise the real and continuing failure of theorists to confront the fact that the human race consists of persons of two sexes. They are by this means able to ignore the fact that there are *some* socially relevant physical differences between women and men, and the even more important fact that the sexes have had very different histories, very different assigned social roles and "natures," and very different degrees of access to power and opportunity in all human societies up to and including the present.

False gender neutrality is not a new phenomenon. Aristotle, for example, used *anthropos*—"human being"—in discussions of "the human good" that turn out not only to exclude women but to depend on their subordination. Kant even wrote of "all rational beings as such" in making arguments that he did not mean to apply to women. But it was more readily apparent that such arguments or conceptions of the good were not about all of us, but only about male heads of families. For their authors usually gave at some point an explanation, no matter how inadequate, of why what they were saying did not apply to women and of the different characteristics and virtues, rights, and responsibilities they thought women ought to have. Nevertheless, their theories have often been read as though they pertain (or can easily be applied) to all of us. Feminist interpretations of the last fifteen years or so have revealed the falsity of this "add women and stir" method of reading the history of political thought.[15]

The falseness of the gender-neutral language of contemporary political theorists is less readily apparent. Most, though not all, contemporary moral and political philosophers use "men and women," "he or she," "persons," or the increasingly ubiquitous "self." Sometimes they even get their computers to distribute masculine and feminine terms of reference randomly.[16] Since they do not explicitly exclude or differentiate women, as most theorists in the past did, we may be tempted to read their theories as inclusive of all of us. But we cannot. Their merely terminological responses to feminist challenges, in spite of giving a superficial impression of tolerance and inclusiveness, often strain credulity and sometimes result in nonsense. They do this in two ways: by ignoring the irreducible biological differences between the sexes, and/or by ignoring their different assigned social roles and consequent power differentials, and the ideologies that have supported them. Thus gender-neutral terms frequently obscure the fact that so much of the real experience of "persons," so long as they live in gender-structured societies, *does* in fact depend on what sex they are.

False gender neutrality is by no means confined to the realm of theory. Its harmful effects can be seen in public policies that have directly affected large numbers of women adversely. It was used, for example, in the Supreme Court's 1976 decision that the exclusion of pregnancy-related disabilities from employers' disability insurance plans was "not a gender-based discrimination at all." In a now infamous phrase of its majority opinion, the Court explained that such plans did not discriminate against women because the distinction drawn by such plans was between pregnant women and "non-pregnant *persons*."[17]

Examples of false gender neutrality in contemporary political theory will appear throughout this book; I will illustrate the concept here by citing just two examples. Ackerman's *Social Justice in the Liberal State* is a book containing scrupulously gender-neutral language. He breaks with this neutrality only, it seems, to *defy* existing sex roles; he refers to the "Commander," who plays the lead role in the theory, as "she." However, the argument of the book does not address the existing inequality or role differentiation between the sexes, though it has the potential for doing so.* The full impact of Ackerman's gender-neutral language without attention to gender is revealed in his section on abortion: a two-page discussion written, with the exception of a single "she," in the completely gender-neutral language of fetuses and their "parents."[18] The impression given is that there is no relevant respect in which the relationship of the two parents to the fetus differs. Now it is, of course, possible to imagine (and in the view of many feminists, would be desirable to achieve) a society in which differences in the relation of women and men to fetuses would be so slight as to reasonably play only a minor role in the discussion of abortion. But this would have to be a society without gender—one in which sexual difference carried no social significance, the sexes were equal in power and interdependence, and "mothering" and "fathering" a child meant the same thing, so that parenting and earning responsibilities were equally shared. We certainly do not live in such a society. Neither is there any discussion of one in Ackerman's theory, in which the division of labor between the sexes is not considered a matter of social (in)justice. In such a context, a "gender-neutral" discussion of abortion is almost as misleading as the Supreme Court's "gender-neutral" discussion of pregnancy.

A second illustration of false gender neutrality comes from Derek Phillips's *Toward a Just Social Order*. Largely because of the extent of his concern—rare among theorists of justice—with how we are to *achieve and maintain* a just social order, Phillips pays an unusual amount of attention to the family. He writes about the family as the locus for the development of a sense of justice and self-esteem, of an appreciation of the meaning of reciprocity, of the ability to exercise unforced choice, and of an awareness of alternative ways of life.[19] The problem with this otherwise admirable discussion is that, apart from a couple of brief exceptions, the family itself is presented in gender-neutral terms that bear little resemblance to actual, gender-structured life.[20]† It is because of "parental affection," "parental nurturance," and "child rearing" that children in Phillips's families become the autonomous moral

---

*Ackerman's argument about how we arrive at social justice is in most essentials similar to Rawls's. As will become apparent in chapters 5 and 8, I think such methods can be useful in challenging gender and achieving a humanist theory of justice.

†He points out the shortcomings of the "earlier ethic of sacrifice," especially for women. He also welcomes the recent lessening of women's dependence on their husbands, but at the same time blames it for tending to weaken family stability. The falseness of Phillips's gender neutrality in discussing parenting is clearly confirmed later in the book (chaps. 8 and 9), where paid work is "men's" and it is "fathers" who bequeath wealth or poverty on their children.

agents that his just society requires its citizens to be. The child's development of a sense of identity is very much dependent upon being raised by "parental figures who themselves have coherent and well-integrated personal identities," and we are told that such a coherent identity is "ideally one built around commitments to work and love." This all sounds very plausible. But it does not take account of the multiple inequalities of gender. In gender-structured societies—in which the child rearers are women, "parental nurturance" is largely mothering, and those who do what society regards as "meaningful work" are assumed *not* to be primary parents—women in even the best of circumstances face considerable conflicts between love (a fulfilling family life) and "meaningful work." Women in less fortunate circumstances face even greater conflicts between love (even basic care of their children) and any kind of paid work at all.

It follows from Phillips's own premises that these conflicts are very likely to affect the strength and coherence in women of that sense of identity and self-esteem, coming from love and meaningful work, that he regards as essential for being an autonomous moral agent. In turn, if they are mothers, it is also likely to affect their daughters' and sons' developing senses of their identity. Gender is clearly a major obstacle to the attainment of a social order remotely comparable to the just one Phillips aspires to—but his false gender-neutral language allows him to ignore this fact. Although he is clearly aware of how distant in some other respects his vision of a just social order is from contemporary societies,[21] his use of falsely gender-neutral language leaves him quite unaware of the distance between the type of family that might be able to socialize just citizens and typical families today.

The combined effect of the omission of the family and the falsely gender-neutral language in recent political thought is that most theorists are continuing to ignore the highly political issue of gender. The language they use makes little difference to what they actually do, which is to write about men and about only those women who manage, in spite of the gendered structures and practices of the society in which they live, to adopt patterns of life that have been developed to suit the needs of men. The fact that human beings are born as helpless infants—not as the purportedly autonomous actors who populate political theories—is obscured by the implicit assumption of gendered families, operating outside the range of the theories. To a large extent, contemporary theories of justice, like those of the past, are about men with wives at home.

Gender as an Issue of Justice

For three major reasons, this state of affairs is unacceptable. The first is the obvious point that women must be fully included in any satisfactory theory of justice. The second is that equality of opportunity, not only for women but for children of both sexes, is seriously undermined by the current gender injustices of our society. And the third reason is that, as has already been suggested, the family—currently the linchpin of the gender structure—must be just if we are to have a just society, since it is within the family that we first come to have that sense of ourselves and our relations with others that is at the root of moral development.

COUNTING WOMEN IN

When we turn to the great tradition of Western political thought with questions about the justice of the treatment of the sexes in mind, it is to little avail. Bold feminists like Mary Astell, Mary Wollstonecraft, William Thompson, Harriet Taylor, and George Bernard Shaw have occasionally challenged the tradition, often using its own premises and arguments to overturn its explicit or implicit justification of the inequality of women. But John Stuart Mill is a rare exception to the rule that those who hold central positions in the tradition almost never question the justice of the subordination of women.[22] This phenomenon is undoubtedly due in part to the fact that Aristotle, whose theory of justice has been so influential, relegated women to a sphere of "household justice"—populated by persons who are not fundamentally equal to the free men who participate in political justice, but inferiors whose natural function is to serve those who are more fully human. The liberal tradition, despite its supposed foundation of individual rights and human equality, is more Aristotelian in this respect than is generally acknowledged.[23] In one way or another, almost all liberal theorists have assumed that the "individual" who is the basic subject of the theories is the male head of a patriarchal household.[24] Thus they have not usually considered applying the principles of justice to women or to relations between the sexes.

When we turn to contemporary theories of justice, however, we expect to find more illuminating and positive contributions to the subject of gender and justice. As the omission of the family and the falseness of their gender-neutral language suggest, however, mainstream contemporary theories of justice do not address the subject any better than those of the past. Theories of justice

14

that apply to only half of us simply won't do; the inclusiveness falsely implied by the current use of gender-neutral terms must become real. Theories of justice must apply to all of us, and to all of human life, instead of *assuming* silently that half of us take care of whole areas of life that are considered outside the scope of social justice. In a just society, the structure and practices of families must afford women the same opportunities as men to develop their capacities, to participate in political power, to influence social choices, and to be economically as well as physically secure.

Unfortunately, much feminist intellectual energy in the 1980s has gone into the claim that "justice" and "rights" are masculinist ways of thinking about morality that feminists should eschew or radically revise, advocating a morality of care.[25] The emphasis is misplaced, I think, for several reasons. First, what is by now a vast literature on the subject shows that the evidence for differences in women's and men's ways of thinking about moral issues is not (at least yet) very clear; neither is the evidence about the source of whatever differences there might be.[26] It may well turn out that any differences can be readily explained in terms of roles, including female primary parenting, that are socially determined and therefore alterable. There is certainly no evidence—nor could there be, in such a gender-structured society—for concluding that women are somehow naturally more inclined toward contextuality and away from universalism in their moral thinking, a false concept that unfortunately reinforces the old stereotypes that justify separate spheres. The capacity of reactionary forces to capitalize on the "different moralities" strain in feminism is particularly evident in Pope John Paul II's recent Apostolic Letter, "On the Dignity of Women," in which he refers to women's special capacity to care for others in arguing for confining them to motherhood or celibacy.[27]

Second, as I shall explain in chapter 5, I think the distinction between an ethic of justice and an ethic of care has been overdrawn. The best theorizing about justice, I argue, has integral to it the notions of care and empathy, of thinking of the interests and well-being of others who may be very different from ourselves. It is, therefore, misleading to draw a dichotomy as though they were two contrasting ethics. The best theorizing about justice is not some abstract "view from nowhere," but results from the carefully attentive consideration of *everyone's* point of view. This means, of course, that the best theorizing about justice is not good enough if it does not, or cannot readily be adapted to, include women and their points of view as fully as men and their points of view.

15

GENDER AND EQUALITY OF OPPORTUNITY

The family is a crucial determinant of our opportunities in life, of what we "become." It has frequently been acknowledged by those concerned with real equality of opportunity that the family presents a problem.[28] But though they have discerned a serious problem, these theorists have underestimated it because they have seen only half of it. They have seen that the disparity among families in terms of the physical and emotional environment, motivation, and material advantages they can give their children has a tremendous effect upon children's opportunities in life. We are not born as isolated, equal individuals in our society, but into family situations: some in the social middle, some poor and homeless, and some superaffluent; some to a single or soon-to-be-separated parent, some to parents whose marriage is fraught with conflict, some to parents who will stay together in love and happiness. Any claims that equal opportunity exists are therefore completely unfounded. Decades of neglect of the poor, especially of poor black and Hispanic households, accentuated by the policies of the Reagan years, have brought us farther from the principles of equal opportunity. To come close to them would require, for example, a high and uniform standard of public education and the provision of equal social services—including health care, employment training, job opportunities, drug rehabilitation, and decent housing—for all who need them. In addition to redistributive taxation, only massive reallocations of resources from the military to social services could make these things possible.

But even if all these disparities were somehow eliminated, we would still not attain equal opportunity for all. This is because what has not been recognized as an equal opportunity problem, except in feminist literature and circles, is the disparity *within* the family, the fact that its gender structure is itself a major obstacle to equality of opportunity. This is very important in itself, since one of the factors with most influence on our opportunities in life is the social significance attributed to our sex. The opportunities of girls and women are centrally affected by the structure and practices of family life, particularly by the fact that women are almost invariably primary parents. What nonfeminists who see in the family an obstacle to equal opportunity have *not* seen is that the extent to which a family is gender-structured can make the sex we belong to a relatively insignificant aspect of our identity and our life prospects or an all-pervading one. This is because so much of the social construction of gender takes place in the family, and particularly in the institution of female parenting.

16

Moreover, especially in recent years, with the increased rates of single motherhood, separation, and divorce, the inequalities between the sexes have *compounded* the first part of the problem. The disparity among families has grown largely because of the impoverishment of many women and children after separation or divorce. The division of labor in the typical family leaves most women far less capable than men of supporting themselves, and this disparity is accentuated by the fact that children of separated or divorced parents usually live with their mothers. The inadequacy—and frequent nonpayment—of child support has become recognized as a major social problem. Thus the inequalities of gender are now directly harming many children of both sexes as well as women themselves. Enhancing equal opportunity for women, important as it is in itself, is also a crucial way of improving the opportunities of many of the most disadvantaged children.

As there is a connection among the parts of this problem, so is there a connection among some of the solutions: much of what needs to be done to end the inequalities of gender, and to work in the direction of ending gender itself, will also help to equalize opportunity from one family to another. Subsidized, high-quality day care is obviously one such thing; another is the adaptation of the workplace to the needs of parents. These and other relevant policy issues will be addressed in chapter 8.

THE FAMILY AS A SCHOOL OF JUSTICE

One of the things that theorists who have argued that families need not or cannot be just, or who have simply neglected them, have failed to explain is how, within a formative social environment that is *not* founded upon principles of justice, children can learn to develop that sense of justice they will require as citizens of a just society. Rather than being one among many co-equal institutions of a just society, a just family is its essential foundation.

It may seem uncontroversial, even obvious, that families must be just because of the vast influence they have on the moral development of children. But this is clearly not the case. I shall argue that unless the first and most formative example of adult interaction usually experienced by children is one of justice and reciprocity, rather than one of domination and manipulation or of unequal altruism and one-sided self-sacrifice, and unless they themselves are treated with concern and respect, they are likely to be considerably hindered in becoming people who are guided by principles of justice. Moreover, I claim, the sharing of roles by men and women, rather than the division of roles between them, would have a further positive impact because the experience of *being* a physical and psychological nurturer—whether of a child or of another adult—would increase that capacity to identify with and fully comprehend the viewpoints of others that is important to a sense of justice. In a society that minimized gender this would be more likely to be the experience of all of us.

Almost every person in our society starts life in a family of some sort or other. Fewer of these families now fit the usual, though by no means universal, standard of previous generations, that is, wage-working father, homemaking mother, and children. More families these days are headed by a single parent; lesbian and gay parenting is no longer so rare; many children have two wage-working parents, and receive at least some of their early care outside the home. While its forms are varied, the family in which a child is raised, especially in the earliest years, is clearly a crucial place for early moral development and for the formation of our basic attitudes to others. It is, potentially, a place where we can *learn to be just*. It is especially important for the development of a sense of justice that grows from sharing the experiences of others and becoming aware of the points of view of others who are different in some respects from ourselves, but with whom we clearly have some interests in common.

The importance of the family for the moral development of individuals was far more often recognized by political theorists of the past than it is by those of the present. Hegel, Rousseau, Tocqueville, Mill, and Dewey are obvious examples that come to mind. Rousseau, for example, shocked by Plato's proposal to abolish the family, says that it is

> as though there were no need for a natural base on which to form conventional ties; as though the love of one's nearest were not the principle of the love one owes the state; as though it were not by means of the small fatherland which is the family that the heart attaches itself to the large one.[29]

Defenders of both autocratic and democratic regimes have recognized the political importance of different family forms for the formation of citizens. On the one hand, the nineteenth-century monarchist Louis de Bonald argued against the divorce reforms of the French Revolution, which he claimed had weakened the patriarchal family, on the grounds that "in order to keep the state out of the hands of the people, it is necessary to keep the family out of the hands of women and children."[30] Taking this same line of thought in the opposite direction, the U.S. Supreme Court decided in 1879 in *Reynolds v. Nebraska* that familial patriarchy fostered despotism and was therefore intolerable. Denying Mormon men the freedom to practice polygamy, the Court asserted that it was an offense "subversive of good order" that "leads to the patriarchal principle, . . . [and] when applied to large communities, fetters the people in stationary despotism, while that principle cannot long exist in connection with monogamy."[31]

However, while de Bonald was consistent in his adherence to an hierarchical family structure as necessary for an undemocratic political system, the Supreme Court was by no means consistent in promoting an egalitarian family as an essential underpinning for political democracy. For in other decisions of the same period—such as *Bradwell v. Illinois*, the famous 1872 case that upheld the exclusion of women from the practice of law—the Court rejected women's claims to legal equality, in the name of a thoroughly patriarchal, though monogamous, family that was held to require the dependence of women and their exclusion from civil and political life.[32] While bigamy was considered patriarchal, and as such a threat to republican, democratic government, the refusal to allow a married woman to employ her talents and to make use of her qualifications to earn an independent living was not considered patriarchal. It was so far from being a threat to the civil order, in fact, that it was deemed necessary for it, and as such was ordained by both God and nature. Clearly, in both *Reynolds* and *Bradwell*, "state authorities enforced family forms preferred by those in power and justified as necessary to stability and order."[33] The Court noticed the despotic potential of polygamy, but was blind to the despotic potential of patriarchal monogamy. This was perfectly acceptable to them as a training ground for citizens.

Most theorists of the past who stressed the importance of the family and its practices for the wider world of moral and political life by no means insisted on congruence between the structures or practices of the family and those of the outside world. Though concerned with moral development, they bifurcated public from private life to such an extent that they had no trouble reconciling inegalitarian, sometimes admittedly unjust, relations founded upon sentiment within the family with a more just, even egalitarian, social structure outside the family. Rousseau, Hegel, Tocqueville—all thought the family was centrally important for the development of morality in citizens, but all defended the hierarchy of the marital structure while spurning such a degree of hierarchy in institutions and practices outside the household. Preferring instead to rely on love, altruism, and generosity as the basis for family relations, none of these theorists argued for *just* family structures as necessary for socializing children into citizenship in a just society.

The position that justice within the family is irrelevant to the development of just citizens was not plausible even when only men were citizens. John Stuart Mill, in *The Subjection of Women*, takes an impassioned stand against it. He argues that the inequality of women within the family is deeply subversive of justice in general in the wider social world, because it subverts the moral potential of men. Mill's first answer to the question, "For whose good are all these changes in women's rights to be undertaken?" is: "the advantage of having the most universal and pervading of all human relations regulated by justice instead of injustice." Making marriage a relationship of equals, he argues, would transform this central part of daily life from "a school of despotism" into "a school of moral cultivation."[34] He goes on to discuss, in the strongest of terms, the noxious effect of growing up in a family not regulated by justice. Consider, he says, "the self-worship, the unjust self-preference," nourished in a boy growing up in a household in which "by the mere fact of being born a male he is by right the superior of all and every one of an entire half of the human race." Mill concludes that the example set by perpetuating a marital structure "contradictory to the first principles of social justice" must have such "a perverting influence" that it is hard even to imagine the good effects of changing it. All other attempts to educate people to respect and practice justice, Mill claims, will be superficial "as long as the citadel of the enemy is not attacked." Mill felt as much hope for what the family might be as he felt despair at what it was not. "The family, justly constituted, would be the real school of the virtues of freedom," primary among which was "justice, . . . grounded as before on equal, but now also on sympathetic association."[35] Mill both saw clearly and had the courage to address what so many other political philosophers either could not see, or saw and turned away from.

Despite the strength and fervor of his advocacy of women's rights, however, Mill's idea of a just family structure falls far short of that of many feminists even of his own time, including his wife, Harriet Taylor. In spite of the fact that Mill recognized both the empowering effect of earnings on one's position in the family and the limiting effect of domestic responsibility on women's opportunities, he balked at questioning the traditional division of labor between the sexes. For him, a woman's choice of marriage was parallel to a man's choice of a profession: unless and until she had fulfilled her obligations to her husband and children, she should not undertake anything else. But clearly, however equal the legal rights of husbands and wives, this position largely undermines Mill's own insistence upon the importance of marital equality for a just society. His acceptance of the traditional division of labor, without making any provision for wives who were thereby made economically dependent upon their husbands, largely undermines his insistence upon family justice as the necessary foundation for social justice.

Thus even those political theorists of the past who have perceived the family as an important school of moral development have rarely acknowledged the need for congruence between the family and the wider social order, which suggests that families themselves need to be just. Even when they have, as with Mill, they have been unwilling to push hard on the traditional division of labor within the family in the name of justice or equality.

Contemporary theorists of justice, with few exceptions, have paid little or no attention to the question of moral development—of how we are to *become* just. Most of them seem to think, to adapt slightly Hobbes's notable phrase, that just men spring like mushrooms from the earth.[36] Not surprisingly, then, it is far less often acknowledged in recent than in past theories that the family is important for moral development, and especially for instilling a sense of justice. As I have already noted, many theorists pay no attention at all to either the family or gender. In the rare case that the issue of justice within the family is given any sustained attention, the family is not viewed as a potential school of social justice.[37] In the rare case that a theorist pays any sustained attention to the development of a sense of justice or morality, little if any attention is likely to be paid to the family.[38] Even in the rare event that theorists pay considerable attention to the family *as* the first major locus of moral socialization, they do not refer to the fact that families are almost all still thoroughly gender-structured institutions.[39]

Among major contemporary theorists of justice, John Rawls alone treats the family seriously as the earliest school of moral development. He argues that a just, well-ordered society will be stable only if its members continue to develop a sense of justice. And he argues that families play a fundamental role in the stages by which this sense of justice is acquired. From the parents' love for their child, which comes to be reciprocated, comes the child's "sense of his own value and the desire to become the sort of person that they are."[40] The family, too, is the first of that series of "associations" in which we participate, from which we acquire the capacity, crucial for a sense of justice, to see things from the perspectives of others. As I shall show, this capacity—the capacity for empathy—is essential for maintaining a sense of justice of the Rawlsian kind. For the perspective that is necessary for maintaining a sense of justice is not that of the egoistic or disembodied self, or of the dominant few who overdetermine "our" traditions or "shared understandings," or (to use

Nagel's term) of "the view from nowhere," but rather the perspective of every person in the society for whom the principles of justice are being arrived at. As I shall argue, the problem with Rawls's rare and interesting discussion of moral development is that it rests on the unexplained *assumption* that family institutions are just. If gendered family institutions are *not* just, but are, rather, a relic of caste or feudal societies in which responsibilities, roles, and resources are distributed, not in accordance with the principles of justice he arrives at or with any other commonly respected values, but in accordance with innate differences that are imbued with enormous social significance, then Rawls's theory of moral development would seem to be built on uncertain ground. This problem is exacerbated by suggestions in some of Rawls's most recent work that families are "private institutions," to which it is not appropriate to apply standards of justice. But if families are to help form just individuals and citizens, surely they must be *just families*.

In a just society, the structure and practices of families must give women the same opportunities as men to develop their capacities, to participate in political power and influence social choices, and to be economically secure. But in addition to this, families must be just because of the vast influence that they have on the moral development of children. The family is the primary institution of formative moral development. And the structure and practices of the family must parallel those of the larger society if the sense of justice is to be fostered and maintained. While many theorists of justice, both past and present, appear to have denied the importance of at least one of these factors, my own view is that both are absolutely crucial. A society that is committed to equal respect for all of its members, and to justice in social distributions of benefits and responsibilities, can neither neglect the family nor accept family structures and practices that violate these norms, as do current gender-based structures and practices. It is essential that children who are to develop into adults with a strong sense of justice and commitment to just institutions spend their earliest and most formative years in an environment in which they are loved and nurtured, *and* in which principles of justice are abided by and respected. What is a child of either sex to learn about fairness in the average household with two full-time working parents, where the mother does, at the very least, twice as much family work as the father? What is a child to learn about the value of nurturing and domestic work in a home with a traditional division of labor in which the father either subtly or not so subtly uses the fact that he is the wage earner to "pull rank" on or to abuse his wife? What is a child to learn about responsibility for others in a family in which, after many years of arranging her life around the needs of her husband and children, a woman is faced with having to provide for herself and her children but is totally ill-equipped for the task by the life she agreed to lead, has led, and expected to go on leading?

In the next five chapters, I shall analyze a number of recent, influential political theories, paying special attention to women and gender. In chapter 2, I shall examine and rebut two claims whose validity would undercut much of my subsequent argument. One is that justice is not a primary virtue for the family—an intimate group that is characterized by harmony of interests and that can reasonably be expected to be better than just. The other is the claim that the "nature" of sexual difference renders the demand that families be just not only unreasonable but harmful; families are naturally and necessarily unjust. Next, in chapters 3, 4, and 5, I shall analyze a number of recent theories that set out to answer the question, "What is just?" in very different ways. In chapter 3, I discuss those theories that center on traditions, or on the "shared meanings" of a culture. In chapter 4, I look at the libertarian argument that the assets of individuals and whatever flows from them are to be regarded as the absolute property of those individuals, such that any social redistributions are unjust because they are violations of their rights. In chapter 5, I turn to the argument that reasonable principles of social justice can be arrived at only through the deliberations of persons so situated as to be unaware of their own particular interests in the outcome.

I shall analyze each of these types of theory from a feminist perspective— one that treats women, as well as men, as full human beings to whom a theory of social justice must apply. I shall show how some of them (the tradition-based and the libertarian) are completely demolished by the imposition of this demand, but that more egalitarian theories, though unsatisfactory as they stand, have considerable potential for the development of a fully humanist theory of justice. What impedes this potential from being developed, however, is the adherence to that dichotomizing of public from private spheres that, as we saw earlier, tends to lead to the exclusion of marriage and the family from most discussions of justice. Thus, in chapter 6, I show how arguments that have been developed primarily by feminists, but to which others have contributed, expose the artificial nature of the dichotomy between the sphere of private, domestic life and that of the state and marketplace. Once we see that the separation of private from public is largely an ideological construct, having little relevance to actual human social life, we will see more clearly not only the potential but also the necessity for applying the standards of justice to the family.

In the last two chapters, I show that the family in the specific forms in which it exists in our society is not just, and then suggest how it might become more just. Chapter 7 consists of an argument, grounded in current empirical evidence, that gender-structured marriage and family life as practiced in the United States today are far from meeting most currently accepted standards of social justice. It provides evidence for the view sketched at the outset of this introductory chapter—that gender-structured marriage is an institution that makes women economically and socially vulnerable. Finally, chapter 8 contains some suggestions for public policy changes that might substantially alleviate the present injustices of gender. I make use of some of the best methods of thinking about justice that I have looked at in previous chapters. And I take seriously into account the fact that the social significance of sexual difference is a contentious issue in our society. My proposals, centered on the family but also on the workplace and other social institutions that currently reinforce the gender structure, will suggest some ways in which we might make our way toward a society much less structured by gender, and in which any remaining, freely chosen division of labor by sex would not result in injustice. In such a society, in all the spheres of our lives, from the most public to the most personal, we would strive to live in accordance with truly humanist principles of justice.

2

The Family:
Beyond Justice?

The substantial inequalities that continue to exist between the sexes in our society have serious effects on the lives of almost all women and an increasingly large number of children. Underlying all these inequalities is the unequal distribution of the unpaid labor of the family. Feminists who speak out against the traditional, gender-structured family are often unfairly attacked for being "anti-family." Some who have been so attacked have seemingly capitulated to these accusations and reverted to an unreflective defense of the family.[1] Others have responded more positively, stressing the ongoing need for feminists to "rethink the family"[2] and arguing that the family needs to be just. Moreover, these goals are necessary not only for the sake of women—though the injustice done to them is cause enough for challenging the gender-structured family—but for the sake of social justice as a whole.

In this chapter, I shall take up two different kinds of argument, both leading to the conclusion that to insist that families be internally just is misguided. These arguments have recently been made in widely read and much-praised books: Michael Sandel's *Liberalism and the Limits of Justice* and Allan

25

Bloom's *The Closing of the American Mind*.[3] In the first type of argument, it is claimed that the family is "beyond" justice in the sense of being too elevated for it. In Sandel's view, the family is not characterized by the circumstances of justice, which operate only when interests differ and goods being distributed are scarce. An intimate group, held together by love and identity of interests, the family is characterized by nobler virtues. In the second type of argument, the family is held to be "beyond" justice in the sense that "nature" dictates its hierarchical structure. Bloom acknowledges frankly that the division of labor found within the gender-structured family is unjust, at least by prevailing standards of justice, but holds it to be both grounded in nature and necessary. A great deal of attention has been paid to Sandel's and Bloom's books; both are cherished by antiliberals. The former has flourished within academic circles and the latter, a popular best-seller, largely outside of them. However, it is testimony to the antifeminist climate of the 1980s that, with one notable exception, their claims about justice and the family have been virtually ignored.[4]

Justice and the Idealized Family

The notion that justice is not an appropriate virtue for families was most clearly expressed in the past by Rousseau and Hume. It is currently important because, as we have seen, it seems to be implicit, from their sheer disregard for family life and most aspects of gender, in the work of most contemporary theories of justice. It is rarely argued explicitly these days, but such a case is presented by Michael Sandel in his critique of John Rawls's liberal theory of justice, and I shall focus on this argument here. But first, let us take a brief look at the positions of Rousseau and Hume. On this, as on some other complex issues, Rousseau argues more than one side of the issue. Some of the time, he justifies his conclusion that the governance of the family, unlike that of political society, need not be accountable to its members or regulated by principles of justice by appealing to the notion that the family, unlike the wider society, is founded upon love. Thus unlike a government, he says, the father of a family, "in order to act right, . . . has only to consult his heart."[5] Rousseau concludes that women can, without prejudice to their well-being, be both ruled within the family and denied the right to participate in the realm of politics, where their husbands will represent the interests of the family unit.

Hume argues similarly that the circumstances of family life are such that justice is not an appropriate standard to apply to them. He begins his discussion of justice by pointing out that in situations of "enlarged affections," in which every man "feels no more concern for his own interest than for that of his fellows," justice is useless, because unnecessary. He regards the family as one of the clearest instances of such enlarged affections, in which justice is inappropriate because "all distinction of property be, in a great measure, lost and confounded. . . . Between married persons, the cement of friendship is by the laws supposed so strong as to abolish all division of possessions; and has often, in reality, the force ascribed to it."[6] The message is similar to Rousseau's: the affection and unity of interests that prevail within families make standards of justice irrelevant to them.

In his critique of Rawls, Sandel explicitly takes up and builds on Hume's vision of family life, in order to make the case that there are important social spheres in which justice is an inappropriate virtue. A central piece of his argument against Rawls, which he presents as a case against liberal accounts of justice in general, is based on a denial of Rawls's claim that justice is the primary moral virtue.[7] This claim depends on the assumption that human society is characterized by certain "circumstances of justice." These include, first, the condition of moderate scarcity of resources, and second, the fact that, while persons have some similar or complementary needs and interests, they also have "different ends and purposes, and . . . make conflicting claims on the natural and social resources available."[8] Does Rawls think the circumstances of justice apply *within* families? It seems—although he has not held consistently to this position—that he is one of the few theorists of justice who do. As I shall show in chapter 5, he goes on to *assume*, rather than to *argue*, that the family "in some form" is just. But it is clear from both his statement of this assumption and his initial inclusion of the family as part of the "basic structure of society" that (in A *Theory of Justice*, at least) he does not consider the family to be outside the circumstances of justice.

Sandel, however, argues that Rawls's claim for the primacy of justice is undermined by the existence of numerous social groupings in which the circumstances of justice do *not* predominate. Among such groupings, characterized by their "more or less clearly-defined common identities and shared purposes," the family "may represent an extreme case."[9] He argues that the existence of such associations refutes in two respects Rawls's claim that justice is the first or primary virtue of social institutions. First, he agrees with Hume that in such "intimate or solidaristic associations . . . the values and aims of the participants coincide closely enough that the circumstances of justice prevail to a relatively small degree." In "a more or less ideal family situation," spontaneous affection and generosity will prevail.[10] Second, not only will justice not be the prevailing virtue in such associations, but if they were to begin to operate in accordance with principles of justice, an overall moral improvement would by no means necessarily result. Instead, the loss of certain "'nobler virtues, and more favourable blessings'" could mean that "in some cases, justice is not a virtue but a vice."[11] Given such a possibility, the moral primacy of justice is demonstrated to be unfounded. Instead of being the primary virtue, as Rawls claims, in some situations justice is "a remedial virtue," called upon to repair fallen conditions.[12]

In both its eighteenth- and its twentieth-century manifestations, the argument that human associations exemplified by the family challenge the primacy of justice rests, in two respects, on faulty foundations. It misapprehends what is meant by the claim that justice is the first or primary virtue of social institutions; and it idealizes the family. When Rawls claims the primacy of justice, he does not mean that it is the highest or noblest of virtues. Rather, he means that it is the most fundamental or essential. This is implied by the simile he employs on the opening page of A *Theory of Justice*:

> Justice is the first virtue of social institutions, as truth is of systems of thought. A theory however elegant or economical must be rejected or revised if it is untrue; likewise laws and institutions no matter how efficient and well-arranged must be reformed or abolished if they are unjust.[13]

In the same way that theories can have qualities other than truth, some of which—brilliance or social utility, for example—might be more elevated than mere truth, so can social institutions have other moral qualities, some of which might be more elevated than mere justice. The point is that justice takes primacy because it is the most *essential*, not because it is the *highest*, of virtues. In fact, Rawls states explicitly his belief that there are moral principles and sentiments that are higher and nobler than justice. He refers to "supererogatory actions," such as "acts of benevolence and mercy, of heroism and self-sacrifice," as stemming from "higher-order moral sentiments that serve to bind a community of persons together."[14] He also indicates on several occasions that the members of families do commonly exhibit such higher moral virtues in relation to one another. But he considers that only

28

saints and heroes, not ordinary persons, can *consistently* adhere to such standards of morality, which can require considerable sacrifice of self-interest, narrowly construed.[15] Furthermore, it is clear that, in Rawls's view, such moralities of supererogation, while they require *more* than the norms of right and justice, do not in any way contradict them. This is so both because their aims are continuous with these principles but extend beyond what they require and because such moralities need to rely upon the principles of justice when the claims of the goods they seek conflict.[16] Thus justice is first or primary among virtues in that such admittedly higher forms of morality depend upon it, both conceptually and in practice, in ways that it does not depend upon them.

When these points are taken into consideration, we can see that both the argument against the moral primacy of justice and that against justice as a central virtue for the family lose their force. The morality that often prevails in communities or associations that are governed in large part by affection, generosity, or other virtues morally superior to justice is a form of supererogation; individuals' narrowly construed interests give way to their concern for common ends or the ends of others they care about a great deal. Nevertheless, it is essential that such higher moral sentiments and actions, within the family as well as in society at large, be underwritten by a foundation of justice. Justice is needed as the primary, meaning most fundamental, moral virtue *even* in social groupings in which aims are largely common and affection frequently prevails.

We can learn more about why justice is a necessary virtue for families by examining the second flaw in Sandel's argument, which is that it relies upon an idealized, even mythical, account of the family. The picture drawn is, in fact, very close to Rawls's example of a circumstance in which he too agrees that justice is superfluous: "an association of saints agreeing on a common ideal."[17] But viewed realistically, human associations, including the family, do not operate so felicitously. And a theory of justice must concern itself not with abstractions or ideals of institutions but with their realities. If we were to concern ourselves only with ideals, we might well conclude that wider human societies, as well as families, could do without justice. The ideal society would presumably need no system of criminal justice or taxation, but that does not tell us much about what we need in the world we live in.

The vision of the family as an institution far above justice pays too little attention to what happens within such groupings when, as is surely common, they fail to meet this saintly ideal. Even a brief glance at the example that

29

Hume regards as the paradigm setting for the exercise of moral virtues nobler than justice should serve to make us less than comfortable with his and Sandel's dismissal of the need for justice in such settings. The unity of the eighteenth-century family—enshrined in the ideology of the time and revived in the 1970s by family historians[18]—was based on the legal fiction of "coverture." The *reason* that, as Hume puts it, "the laws supposed . . . the cement of friendship [between married persons] so strong as to abolish all division of possessions," was that upon marrying, women became legal nonpersons. Contrary to what Hume's words suggest, the common law did not institute the shared or common ownership of the property of spouses. Rather, it automatically transferred all of a wife's personal property—as well as control over, and the income from, her real property—into the hands of her husband. As John Stuart Mill was later to put it: "the two are called 'one person in law,' for the purpose of inferring that whatever is hers is his, but the parallel inference is never drawn that whatever is his is hers."[19] Hume and others justified coverture by reference to the "enlarged affections" and unity of the family. This same idealized vision of the family as "the place of Peace; the shelter, not only from all injury, but from all terror, doubt, and division," as John Ruskin depicted it, was central to the arguments made by the opponents of married women's rights in the nineteenth century.[20] But *we* must realize that questions of distributive justice were not considered important in the context of this type of family because not only the wife's property but her body, her children, and her legal rights belonged to her husband. To revert in the late twentieth century to this account of family life in order to argue that the circumstances of justice are not so socially pervasive as liberals like Rawls think they are is not only grossly ahistorical. It does not allow for the fact that the account was a myth, and a far from harmless one. It served as the ideology that veiled the *in*justice called coverture.

What this example can teach us about justice and the family is that while it is quite possible for associations to appear to operate according to virtues nobler than justice, and thus to be morally preferable to those that are *just* just, we need to scrutinize them closely before we can conclude that this is really the case. In particular, we need to ask whether their members are entitled to their fair shares of whatever benefits and burdens are at issue when and insofar as the circumstances of justice arise—when interests or ends conflict and some resources are scarce (as tends to happen at least some of the time, except in communities of saints with common ends). Thus even if wives never had occasion to ask for their just share of the family property, due to the generosity and spontaneous affection of their husbands, we would be unable to assess the families in which they lived from a moral point of view unless we knew whether, if they did ask for it, they would be considered entitled to it. It is not difficult to imagine the kind of response that would have been received by most eighteenth-century wives if they had asked for their just shares of the family property! This should make us highly skeptical of reliance on the supposedly higher virtues embodied by such institutions.

It is clear from the facts that I pointed to in chapter 1, and shall later give a more thorough account of, that Sandel's argument against the primacy of justice also depends on a highly idealized view of the *contemporary* family. "Enlarged affections" are by no means the only feelings that occur, and are acted upon, in families. Since the 1970s, it has been "discovered" that a great deal of violence—much of it serious, some of it fatal—occurs within families. Our courts and police are increasingly preoccupied with family assault and with the sexual abuse of weaker family members by more powerful ones. The family is also an important sphere of distribution. In the "more or less ideal family situation," Sandel says, the appeal to fairness is "preempted by a spirit of generosity in which I am rarely inclined to claim my fair share," and "the questions of what I get and what I am due do not loom large in the overall context of this way of life."[21] The implication seems to be that there are not likely to be *systematic* injustices. No account is taken of the fact that the socialization and role expectations of women mean that they are generally more inclined than men not to claim their fair share, and more inclined to order their priorities in accordance with the needs of their families. The supererogation that is expected in families often occurs at women's expense, as earlier ideologists of the family were well aware; Ruskin continues his vision by exhorting women to be "enduringly incorruptibly good; instinctively infallibly wise . . . , not for self-development but for self-renunciation."[22]

In fact, many social "goods," such as time for paid work or for leisure, physical security, and access to financial resources, typically are unevenly distributed within families. Though many may be "better than just," at least most of the time, contemporary gender-structured families are *not* just. But they *need* to be just. They cannot rely upon the spirit of generosity—though they can still aspire to it—because the life chances of millions of women and children are at stake. They need to be just, too, if they are to be the first schools of moral development, the places where we first learn to develop a sense of justice. And they need to be just if we are even to begin to approach the equality of opportunity that our country claims as one of its basic ideals.

31

It seems to be assumed by those who have held the position I have been criticizing that justice somehow takes away from intimacy, harmony, and love. But why should we suppose that harmonious affection, indeed deep and long-lasting love, cannot co-exist with ongoing standards of justice? Why should we be forced to choose and thereby to deprecate the basic and essential virtue, justice, by playing it off against what are claimed to be higher virtues? We are surely not faced with such a choice if, viewing human groupings like the family realistically, we insist that they be constructed upon a basis of justice. For this need not mean that we cannot also hope and expect more of them. We need to recognize that associations in which we *hope* that the best of human motivations and the noblest of virtues will prevail are, in fact, morally superior to those that are *just* just only if they are firmly built on a foundation of justice, however rarely it may be invoked. Since this is so, the existence of associations like families poses no problem for the moral primacy of justice. If they normally operate in accordance with spontaneous feelings of love and generosity, but provide justice to their members when, as circumstances of justice arise, it is needed, then they are just and better than just. But if they do not provide justice when their members have reason to ask it of them, then despite their generosity and affection, they are worse.

Thus, it is only when the family is idealized and sentimentalized that it can be perceived as an institution that undermines the primacy of justice. When we recognize, as we must, that however much the members of families care about one another and share common ends, they are still discrete persons with their own particular aims and hopes, which may sometimes conflict, we must see the family as an institution to which justice is a crucial virtue. When we recognize, as we surely must, that many of the resources that are enjoyed within the sphere of family life—leisure, nurturance, money, time, and attention, to mention only a few—are by no means always abundant, we see that justice has a highly significant role to play. When we realize that women, especially, are likely to change the whole course of their lives because of their family commitments, it becomes clear that we cannot regard families as analogous to other intimate relations like friendship, however strong the affective bonding of the latter may be. And now that it cannot be assumed, as it was earlier, that marriage is for life, we must take account of the fact that the decreasing permanence of families renders issues of justice within them more critical than ever. To substitute self-sacrifice and altruism for justice in the context of a unity that may dissolve before one's very eyes, without one's consent and to the great detriment of those one cares most about, would perhaps be better labeled lack of foresight than nobility.

The Unjust Family as Natural and Socially Necessary

While in Rousseau's *idealized* vision of family life, dependent, secluded, and subordinated wives could rely on their husbands' loving care and protection, he at times recognized the folly of trusting this account of family life. In his own fictional depictions, husbands and fathers fall far short of this ideal; they frequently neglect, abuse, and abandon those they are supposed to take care of.[23] Rousseau himself sent all his children off to foundling homes, against his wife's will. However, in spite of his own recognition of the fragility of the myth on which it was based, he could see no alternative to the dependent position of women that he regarded as imposed by nature. The "very law of nature," in Rousseau's view, leaving men uncertain of the paternity of the children they are expected to maintain, dictates that women are "at the mercy of men's judgments."[24] In Book 5 of *Emile*, having described in detail Sophie's careful preparation for a life of coquettish subordination to the multiple needs and whims of her husband, Rousseau frankly admits the injustice of it all:

> As she is made to obey a being who is so imperfect, often so full of vices, and always so full of defects as man, she ought to learn early to endure even injustice and to bear a husband's wrongs without complaining. It is not for his sake, it is for her own, that she ought to be gentle. The bitterness and the stubbornness of women never do anything but increase their ills and the bad behavior of their husbands.[25]

Thus, nature necessitates women's subjection to men, and the imperfections of men's nature necessitate the reinforcement of women's natural propensity for enduring injustice. The good of society and the continuation of the species make inevitable the rigid division of labor between the sexes and the subordination of women. Rather than delving further into Rousseau's reasons for believing this to be the case, let us now turn to the same argument as it appears in Allan Bloom's 1987 version. For two main reasons, it is important to pay attention to Bloom's variety of antifeminism: it is a strongly articulated, though somewhat extreme, version of notions that have considerable currency in powerful circles these days; and Bloom, because of his own political agenda, admits freely that the maintenance of sex roles in the family is inconsistent with liberal-democratic standards of justice.

The ostensible theme of Bloom's *The Closing of the American Mind* is that American liberal democracy is disintegrating because its universities are failing to educate the young elite. Without the education in rational thinking that can be provided only by serious study of the great books of Western philosophy and literature, young people are aimlessly wandering in the chaos of relativism—tolerance gone wild—that plagues our society. A major enemy, in Bloom's account of what has gone wrong since the early 1960s (when he thinks things were still basically on track), is feminism. For, while "nature should be the standard by which we judge our . . . lives," feminism is "not founded on nature," defying as it does women's natural biological destiny.[26] Feminism is much to blame both for undermining the prestige of the great books and for hastening the decline of the already beleaguered family.

Bloom's arguments on both issues depend on completely unsubstantiated statements of alleged "fact." We are told, for example, that even in "relatively happy" homes, "the dreariness of the family's spiritual landscape passes belief," that "central to the feminist project is the suppression of modesty," that "there are two equal careers in almost every household composed of educated persons under thirty-five," and that, due to feminist activism, "offensive authors" are being expunged from college courses or included only to demonstrate the great books' distorting prejudices about women.[27] No evidence is cited for these or other such general allegations, which many of us who live in families, are active in the feminist movement, struggle to maintain our careers in the context of unequal family demands, or teach the great books know to be preposterous. The fact that Bloom's book, with its multiple inaccuracies and its disdain for evidence, topped the *New York Times'* nonfiction best-seller list throughout the summer of 1987 is, to my way of thinking, the clearest sign yet that there is indeed *something* wrong with American higher education.

At times, in Bloom's lament about the decline of the family, there appear hints of the idealized, better-than-just version of it. He writes of the family as "the intermediary . . . that gave men and women unqualified concern for at least some others," thereby tempering individualism. But most of his argument runs counter to this notion. He assumes that men are by nature selfish creatures, who could not even be imagined as having "unqualified concern" for anyone but themselves. The problem, as Bloom sees it, is that "women are no longer willing to make unconditional and perpetual commitments on un-equal terms." Arguing that feminism has eroded the family by its resistance to traditional sex roles, he says that it "ends, as do many modern movements that seek abstract justice, in forgetting nature and using force to refashion human beings to secure that justice."[28]*

Closely following Rousseau throughout his argument, he claims that if women refuse to be full-time mothers, men will refuse to be fathers at all, be-cause they will no longer be gaining enough of what they expect from family life to have any commitment to it. Nature, according to Bloom, makes mother-hood entirely different from fatherhood. Men have no natural desire or need for children. But women naturally want children, and therefore must take care of them. In order to get their children's fathers to support them while they do this, women must charm men into marriage (largely by withholding sex), and then must cater to their needs and take care of them. Recognizing the natural basis of their dependence, women should not develop careers, for this causes struggle and threatens family unity. They must accept the fact that "nothing can effectively make most men share equally the responsibilities of childbear-ing and child-rearing." Bloom acknowledges that, by the egalitarian standards of modernity, this inequality of women is unjust.[29] But the writers of the great books all knew it to be natural and therefore necessary, which is why, by Bloom's own admission, they are all sexist. The only ones who do not *seem* to agree with Bloom about the proper role of women are either not great (Mill) or did not mean what they said (Plato).

As Bloom says, feminist scholars during the last fifteen years or so have challenged many of the works that make up the tradition of what one has wit-tily called "malestream thought."[30] But the sexism of the great books has not been wantonly, angrily, and arbitrarily assaulted, as Bloom would like his read-ers to think. It has been carefully argued about. Feminists have brought the test of rational thought to what the great books have said about women and the family, and in many cases shown their assumptions to be unfounded and their arguments irrational. We have not, as Bloom alleges, gone on to con-clude that these authors are worthless thinkers, to be relegated to the intellec-tual junkheap. We have, however, insisted that it would be wrong (not least because it is intellectually dishonest) to continue to teach their works as though they did not believe such things, or as though their statements about women were aberrations that can be conveniently forgotten because they

---

*He does not explain how feminists have used force in pursuit of their aims. By chaining themselves to railings, or by learning self-defense, perhaps?

have no effect on the "important" things the philosophers had to say. We have faced up to the challenge of learning what we can from great minds of the past and teaching it to our students, when most people in our society are no longer prepared to think about women in the ways they did.

What might happen if Bloom's complaint that feminism has undermined the teaching of the great books were transformed into policy? Would existing feminist criticisms, however rational, be banned? If so, would women (who would soon begin again to raise similar questions and to make similar objections) have to be forbidden from both teaching and studying in institutions of higher education? Who knows to what lengths we might have to go in order to protect the sexism of Aristotle, Rousseau, and Nietzsche from rational scrutiny. The world of Margaret Atwood's *The Handmaid's Tale*, in which women, as reproductive vessels, are no longer taught to read or write, might well be the logical conclusion of Bloom's train of thought.[31] From his point of view, there would appear to be nothing wrong with women's being uneducated, as long as they were dependent upon men and relatively powerless within the family, as he recommends.

Like many other antifeminists, Bloom relies heavily on "nature" and especially on reproductive biology to argue for the rationality and necessity of traditional sex roles. As we have seen, he uses the old trick of making child rearing by males look absurd by fusing it with male childbearing. He says that nature dictates, via female lactation, that women must stay home with children. Stooping to puerile humor, he remarks that paternity leave is "contrived and somewhat ridiculous," since the law cannot make male nipples give milk.[32] He does not seem to realize that the great majority of infants in the United States are at least partly bottle-fed, that nursing an infant is only a tiny part of raising a child, that flexibility of working and child-care conditions can allow wage-earning mothers both to breast-feed their infants and to share the care of them equally with fathers.

Bloom does not *want* to realize any of these things, of course. His fundamental case against feminist attempts to share more fairly the unpaid responsibilities of the family is that it undermines masculinity. "Here," he says, "is where the whole business turns nasty." (He means, of course, that the implications of feminism turn nasty; to my way of thinking it is his argument that gets rather nasty at this point.) He continues:

> The souls of men—their ambitious, warlike, protective, possessive character— must be dismantled in order to liberate women from their domination.

> Machismo—the polemical description of maleness or spiritedness, which was the central *natural* passion in men's souls in the psychology of the ancients, the passion of attachment and loyalty—was the villain, the source of the difference between the sexes. . . . With machismo discredited, the positive task is to make men caring, sensitive, even nurturing, to fit the restructured family. . . . And it is indeed possible to soften men. But to make them "care" is another thing, and the project must inevitably fail.[33]

The reason it must fail, he alleges, is that men cannot be forced to give up their natural selfishness, especially at a time when women are being more selfish. I need not go into just how wrong Bloom is about the ancients' view of male spiritedness; Martha Nussbaum has shown far better than I could how many of them, including those Bloom judges to be the best, believed that the needs of society required that such passions be modified.[34] But it is important to discuss his reliance upon what is natural.

"Nature," Bloom states, "should be the standard by which we judge our own lives and the lives of peoples. That is why philosophy . . . is the most important human science."[35] But what on earth, we must ask, is "nature"? And how is philosophy to help us discover it? It is unfortunate that Bloom is so contemptuous of Mill, who made arguments well worthy of his consideration about the political uses and abuses of *nature* and *the natural*.[36] One of the major sources of irrationality, Mill says, is that these words are sometimes used to mean the way things would be without human intervention and sometimes to mean the way things ought to be, as though the two are somehow synonymous. These words, Mill argues, have been used with such confusion and such proliferation of meanings that they have become "one of the most copious sources of false taste, false philosophy, false morality, and even bad law."[37] As we have seen, much of past and present feminism has dealt extensively with the subject of how "nature," and biological determinism in particular, has been used to oppress women.

Bloom, despite his reverence for philosophy, seems to feel no need to make arguments about what nature is or why it is good. He uses the words *nature* and *natural*—words crucial to his book's potential coherence, in a multitude of different ways, without ever defining them.* Unlike some scholars, such as Ruth Bleier and Anne Fausto-Sterling, who have given much thought to the

---

*One of the first uses in the book gives us an immediate clue to its author's misogyny: in the preface we learn that "nature, not the midwife" is the cause of the delivery of babies (p. 20). Where, we might ask, is the mother? One of the oddest uses comes on p. 105, where Bloom blames the sexual revolution and feminism for producing "an odd tension in which all the moral restraints governing nature disappeared, but so did nature." It is difficult to see why any tension should result from the lack of restraints on something that has disappeared.

matter,[38] he seems quite confident that he knows where the "natural" (which in this context seems to mean "biological") differences between the sexes begin and end. Yet he persists in the belief that child rearing as a whole is "naturally" women's responsibility. "Biology forces women to take maternity leaves," he pronounces. And he greets with sarcasm and deprecation women's claim that we ourselves should have a major say in what constitutes "the feminine nature."[39]* Frequently falling into the fallacious way of thinking that Mill warns against, Bloom never confronts all the things that contemporary people, or even the Greeks, would have had to give up to return to nature, in the sense of letting biology take its course. He ridicules liberals whose concern for the natural environment leads them to protest the extinction of the snail darter, but who also defend the right to abortion. However, he has nothing to say about the fact that modern medicine and innumerable other life-preserving and life-enhancing aspects of modern life are manifest departures from the notion that biology is destiny. Most of the time, it is difficult to discern any consistent meaning in Bloom's references to "the natural," except that it is whatever preserves the dominance of the white male elite and enables its members, by philosophizing, to come to terms with their own mortality.

Ultimately, the only comprehensible way to read Bloom's book is the same way he wants us to read the *Republic*. According to Bloom, who ignores all reasoning to the contrary, Plato made the ridiculous proposal that the elite women should be treated equally with the men only in order to demonstrate the impossibility of his entire project. Bloom's own book about education purports, on one level at least, to be about the preservation of liberal democracy. But he is really, of course, a vehement defender of aristocracy. Among the reasons for his contempt for today's students is his (unfounded) belief that their instincts are wholly egalitarian: "Whenever they meet anyone," he alleges, "considerations of sex, color, religion, family, money, nationality, play no role in their reactions."[40] (Doubtless, both most of the students and the administrators of the colleges and universities now fraught with racist and sexist conflict might like to be reassured by Bloom's words, but the evidence before their eyes belies them.) His own belief in an aristocracy based on race, sex, and other natural indicators of "excellence" is evident over and over again in the book, such as

---

*He says of the "recent feminist discussion" of the differences between men and women that "the feminine nature is a mystery to be worked out on its own, which can now be done because the male claim to it has been overcome."

when he remarks—seemingly with deliberate intent to insult—that the black students in the major universities "have, by and large, proved indigestible," or when he explains that white males still predominate in the natural sciences because it is only there that standards of excellence have not been eroded by affirmative action policies.[41]

As we should expect, *The Closing of the American Mind* can be read coherently only as a Straussian text, its superficial meaning veiling a deeper message.* It has obvious parallels in subject matter, and even in its ordering, with Plato's *Republic*. Here, as with Plato, the treatment of sexual relations and the family is of critical importance in unlocking the author's real meaning. Bloom does not take the risk, as he thinks Plato does, of "joking" about how women can be equal. Perhaps he fears that—as he thinks Plato was until the Straussian interpretation, and still is by most of us—he will be misread as meaning what he says. Instead, Bloom thinks he has shown that the equality of women would be impossible, ridiculous, unnatural, and socially devastating. By liberal democratic standards, then, a fundamental injustice must remain at the very foundation of the society. But this, more clearly than anything else, must show that all the other pretensions to human equality are equally doomed, the whole egalitarian enterprise of modernity misguided, and aristocracy vindicated.

For those of us who *are* still attached to democracy, to an egalitarian liberalism, and to feminism, Bloom's conclusions need hold no fearful portents. For the egalitarian family is not an absurd impossibility, but rather a necessary component of the society that we want to build. The things that make traditional families unjust are not matters of natural necessity, as reactionaries like Bloom would like to have us believe. There is surely nothing in our natures that requires men not to be equal participants in the rearing of their children. Bloom says they won't do it because they are naturally selfish. Even if he were right, which I very strongly doubt, since when did we shape public policy around people's faults? Our laws do not allow kleptomaniacs to shoplift, or those with a predilection for rape to rape. Why, then, should we allow fathers who refuse to share in the care of their children to abdicate their responsibilities? Why should we allow the

---

*This method of political philosophizing originated with the work of Leo Strauss, who taught at the University of Chicago in the post–World War II years. The method depends heavily on the belief that all the great books of Western philosophy are written with two levels of meaning, one of which is easily accessible, the other—almost always containing a highly inegalitarian message—accessible only to the learned few, the "men of excellence." Not surprisingly, there are few female or black Straussians.

continuance of the peculiar contract that marriage has become, in which legal equality is assumed but actual inequality persists because women, whether or not they work for wages, are considerably hampered in developing skills or economic security, being caught up in doing the great bulk of the family's unpaid work? Why should we allow an injustice that is clearly harming large numbers of children, as well as women, to persist at the foundation of our political order?

3

Whose Traditions?
Which Understandings?

The past decade has witnessed the renewed appeal of traditional values and traditional culture. In particular, and in part in reaction to feminism, it has included an attempt to restore or recover the traditional family, perceived as a lost or dying institution. Some prominent examples include the Family Protection Act introduced into Congress in 1981, one of whose clauses would have prohibited the use of federal funds to question traditional sex roles, and the pope's 1988 statement that a woman's vocation is either motherhood or celibacy.[1]

Appealing to tradition and grieving for its loss has been evident in popular periodicals and rhetoric and more academic works. These range from a full-page advertisement for *Good Housekeeping* magazine in the *New York Times*, glorifying the "traditional" woman, and George Bush's stress in the 1988 presidential campaign on the family and its "traditional values," to popular academic books such as Christopher Lasch's *Haven in a Heartless World*, Robert Bellah's *Habits of the Heart*, Edward Shils's *Tradition*, and, as discussed in the previous chapter, Allan Bloom's *The Closing of the American Mind*.[2] Shils is particularly explicit about the connections between tradition and the patriarchal family.[3] At the extreme, "traditional" marriage has been invoked to argue against both the legal recognition of rape within marriage and the provision of shelters for battered wives.*

Contemporary with this general nostalgia for tradition has been the parallel movement in some theories of social justice toward reliance upon traditions, or "shared understandings." This has been closely linked with a sustained assault on liberal moral and political theories that attempt to invent or to formulate principles of justice from positions that the traditionalists regard as outside particular social contexts. Focusing their attacks primarily on the work of John Rawls, a number of these theorists, known as "communitarians," have argued that attempts to disengage moral or political theories from the thinking of actual people living at specific times and in particular communities are doomed to failure or irrelevance.[6] In place of such theories, they aim to construct theories of justice by interpreting some combination of our traditions, the values latent or deeply rooted in our communities, or the meanings or understandings we share.

There is a ghostly element to the debate between liberals and communitarians, since the latter—including Alasdair MacIntyre, Michael Sandel, and Charles Taylor—have not yet come up with any kind of developed theory. Michael Walzer, who *has* developed a theory of justice, is only in part a communitarian, though he is similarly critical of Rawls's approach to justice. His reliance on "shared meanings" or "understandings" is in some respects akin to communitarian ideas and, as I shall argue in this chapter, shares some of their problems.[7] Whereas the implications of most communitarian arguments are reactionary and inegalitarian, however, Walzer interprets shared meanings or understandings in ways that lead to the defense of far more egalitarian conclusions. And whereas MacIntyre thinks that in contemporary times we have become incoherent, share no moral understandings, and need to rediscover philosophical traditions that have been lost, Walzer thinks that communities of ordinary people do have shared understandings, though they may be latent and need to be brought fully to consciousness. He sees this bringing forth of latent meanings as the task of the social critic.

As I shall argue here, both these ways of thinking have serious deficiencies. The appeal to "our traditions" and the "shared understandings" approach are

---

*Opposing the enforcement of rape laws against husbands, Alaska Senator Paul Fischer said in 1985: "I don't know how you can have a sexual act and call it forcible rape in a marriage situation. . . . I still believe in the old traditional bond of marriage."[4] U.S. Senator Gordon Humphrey (N.H.) argued in 1980 against funding "so-called 'homes' for battered women," on the grounds that "the federal government should not fund missionaries who would war on the traditional family or on local values."[5]

both incapable of dealing with the problem of the effects of *social domination* on beliefs and understandings. They therefore prove to be useless or distorting ways of thinking when we include women as fully human subjects in our theorizing about justice or try to assess gender by the standards of justice. But a number of feminist theorists and scholars of moral development have come to look on communitarianism as an ally in their struggle against what they see as a masculinist abstraction and emphasis on justice, impartiality, and universality. They see such theories and conceptions of the self and its relation to context and community as more akin than theories of justice and rights to women's moral needs and concerns.[8] As the argument of this chapter shows, feminists need to be wary of such alliances.

Rationality and Justice in the Context of Traditions

Defenders of traditions make different kinds of claims about their significance. Some claim that adherence to traditions is necessary if our lives are to be grounded and to have coherence, or that it helps to prevent us from feeling alienated and empty. While agreeing with them, MacIntyre makes much stronger claims. He says that only by turning to and immersing ourselves in the knowledge of traditions—specifically, those that form the background to Western culture—can we achieve sound reasoning about *justice*. He accuses three centuries of theorists of liberal individualism of having failed to come up with any "coherent rationally defensible statement" of their point of view, citing as evidence their continued disagreements about specific issues.[9] And he promises to provide better answers. By immersing himself in traditions and studying the narrative of their histories, by evaluating them in relation to one another, he claims to be able to come up with the rational answers we need when we confront, in many situations in life, the question, "What am I to do?"[10]

In his 1981 book, *After Virtue*, MacIntyre aims to show that we must turn to what he calls "the classical tradition" of ethics, revolving around the concept of the virtues, if we are to be rescued from what he regards as the incoherence of modern moral language and practice. In contrast with liberal theories that value "the capacity to detach oneself from any particular standpoint or point of view,"[11] what characterizes the ethics of tradition, centered

43

on Aristotle, is its thorough rootedness in the context of a particular social order. Specific social roles are the most fundamental assumptions on which the traditions build, and their ethics center on the virtues that are necessary for the performance of these roles.

More recently, in his 1988 book, *Whose Justice? Which Rationality?* MacIntyre promises to address that crucial question left unanswered in his earlier defense of a tradition-based morality of the virtues. He will, he says, supply "an account of what rationality is, in the light of which rival and incompatible evaluations of the arguments of *After Virtue* could be adequately accounted for."[12] After a lengthy exposition of the history of three ethical traditions he finds, after a few sentences of argument, that Thomas Aquinas's synthesis of the Aristotelian and the Augustinian Christian traditions best exemplifies rationality and justice. As he admits, he has arrived, at the end of the book, at the starting point for his own moral theorizing. Presumably another book will follow.

In spite of its unfinished nature, MacIntyre's work has become an influential defense of tradition-based thinking about social justice. It is treated, in some circles at least, as a worthy critique of contemporary liberalism. Most of those who discuss it seem far more interested in its methodology than in its political implications. Few reviewers or critics have confronted the pervasive elitism of MacIntyre's defense of tradition as a basis for justice, and its equally pervasive sexism has scarcely been mentioned.[13] In fact, one moral philosopher has suggested that MacIntyre be recognized as an "honorary woman," because of the contextuality of his ethics.[14] I shall offer here a much-needed critique, showing how a primarily feminist analysis can serve to uncover a more general and basic problem of this way of thinking—its incapacity to deal critically with the fact and the effects of domination.

MacIntyre's language in both *After Virtue* and *Whose Justice?* is a clear case of the false gender neutrality that I exposed and explained in chapter 1. He writes of "men and women," or "he or she," in contexts where to do so is patently absurd. He uses these terms, for example, when discussing the quest of classical Athenian citizens for riches, power and prestige, although in fact Athenian women were not citizens with access to any of these things. Occasionally, where the use of gender-neutral terms might seem so absurd as to strike even the most insensitive reader, MacIntyre reverts to the use of *men, boys*, and *he*.[15] Sometimes in his discussions of Aristotle's conception of the *polis*, MacIntyre so closely intertwines references to "the good man" or "he" with references to "the virtuous person," "the human individual," or "he or she" that one is left with the impression that it is his conscious intention to make the reader forget about the exclusionary nature of Aristotle's views about who could lead "the good life for a human being."[16] MacIntyre uses these terms to discuss Aristotle's question, "What is the good life for man?" in spite of the fact that Aristotle's answer to this question was a life that he thought women (as well as slaves and manual workers) were necessarily excluded from, and one that depended in large part on the performance by these excluded people of subordinate functions.[17] Again, in the context of the Adam and Eve story and Augustine's conception of the will, MacIntyre persistently employs gender-neutral language, even though Christian (especially Catholic) theology has assigned to Eve the primary blame for the fall from grace. The same thing happens all through his discussion of Aquinas's theory, even though he notes in passing that "in the household and family structures of which he knew everyone else acted as the agent of the male head of household."[18]

This use of gender-neutral language in the discussion of traditions and societies in which sex difference was a central and determining feature that justified the subordination of women continues throughout MacIntyre's recent work. It is particularly striking in a passage in which he presents human life as a narrative, in which each character's role is largely predetermined. Given this, he says, unless children are educated into the virtues through being told the stories of their moral tradition, they will be left "unscripted, anxious stutterers in their actions as in their words." And what stories are these? Stories "about wicked stepmothers, lost children, good but misguided kings, wolves that suckle twin boys, youngest sons who receive no inheritance but must make their own way in the world and eldest sons who waste their inheritance on riotous living and go into exile to live with the swine." These are the stories that teach children "the cast of characters . . . in the drama into which they have been born and what the ways of the world are."[19] Despite his use of the gender-neutral word *children*, MacIntyre fails entirely to notice that the vast preponderance of the cast is male, and that the only explicitly female characters mentioned are a wicked stepmother and a suckling wolf. Faced with this choice of roles—human but wicked, nurturing but bestialized—surely girls are more likely to be rendered "unscripted, anxious stutterers" by being *subjected to* than by being deprived of such stories. For these stories, as well as many others in "our" mythology, are themselves basic building blocks of male domination.

Why should we expect to find rationality and justice embodied in traditions? And how are we to determine which traditions best represent justice and rationality? As we shall see, MacIntyre does not provide satisfactory or consistent answers to these questions, even within the framework of his own theorizing. One of the most serious problems of his theory issues from his claim that traditions are best tested when, often because of social change, they confront what he calls "epistemological crises," which are marked by the "dissolution of historically founded certitudes."[20] For he fails to provide an account of the rationality of the traditions on which his theory relies that responds to one of the most serious epistemological crises of our time: the challenge of feminism, which has resulted from the full realization by some of us of the extent to which "our" theories and traditions are deeply infused with patriarchalism. Indeed, as I shall show, the tradition that, according to MacIntyre, provides us with the best account of justice and rationality compounds the misogyny and sexism of two of the traditions in Western culture that have been most hostile to the idea of the full humanity of women.

First, let us look at how MacIntyre thinks we are to evaluate against each other the claims to rationality and justice of the various traditions. He does not claim that all traditions have embodied rational enquiry, much less that they have done so equally. In some instances, he acknowledges, those Enlightenment thinkers who dismissed tradition as "the antithesis of rational enquiry" were in the right.[21] How, then, are we to judge among them which tradition is more rational than others? MacIntyre's argument about how we can find justice and rationality "embodied" in social and intellectual tradition is "essentially historical. To justify," he says, "is to narrate how the argument has gone so far."[22] In order to do this, we need to be able to understand the arguments of the traditions in their historical context. The bulk of *Whose Justice? Which Rationality?* traces three traditions, each part of the background culture of our own culture, each of which MacIntyre takes to exemplify "the concept of tradition-constituted and tradition-constitutive rational enquiry," and each of which has argued with and/or been allied or synthesized with at least one of the others.[23] They are the Aristotelian tradition, with its origins in Homer and its culmination in Aquinas; the tradition of Augustinian Christianity; and the blending of Calvinist Augustinianism with Renaissance Aristotelianism that became the tradition of the Scottish Enlightenment (ultimately subverted by Hume). MacIntyre also claims that liberalism, founded in antagonism to traditional ways of thinking, has, despite itself, become a tradition. It is of course his least preferred, and his account of it is both perfunctory and distorted.

Whose Traditions? Which Understandings?

After nearly four hundred pages of historical narrative, MacIntyre finds it necessary to remind the reader, in the last few pages of the book, that what he is after is an account of *which* tradition best embodies justice and rationality.[24] This is a necessary reminder since in presenting his account of the three traditions, MacIntyre has *not* engaged in the sort of discussion of their major arguments that he then tells us is required, if we are to be able to evaluate them; he barely scratches the surface of any such questions. He does tell the reader, mostly in the last, brief chapter, how this should be done. But his account of how we are to arrive at justice and rationality, and thence to resolve difficult moral issues, is fraught with serious problems.

Traditions mature, improving their accounts of justice and practical rationality, MacIntyre argues, at times of social change. At such times, traditions are tested, and "a tradition becomes mature just insofar as its adherents confront and find a rational way through or around those encounters with radically different and incompatible positions." Here, he stresses the importance of being ready to concede that the conceptual resources of one's tradition are inadequate, and of being sensitive to the distortions that may occur when one tries to encompass theses from another tradition into one's own. It is, he says, part of the nature of traditions that their adherents cannot know in advance, whatever their own convictions, in what condition their tradition will emerge from such conflict.[25] At the same time, MacIntyre stresses the impossibility of trying to evaluate, or decide among, traditions by trying to get outside them. "We have learned," he says, " . . . that the resources of adequate rationality are made available to us only in and through traditions." To be outside all traditions is "to be a stranger to enquiry, . . . in a state of intellectual and moral destitution."[26] But how is one to begin? If one can think rationally only from the standpoint of tradition, but is confronted by the claims of rival traditions, *which* tradition is it rational for one to adopt?

Here, MacIntyre gives an extraordinarily subjectivist response: "The initial answer is: that will depend upon *who you are and how you understand yourself*" (emphasis added).[27] Not only the resolutions but the moral problems themselves will vary with the historical, social, and cultural situation, and with the history of belief and attitude, of each particular person. So first a person decides, or perhaps discovers, often with "a shock of recognition," on this basis, of what tradition "his or her life so far forms an intelligible part."[28] He or she is then required, by the demands of rationality, both to engage in the ongoing arguments within that tradition and to test his or her relationship to this particular tradition by engaging in the arguments of that tradition with one or more of its rivals. The latter task not only necessitates the acquisition of a "second first language" but also requires "a work of the imagination whereby the individual is able to place him or herself imaginatively within the scheme of belief inhabited by those whose allegiance is to the rival tradition, so as to perceive and conceive the natural and social worlds as they perceive and conceive them."[29] Only by first adopting a tradition, and then engaging in such argumentative dialogue, such conversation between traditions, can one come to a satisfactory and defensible account of justice and practical rationality.

Some of the problems with this tradition-based theory of justice are of a general nature.* Before we even reach the stage of confronting these problems, however, we encounter one that is particularly clear when we approach the theory from a feminist perspective. This is MacIntyre's entirely subjectivist account of how "we" find an intelligible and justifiable tradition to which we can respond. He suggests that "the individual educated into self-knowledge of his or her own incoherence [be invited] to acknowledge in which of these rival modes of moral understanding he or she finds him or herself most adequately explained and accounted for."[30] MacIntyre, though he describes himself in the first chapter as an Augustinian Christian, pronounces by the last chapter that it is the Thomistic tradition whose rationality he has found best confirmed by its encounters with other traditions. In it he finds

---

*First, MacIntyre is careful to insist that in order to engage in dialogue, one does not *really* adopt the beliefs or standpoint of the adherents to a rival tradition; one merely pretends to, as an actor impersonates, speaking in the voice of a character (*Whose Justice?* p. 395). And he *must* insist on this, because he has earlier stated very clearly that "genuinely to adopt the standpoint of a tradition thereby *commits one to its view of what is true and false and, in so committing one, prohibits one from adopting any rival standpoint*" (*Whose Justice?* p. 367 [emphasis added]). But doesn't this completely subvert the point of dialectic between traditions, and contradict the argument that in such an encounter an adherent of one might become convinced of the superior rationality of the other? (*Whose Justice?* pp. 387–88 and chap. 20, passim.)

Second, while MacIntyre castigates liberals, operating outside of traditions, for failure to reach agreement about fundamental specific moral questions, he himself fails even to engage in sustained argument about such specific questions, much less come up with answers. If he were to do so, it would surely become obvious that one tradition may have the most rational answer to one moral problem, and another tradition a more rational answer to another. There is surely no reason to believe that any one tradition will have *all* the most rational answers. For his castigation of modernity, and especially liberals, for such failure see, for example, *Whose Justice?* pp. 1–4, 332–35.

Ten pages from the end of the book (p. 393), he reminds us of the importance of such contemporary moral dilemmas as conscientious objection and affirmative action, yet still fails to indicate just what his traditions have to contribute to such discussions. The only specific issue that comes up recurrently, in the context of various traditions, in *After Virtue* and *Whose Justice?* is that of whether rights to private property precede or follow from discussions of distributive justice. This is of course a moral issue of the greatest importance; the problem is that MacIntyre never really engages the question itself, or debates the various traditions' answers to it. It seems extraordinary, in the context of contemporary moral issues of the magnitude of nuclear deterrence or abortion, that MacIntyre's central examples of epistemological crises that tested traditions against one another are theological, metaphysical, and scientific, *not* primarily moral or political ones. *Whose Justice?* pp. 362–63.

himself "most adequately explained and accounted for." Certainly, most twentieth-century men would not agree. However, women—at least those of us whose understanding of who we are centers on or even includes the statement "I am a woman"—will be even more obviously confounded by the set of traditions MacIntyre presents in his book and by his general argument about arriving at justice and moral reasoning by encounters with such traditions. Let us now look from a woman's point of view at some of the traditions MacIntyre finds preferable to liberalism.

Whose Traditions?

MacIntyre presents, most of the time, a benign portrait of the three traditions he prefers to liberalism, and of the societies in which they were embedded. This starts with the Homeric world view, which he evaluates differently from many who have studied it. According to him, the wars fought by the Homeric heroes were to protect and bring prosperity to their households and local communities, whose members therefore all benefited from their warrior elites' virtues of physical strength, courage, intelligence, and prosperity. He is only momentarily puzzled by the paradox raised by this rather one-sided interpretation of Homer—that in order to achieve contentment and prosperity both for themselves and for those left at home, the heroes "pursue a course whose characteristic end is death."[31] Other interpretations of Homer, in which the hero's own success and immortal fame are recognized as the driving forces, do not raise any such paradoxes.[32] Though MacIntyre emphasizes the connection of role and status with privileges and duties, his benign interpretation de-emphasizes both the social hierarchy of heroic societies and the heavy sanctions that reinforced it.[33] Those who stayed at home, and their points of view, are virtually ignored.

This is particularly noticeable the few times that MacIntyre mentions Homeric women. "Andromache and Hector, Penelope and Odysseus are friends (*philos*)," MacIntyre asserts, "as much as are Achilles and Patroclus," but he does not point out here that this indicates no necessary similarity between the two relationships, since to call someone a friend in the Homeric context could simply indicate kinship.[34] He acknowledges that women's virtues were different from men's, consisting primarily in their physical attractions and their fidelity. But he does not confront the fact that women's virtues were defined in relation to men, whereas men's virtues were not defined in relation to women. Neither does he see that this entails no possibility of equality, or friendship based on equality, between the sexes. Mortal women appear most often in Homer as causes of conflict between men or armies, or as part of the booty. For a clearer picture than MacIntyre provides, we must turn to M. I. Finley, who writes:

> There is no mistaking the fact that Homer fully reveals what remained true for the whole of antiquity, that women were held to be naturally inferior and therefore limited in their function to the production of offspring and the performance of household duties, and that the meaningful social relationships and the strong personal attachments were sought and found among men.[35]

As for the rest of the social hierarchy, MacIntyre does not mention the free members of the non-elite classes, who could not possess the virtues no matter what they did. When he writes that "the word *aretê* . . . is in the Homeric poems used for excellence of any kind," the *reader* must provide the caution "except excellence in any activity not valued by the male elite." It is not until his later chapter on classical Greek society, wishing to make it appear more egalitarian, that MacIntyre makes explicit the fact that "virtue" and "honor" in Homer are the virtue of and the honor due to a warrior king.[36] Slaves, MacIntyre admits, were not much better off than the dead, but he defines them as "outside the heroic community." Having defined the community so as to exclude its slaves, he claims that the Homeric virtues were those qualities that protected and furthered the interests of the community as a whole.

Even with slaves excluded, this interpretation of heroic Greece as a communitarian culture with a tradition of shared values is not convincing. What evidence is there that the warrior kings fought their wars and cultivated their virtues primarily for the sake of the community and its households, rather than that the household was viewed largely as the economic and reproductive base for wars fought primarily to bring glory, wealth, and immortal fame to the heroes? If Odysseus's success as a warrior was for the sake of his household and community, why did he spend ten years on the journey home from a nine-year-long war? Was the Trojan War itself really embarked on for the sake of the warriors' households and kinship groups, or was it rather an essentially masculine war of revenge for the honor of a king, who had been slighted by his wife's defection? MacIntyre neither asks nor answers such questions. But other commentators, such as M. I. Finley, A. W. H. Adkins, and Nancy Hartsock, freely acknowledge that the Homeric epics depict a society in which most people were perceived as existing for the sake of the male elite, and in which what are presented as "the virtues" were reserved for these few.

The core problem with MacIntyre's account of Homeric society lies in his accounts of all the societies in which his traditions flourished. It is his failure to ask: "By what ethical standard can its entire social structure be defended?" At one point he comes close to asking this vital question, when he compares the evaluative rules and terms of the *Iliad* to the rules of a game, such as chess. This analogy, he admits, is dangerous as well as illuminating, because games are played for a number of purposes. Surely the implication is that these purposes must themselves be subject to ethical scrutiny, which would seem especially called for when the "game" requires a social structure of hierarchy and domination. Having raised the problem, however, MacIntyre immediately dismisses it:

> There is nothing to be made of the question: for what purpose do the characters in the *Iliad* observe the rules that they observe and honour the precepts which they honour? It is rather the case that it is only within their framework of rules and precepts that they are able to frame purposes at all.

For MacIntyre, this very feature of the heroic ethic makes it vastly preferable to the stance of "some modern moral philosophers" who value "the capacity to detach oneself from any particular standpoint or point of view, to step backwards, as it were, and view and judge that standpoint or point of view from the outside. In heroic society there is no 'outside' except that of the stranger."[37]

It is important to recognize that MacIntyre's cavalier dismissal of the importance of objectivity in ethics is clearly linked to the fact that he assumes that if "we" were members of heroic society, we would be *heroes*. Asking "what relevance can [the heroic virtues] possess for us?" since "nobody now can be a Hector or a Gisli," he gives no thought to the far greater probability, if one were transported back, of being not a hero but, though not a stranger, an outsider to his or her culture's highest virtues—a slave, an ordinary male member of the underclass, or (more probably still) a woman. This is why he can be so dismissive of what he calls the "outside" point of view, which takes into account the viewpoint of those excluded from the dominant group. But it seriously damages his reliance on the Homeric ethic and, as we shall see, on the other traditional ethics on which he depends for his theory of justice. If it is the case, as MacIntyre claims, that "heroic society is still inescapably a part

51

of us all,"[38] then we must confront the fact that its ethic reflected not "shared values" but the dominance of a male warrior elite. Given this, it is especially urgent that we evaluate both the society and its ethic from the points of view of *all* its members.

This is equally the case with classical Greek society. It is particularly important with Aristotle's ethics, central to the tradition that MacIntyre thinks can rescue us from the mires into which, he alleges, contemporary moral philosophy has led. He concludes in *After Virtue* that "the Aristotelian tradition can be restated in a way that restores intelligibility and rationality to our moral and social attitudes and commitments."[39] And in *Whose Justice?* he takes the equally strong stand that "the importance of other subsequent moral and political philosophies will turn on whether they do or do not impugn, vindicate, or correct and supplement Aristotle's answers to Plato's questions."[40] Here again, MacIntyre does not confront the pivotal fact that "the good life" not only excludes but *depends* upon the exclusion of the great majority of people, including all women.

What does MacIntyre find so compelling about the Aristotelian ethic? First, that it rejects the false distinction between fact and value, and equates the good with the realization of man's essential nature. It presupposes "some account of the essence of man as a rational animal and above all some account of the human *telos*." To act in accordance with its virtues enables us "to realise our true nature and to reach our true end. To defy them will be to be frustrated and incomplete, to fail to achieve that good of rational happiness which it is peculiarly ours as a species to pursue." MacIntyre indicts the Enlightenment for, among other things, rejecting any such teleological view of human nature. Second, he values the Aristotelian tradition's functional concept of a man, rooted in particular forms of social life: "according to that tradition to be a man is to fill a set of roles each of which has its own point and purpose: member of a family, citizen, soldier, philosopher, servant of God." Again, it was the Enlightenment's error to reject this concept, instead considering it a form of liberation to conceive of man "as an individual prior to and apart from all roles."[41]

As in his discussion of the heroic ethic, here too MacIntyre de-emphasizes the centrality of sexism and elitism in the tradition whose modern relevance he hopes to establish. And in neither book does MacIntyre confront what he as a modern Aristotelian must confront—the far-ranging *implications* of the inherent sexism and elitism of the Aristotelian ethic.[42] On the one hand, aided by falsely gender-neutral language, he writes much of the time as if when Aristotle used the term *anthropos* ("human being") he really did mean it inclusively.[43] He also says that the scope of justice in the post-Homeric city-state necessarily was "the whole life of the community of a *polis*," and that it and the other virtues were aimed at securing "not merely the goods of this or that form of activity, but also the overall good of the *polis*." "The soundness of a particular practical argument, framed in terms of the goods of excellence," he claims, "is independent of its force for any particular person."[44] The impression left by these phrases, and reinforced by the use of gender-neutral language, is that all were at least eligible to participate in such a life and such a good. How else might the soundness of an argument be "independent of its force for any particular person," regardless of whether that person was man or woman, slave or free, manual worker or leisured man?

But of course this impression is false. And so, some of the time, MacIntyre writes in direct contradiction to it. He acknowledges that the ordering of goods in the *polis* was hierarchical, as when he explains that some goods were "valued only for their own sake" and others "only . . . valued as means to some further good," or when he says that in Aristotle's universe "each level of the hierarchy provides the matter in and through which the forms of the next higher level actualize and perfect themselves."[45] It is, we might add, this hierarchy of things and persons, and the goods they produce, that makes Aristotle describe farmers, craftsmen, and day laborers as "necessary conditions" for but not "integral parts" of the best city-state.[46] In *After Virtue*, MacIntyre briefly mentions the fact that many categories of people were excluded from what Aristotle calls "the good life for man." He writes:

> What is likely to affront us—and rightly—is Aristotle's writing off of non-Greeks, barbarians and slaves, as not merely not possessing political relationships, but as incapable of them. . . . [C]raftsmen and tradesmen constitute an inferior class, even if they are not slaves. Hence the peculiar excellences of the exercise of craft skill and manual labour are invisible from the standpoint of Aristotle's catalogue of the virtues.[47]

He completely omits the fact that, in addition to these groups of men, *all* women were excluded by Aristotle from "the good life." In *Whose Justice?*, noting feminist critique of Aristotle, he does briefly discuss the issue, but his response is totally unsatisfactory, even within the context of his own theory.

MacIntyre points out that Aristotle's meritocratic theory of political justice "unfortunately" depends on his belief that farmers, artisans, merchants, and women cannot exercise the virtues "necessary for participation in the active life of the best kind of *polis*."[48] But he does not explain how a modern Aristotelian might overcome this rather large problem. In fact, although the Aristotelian tradition, as presented by MacIntyre, is supposedly aimed at the human good, only those whose productive, reproductive, and daily service needs are fully taken care of by others, and who are therefore free to engage in the highest goods—political activity and intellectual life—are regarded as fully human. This would seem to be a philosophy in need of some considerable adaptation, if it is to be relevant in the late twentieth century! Sometimes MacIntyre seems to be aware of the seriousness of the problem, as when he says: "It is crucial to the structure of Aristotle's extended argument that the virtues are unavailable to slaves or to barbarians and so therefore is the good for man." But just a few pages later, giving no reasons, he refers to Aristotle's "indefensible defence of slavery" as a part of his theory "whose rejection need not carry any large implications for our attitudes to his overall theory."[49] It is by no means clear why this should be so, especially since Aristotle's conceptions of the human *telos* and the good life present serious problems not only for slaves but for the vast majority of people.

In *Whose Justice?* MacIntyre tries to rectify the "mistake" that Aristotle made in excluding women from citizenship. He does not explain how this exclusion is connected with the claims made in Aristotle's biological writings that women are "a deformity, though one which occurs in the ordinary course of nature," and that their very existence is due only to the need for men to be reproduced sexually, so that their (superior) form can be kept separate from their (inferior) matter.[50] Moreover, his response to the problem of the specifically feminist challenge to Aristotle and the Aristotelian legacy is quite inadequate. Arguing that women *can* be included, "without denying [Aristotle's] central claims about the best kind of *polis*," he suggests that it would require their occupational and social roles to be restructured in a way that was inconceivable to Aristotle, but was "envisaged . . . by Plato."[51]

MacIntyre's appeal to Plato presents several serious problems. First, Plato's radical proposals about women were made only for those in the ruling elite of an ideal society that both he and Aristotle thought was impracticable in the real world. Second, Plato's restructuring of the roles of the guardian women in the *Republic* was intrinsically connected with his abolition of the private family.[52] His guardian men and women are "mated" for eugenic breeding purposes, and are not allowed to be attached to their own children, or even to know who they are. This is why Aristotle, having considered it, explicitly rejected Plato's argument about women.[53] Clearly, given Catholic teachings about marriage and sexuality, MacIntyre the Thomist is even less in a position to adopt Plato's abolition of the family as a solution to Aristotle's "mistake" about women. The third problem is that, both in the chapters concerning Aristotle and throughout the rest of the book, MacIntyre clearly *assumes* the continuance of the nuclear family, thereby totally undermining his appeal to Plato's solution.[54]

The last problem with MacIntyre's solution, which is also a problem with his dismissal of Aristotle's defense of slavery, is that it takes no account of the extent to which Aristotle's entire conception of what constitutes "the good life" *depends on* the exclusion from it of the great majority of people. As MacIntyre makes clear, the "supreme good" for a human being, according to Aristotle, consists in the combination of virtuous moral and political activity with contemplative enquiry.[55] And though his tone is different in the case of the exclusion of manual workers than in the case of women and slaves, Aristotle makes it clear that all those who participate in the performance of those necessary but inferior functions such as domestic management, child rearing, and the production of daily necessities cannot live this life of excellence. The kind of redistribution of tasks that MacIntyre suggests as a solution to the problem of the exclusion of women and laborers is simply not acceptable within an Aristotelian framework. For it would result in a citizenry that, because partly occupied with domestic and other manual work, would not be able (as the free and leisured citizens Aristotle envisages would be) to focus entirely on politics and intellectual activity—his "highest life for a human being." Not only his conception of this highest life but his conception of the type of rationality that is required in order to participate in it depend on the performance of all the other functions of life—its "necessary conditions"—by persons who do *not* share in this rationality nor in the virtues required of citizens.

MacIntyre says that he rejects Aristotle's metaphysical biology. But he does not adequately address the problem that then faces him, as an Aristotelian who rejects the belief that not only the nonhuman natural world but also the vast majority of human beings are naturally intended to be the providers of productive and reproductive services for the few. A modern Aristotelian must confront the issue of how "the good life for man" is to be redefined once it is assumed that the differences established by social hierarchies of dominance and submission are *not* natural, and are ethically indefensible. Once "the good life" is really understood to mean the good *human* life, it must be seen to encompass vast aspects of life that are not considered even a part of the subject matter of an ethics that still rests on sexist and elitist assumptions. It must, in the absence of slaves and largely dehumanized workers, discuss how the products and services necessary for human life can be provided in the context of the good life. Likewise, with women not functionally defined by their biology, the raising of children to the point where, and in a way that, they will be able to lead good lives becomes itself necessarily a part of discussion of the good life.

While MacIntyre does not ignore the family, he lists "the making and sustaining of family life" among practices such as playing games and following intellectual pursuits.[56] But this blurs the difference between essential and elective practices and neglects two important facts. First, if it were not for the childbearing, nurturance, and socialization that have taken place within the family, there would be no people to live the good life. Second, throughout recorded history, the institution and practices of the family have been so structured as to render it virtually impossible for women, who have primarily performed these essential human functions, to participate in what men have defined as "the good life for man." MacIntyre's works ignore children and their rearing. Strikingly, not one of those persons whom he lists as exemplars of the virtues was a participating parent.[57*] Despite his insistence that we think in terms of a complete human life—"a concept of a self whose unity resides in the unity of a narrative which links birth to life to death as narrative beginning to middle to end"[58]—his moral subjects, like those of most ethical theories, are apparently born directly into adulthood. And so, in spite of his usage of "men and women" and "he and she," MacIntyre—like the traditions he celebrates—ignores a great deal of what most women since Homeric times have contributed to the human good: the bearing of children and the raising of them to the point where they have the qualities required of human moral subjects, capable of choosing their own mode of the good life, and living it.[†]

MacIntyre's eventual conclusion in *Whose Justice?* is that Thomas Aquinas's synthesis of Aristotle with Augustinian Christianity offers the best, the most defensible account of justice and practical rationality. Thomism is

---

*MacIntyre names St. Benedict, St. Francis of Assisi, St. Theresa, Frederick Engels, Eleanor Marx, Leon Trotsky, and John Stuart Mill. The only one who was a parent at all, Trotsky, was permanently separated from his wife and two daughters after a very short marriage. It does not seem that MacIntyre considers Harriet Taylor *qua* mother of three children an "exemplar of . . . the virtues"; only in her life with Mill, if at all, does she seem to be included. The only child in *After Virtue* is "a highly intelligent seven-year old" who appears in an example where he or she is enticed by the promise of candy into learning to play chess (p. 175).

†We are reminded of this when he discusses some of the Greek's "goods of excellence," especially courage. He points out that the good of the community required, from time to time, that some put their lives at stake in its defense, and in doing so exhibit courage and gain prestige by doing so (*Whose Justice?*, p. 41). But he does not consider for a moment that without women's putting their lives at stake in giving birth, the community would be no more able to sustain itself than if its men were unwilling to go to war.

presented as a version of Aristotelianism that can be applied outside the context of the Greek city-state.[59] The works of Augustine and Aquinas have had immense influence on the development of the Christian tradition, not least on its attitudes toward women and their subordinate roles in church and society. But throughout his discussions of Augustine and Aquinas, aided again by his use of falsely gender-neutral language, MacIntyre ignores the problems that are raised for a potential twentieth-century adherent to these traditions by what they have to say about the nature of women and about just relations between the sexes. In his praise for Aquinas's capacity to synthesize Aristotle's philosophy with Christian theology, he ignores the fact that on these issues, the synthesis compounds the sexism and the misogyny of both.

Theologians and political theorists have paid considerable attention to Augustine's and Aquinas's dispositions of women in recent years, but MacIntyre ignores their work.[60] Augustine's more complex and nuanced conclusions about women's place are well captured in Genevieve Lloyd's phrase "spiritual equality and natural subordination."[61] Perhaps in part because he regarded his mother as an ideal Christian, in part because of the influence of Plato, and in part because of his emphasis on the more egalitarian version of the creation myth,* Augustine believed that men and women were equal in soul and in their capacity to share in the divine life: "not only men but also women might contemplate the eternal reasons of things."[62] However, he also said that, viewed alone, in her quality as man's "help-meet," woman is not, as man alone is, in the image of God; and he referred allegorically to man as higher reason and to woman as lower reason or sensuality. Because of her bodily difference from man and her association with carnality, passion, and therefore sin, as symbolized by Eve's role in the Fall, Augustine saw woman as properly and naturally subordinated to man. In the City of God, woman and man are equal, but in the City of Man woman is man's subject and properly restricted to the domestic sphere or, even better, to celibacy. That these are not mere archaic myths that can safely be ignored was confirmed in 1988, when Pope John Paul II reaffirmed these limitations on women, justifying them, as did Augustine, by the sin of Eve.[63]

In the works of Thomas Aquinas, in which MacIntyre sees the best account of justice and practical rationality to be found in any tradition, the Christian association of women with sin is synthesized with Aristotle's teleological biology. Aquinas places far more emphasis than Augustine on the City

---

*At Genesis 1:27, the Bible says: "And God created man in His own image, in the image of God He created him; male and female created He them."

of Man—the world of politics and the family. Here his reliance on Aristotle is clear, most centrally in his notions that a woman is "a misbegotten male," intended only for the work of reproduction, defective in her reason, and therefore "naturally subject to man, because in man the discretion of reason predominates."[64] As Arlene Saxonhouse sums up his views:

> In Thomas' thought, the body and the soul are not separated, as they are in Augustine's. . . . Since the rational soul is proportionate to the body, the misbegotten body of the female has a soul that is proportionate to it and, therefore, inferior. Thomas concludes that she must be subordinate to the male for her own interest, since, as Aristotle had taught, the inferior must accept the rule of the superior. Like her children, woman benefits when she performs the role in marriage to which her lower capacities are suited.[65]

Apart from one brief mention of Aquinas's assumption that households were male-headed, MacIntyre simply ignores all this. He continually employs gender-neutral language in his discussions of Augustine and Aquinas, just as in those about Homer and Aristotle. Moreover, he contrasts the inclusiveness of the thought of these Christian thinkers with the limitations and exclusions imposed by his historical context on Aristotle's conceptions of justice and practical rationality.[66]

It is by now obvious that many of "our" traditions, and certainly those evaluated most highly by MacIntyre, are so permeated by the patriarchal power structure within which they evolved as to require nothing less than radical and intensive challenge if they are to meet truly humanist conceptions of the virtues. When MacIntyre begins to try to evaluate the rationality of traditions, he says: "The test for truth in the present, therefore, is always to summon up as many questions and as many objections of the greatest strength possible; what can be justifiably claimed as true is what has sufficiently withstood such dialectical questioning and framing of objections."[67] But he reaches his own conclusions about the superiority of the Thomistic synthesis without even subjecting it to what is one of the most crucial tests of it in his time—the challenge of whether this tradition can include women as full human beings.[68]

MacIntyre says that "the initial answer" to questions about practical rationality and justice (questions about "What ought I to do?"), in the light of the claims of the various traditions, "will depend upon who you are and how you understand yourself." Let us, then, imagine a young woman in the United States today taking up MacIntyre's invitation. Let us see whether she will find among his preferred traditions one in which her life will become intelligible and whether, by engaging in conversation with his traditions, she will be helped to become aware of her "incoherence" and to provide an account of it. Let us imagine, at first, that the woman is young, able-bodied, white, heterosexual, married, and that the income of her household is average. Raised in a fairly traditional family, she has nonetheless, like many of her peers, come to have expectations of leading a life that involves both motherhood and wage work. She is contented with her family and other personal relations, but frustrated by the boredom, dead-endedness, and low pay of her wage work, which she stays with because its hours and demands are compatible with the responsibilities she perceives are hers as a wife and mother. She worries that taking up a more demanding though more interesting occupation might strain her marriage and shortchange her children. How will engaging in conversation with the Aristotelian-Christian traditions that MacIntyre prefers to liberalism help her?

To start with, these traditions have no comprehension of her need to be both family member and wage worker. Engaging in conversation with Aristotle will first tell her that her sex is "a deformity in nature," which exists only for the purpose of procreating the male sex, the original and true form of the human being. Engaging in conversation with MacIntyre on Aristotle's exclusion of women from all but domestic life will raise the possibility of Plato's solution: abolish the family. But this woman loves and cherishes her family life and does not relish the idea of living in communal barracks, mating when and with whom she is told to, and not knowing who her children are. And, even if she did, none of the other traditions that MacIntyre suggests she engage in conversation with would tolerate such an idea for an instant. For one thing, they regard sexual activity outside of lifelong marriage as a serious sin. Turning to Augustine, she may be comforted by his conviction that she is the spiritual equal to man, but his equally firm conviction that her physical sexuality makes her necessarily man's inferior is unlikely to help her provide an account of her "incoherence." It seems more likely to exacerbate it. Turning to Thomism—the tradition MacIntyre finds the best embodiment of rationality because of its ability to accommodate Augustinian insights with Aristotelian theorizing—she will encounter the problems of Aristotle and the problems of Augustinian Christianity compounded. For Aquinas synthesizes the Aristotelian view that women are a deformity in nature with the Christian view that women's sexuality is to blame for men's sinful lust. In this tradition, she will find serious consideration being given to questions such as whether women were included in the original Creation and whether, in order to be resurrected, they must be reborn as men. Aquinas is hardly likely to provide the calm coherence for this woman's life that MacIntyre finds in him. And the woman I have imagined presents the *easiest* female test of these traditions, being among the most advantaged of women. If she were poor, black, lesbian, old, disabled, a single parent, or some combination of these, she would surely be even less likely to find herself and her situation rendered more coherent by turning to MacIntyre's traditions.

MacIntyre says that traditions are also to be tested by whether they help persons to answer the real, difficult moral questions they may have to face. Our hypothetical woman's questions may include whether to have an abortion if she accidentally becomes pregnant just as she is completing many years of dedicated and joyful primary parenting and wants to become involved in a fulfilling job; whether to divorce her husband if he has an affair and neglects his family, even though she knows that she and the children are likely to be economically devastated as well as to be faced with the psychological and social stress of divorce; whether to run for office in order to contribute to the solution of political problems about which she has strong convictions, though she knows her children will have less of her time and attention than they are used to. How will MacIntyre's preferred traditions help her, given that with few exceptions the theories that constitute them are unwilling even to grant her the status of full humanity? She is unlikely to conclude from her attempt to engage in conversation with MacIntyre's traditions that she is incoherent, or to find her thinking about justice and practical rationality enhanced. She may indeed conclude, without looking much further into them, that there is something fundamentally incoherent about the traditions themselves and that she will have to look elsewhere for answers to questions about justice and rationality.

FEMINISM AS A TRADITION

In spite of MacIntyre's persistent use of gender-neutral language, it is clear that most women, as well as men who have any kind of feminist consciousness, will not find in any of his traditions a rational basis for moral and political action. Where, then, do we stand? Are we outside all traditions and therefore, in MacIntyre's view at least, "in a state of moral and intellectual destitution"? Can one be anything *but* an outsider to a tradition that excludes one, and some of the things one values most, from what it regards as the best in human life? Can we find, in the history of feminist thought and action, another tradition, that derives much from the liberal tradition MacIntyre distorts and rejects, and that gives an account of rationality and justice superior to that provided by any other? As we saw, he gives conflicting accounts of what a tradition *is*. At times he describes it as a defining context, stressing the authoritative nature of its "texts;" at times he talks of a tradition as "living," as a "not-yet-completed narrative," as an argument about the goods that constitute the tradition.[69]

Feminism is clearly not a tradition in the former sense. Most feminists do not have authoritative texts. We do not assume that we *must* refer back to any particular canons, as medieval scholastics did when citing Aristotle. Feminist theorists disagree with one another on many counts, arguing with both predecessors and contemporaries on all but the most basic issue—our conviction that women are human beings in no way inferior to men, who warrant equal consideration with men in any political or moral theory.

Feminism *is* clearly a tradition, though, in the second sense, that of being a living argument. From Astell, Wollstonecraft, and de Gouges to Thompson, Mill, and Taylor, from Stanton and Anthony to Gilman and Shaw, from Woolf and de Beauvoir to Firestone, Friedan, Oakley, Mitchell, Chodorow, Pateman, and all the other great feminist thinkers of the last two decades, there has been much disagreement about the causes and the nature of the oppression of women, and the solutions to it. But all have agreed that any tradition that does not address these questions, especially if it *cannot* address them because its most fundamental assumptions about what is "the human good" do not even enable these questions to become visible, can no longer be regarded as just or rational.

Of the traditions MacIntyre discusses, only the liberalism he so decisively rejects contains the possibility of encompassing the answers to feminist questions. This is not to say that, as it stands, the liberal tradition has been free of neglect of and rationalizations for women's oppression—far from it.[70] But, as many feminist theorists recognize, a number of the basic tenets of liberalism—including the replacement of the belief in natural hierarchy by a belief in the fundamental equality of human beings, and the placing of individual freedoms before any unified construction of "the good"—have been basic tenets in the development of feminism, too. Though by no means all contemporary feminists are liberals, virtually all acknowledge the vast debts of feminism to liberalism. They know that without the liberal tradition, feminism would have had a much more difficult time emerging. In chapter 5, I shall discuss the arguments of the most influential contemporary liberal theorist of justice, John Rawls, in terms of both their limitations from a feminist point of view and their potential for feminist critique. But now, I turn to Michael Walzer who, like MacIntyre, finds the path to justice in interpretation.

Which Understandings?

In Walzer's recent works, he has argued that principles of justice should be based on the "shared understandings" of each culture.[71] He does not arrive at reactionary conclusions, such as those implied by MacIntyre's adherence to traditions. This is because he both seeks the answers to contemporary questions about justice not in past traditions but in currently shared understandings, and believes that the shared understandings of *our* culture are fundamentally egalitarian ones. This, however, should not blind us to the very real similarities in their methods of thinking about justice. As I shall show in chapter 6, Walzer's *other* criterion for justice—the "separate spheres" criterion, which requires that different social goods be distributed in different ways and independently of each other—is opposed to pervasive inequality and dominance. It has the potential to be a valuable tool for feminist criticism. As I shall argue here, however, the radical potential of the theory is blunted by its reliance on "shared understandings."

Like MacIntyre, Walzer is critical of philosophers who "leave the city . . . [to] fashion . . . an objective and universal standpoint."[72] He too rejects ways of thinking about justice that are not tied to a particular culture, that do not issue from the shared understandings or agreements of actual historical human beings with full knowledge of who they are and where they are situated in society. He argues, instead, for principles of justice in a way that is "radically particularist."[73] Beyond basic rights to life and liberty, he argues, men's and women's rights "do not follow from our common humanity; they follow from shared conceptions of social goods; they are local and particular in character." "Justice" he says, "is relative to social meanings. . . . A given society is just if its substantive life is lived . . . in a way faithful to the shared understandings of the members." And since "social meanings are historical in character," just and unjust distributions change over time.[74] If conclusions

62

about justice are to have "force," Walzer claims, they must not be principles chosen in some hypothetical situation, in which we are deprived of knowledge of our individual characteristics and social situation. They must be arrived at in answer to the question: "What would individuals like us choose, who are situated as we are, who share a culture and are determined to go on sharing it? And this is a question that is readily transformed into, What choices have we already made in the course of our common life? What understandings do we (really) share?"[75]

The difficult issue is whether and how such a relativist criterion for the justice of social arrangements and distributions can have the critical potential Walzer claims for it. *Can* it apply, except where the basic equality of human beings is already assumed? At times, Walzer seems to doubt that it can. He says that if "a just or an egalitarian society . . . isn't already here—hidden, as it were, in our concepts and categories—we will never know it concretely or realize it in fact." The problems of Walzer's relativism are illuminated most clearly by what he says about justice in fundamentally hierarchical systems, such as feudal and caste societies. Such systems are, he says, "constituted by an extraordinary integration of meanings. Prestige, wealth, knowledge, office, occupation, food, clothing, even the social good of conversation: all are subject to the intellectual as well as to the physical discipline of hierarchy." The hierarchy in such systems is determined by a single value—in the case of the caste system, ritual purity, itself dominated by birth and blood—which dominates the distribution of all other social goods, so that "social meanings overlap and cohere," losing their autonomy. In such societies, Walzer acknowledges, where social meanings are integrated and hierarchical, "justice will come to the aid of inequality." Nevertheless, as he must, in light of his shared-understandings or social-meanings criterion for justice, he asserts unambiguously that such societies can meet "(internal) standards of justice."[76] By this criterion, indeed, there are no grounds for concluding that caste societies are any less just than societies that do not discriminate on the basis of inborn status or characteristics.

As Walzer acknowledges, he needs to defend his argument that moral philosophy is best approached through the interpretation of shared meanings against "the charge that it binds us irrevocably to the status quo—since we can only interpret what already exists—and so undercuts the very possibility of social criticism." "Don't the conditions of collective life," he asks, "—immediacy, closeness, emotional attachment, parochial vision—militate against a critical self-understanding?" Doesn't criticism require critical *distance?*[77] In response, he relies on two connected counterarguments. First, he thinks of ideologies, in general, as competing and pluralistic. Groups with different ideologies will win out in turn: "There is no final victory, nor should there be." He adds: "Perhaps the ideology that justifies the seizure [of social goods] is widely believed to be true. But resentment and resistance are (almost) as pervasive as belief. There are always some people, and after a time there are a great many, who think the seizure is not justice but usurpation."[78] Thus the possibility of social change in general rests on the flourishing of dissent. Walzer's second, related line of defense is that "every ruling class is compelled to present itself as a universal class." First comes the work of the affirmers of the dominant culture: "priests and prophets; teachers and sages; storytellers, poets, historians, and writers generally."[79] But as soon as they do their work, the possibility of criticism exists, since they must represent the interests of the ruling group as the common interest of all. Thus their ideas must be presented as universal in form. Since this will set up standards that the rulers will not live up to, given their particular interests, the door is open to social criticism. The best social criticism, Walzer argues, will emerge from this built-in contradiction. It can be found, for example, in the writings and activism of the Italian communist leader Ignazio Silone, who became a revolutionary by "taking seriously the principles taught . . . by [his] own educators and teachers" and using them as a standard to test society, revealing the radical contradiction between its principles and its social practices and institutions.[80]

The weaknesses of both these lines of defense of a theory of justice built on the interpretation of shared meanings are readily exposed when we raise the issue of the justice or injustice of gender. The problem with the first counterargument—the reliance on dissent—is that the closer a social system is to a caste system, in which social meanings overlap, cohere, and are integrated and hierarchical, the less likely it will be that dissenting ideas appear or develop. The more thoroughgoing the dominance, and the more pervasive its ideology across the various spheres, the less chance there is that the whole prevailing system will be questioned or resisted. By arguing that such a system meets "(internal) standards of justice" if it is really accepted by its members, Walzer admits the paradox that the more likely a system is to be able to enshrine the ideology of the ruling group and hence to meet his "shared understandings" criterion for justice, the more *unjust* it will be by his other criterion, since dominance will be all-pervasive within it. The danger of his conception of justice, similar in this respect to the traditionalist conception of

MacIntyre, is that what is just depends heavily upon what people are persuaded of.[81] It cannot cope with a situation of pervasive domination. Even if the social meanings in a fundamentally hierarchical society *were* shared, we should surely be wary of concluding, as Walzer clearly does, that the hierarchy is rendered just by that agreement or lack of dissent.[82]

When Walzer writes of caste societies, with their undifferentiated social meanings, he does so as if they were distant from anything that characterizes our culture. It is only on this assumption that he is able to perceive his two criteria for a just society as being not seriously in conflict in the contemporary context. But when we read his description of caste society, in which an inborn characteristic determines dominant or subordinate status in relation to social goods over a whole range of spheres, we can see that it bears strong resemblances to the gender system that our society still perpetuates to a large extent through the force of its economic and domestic structures and customs and the ideology inherited from its highly patriarchal past. There seem, in fact, to be only two significant differences between the hierarchies of caste and of gender: one is that women have not, of course, been physically segregated from men; the other is that whereas, according to Walzer, "political power seems always to have escaped the laws of caste,"[83] it has rarely escaped the laws of gender.

Like the caste hierarchy, the gender hierarchy is determined by a single value, with male sexuality taking the place of ritual purity. And, also like the caste hierarchy, that of gender ascribes roles, responsibilities, rights, and other social goods in accordance with an inborn characteristic that is imbued by society with tremendous significance. All the social goods listed in Walzer's description of a caste society have been, and many still are, differentially distributed between the sexes. In the cases of prestige, wealth, access to knowledge, office, and occupation, the disparities are fairly obvious. Better and greater amounts of food are often reserved for men in poorer classes and in some ethnic groups; women's clothing has been and still is designed either to constrain their movements or to appeal to men rather than for their own comfort and convenience; and women have been excluded from men's conversation in numerous social contexts, both formal and informal.[84] Although in some cases the disparities between the sexes in terms of social goods have begun to decline in recent years, in other important respects they have increased. In chapter 7, we shall examine the extent to which they persist in the United States today.

As in caste societies, so too in patriarchy has ideology played a crucial part in perpetuating the legitimacy of hierarchy. Though Walzer says in the context of discussing caste societies that "we should not assume that men and women are ever entirely content with radical inequality,"[85] ideology helps us to comprehend the extent to which they often have been and are content. It is not difficult to see how this has operated in the case of gender. When the family is founded in law and custom on allegedly natural male dominance and female dependence and subordination, when religions inculcate the same hierarchy and enhance it with the mystical and sacred symbol of a male god, and when the educational system both excludes women from its higher ranks and establishes as truth and reason the same intellectual bulwarks of patriarchy, the opportunity for competing visions of sexual difference or questioning of gender is seriously limited. In fact, as feminist scholars have recently revealed, the ideology that is embodied in "malestream thought" is undoubtedly one of the most all-encompassing and pervasive ideologies in history.[86]

By now it should be clear that Walzer's second argument against those who question the critical force of his theory is also unsatisfactory. The affirmers of "our" culture, the priests and prophets, teachers and sages, and so on, have been almost uniformly male, and the culture and values they have affirmed have in a multitude of ways reflected the standpoint of men in gendered society. Like MacIntyre and the bearers of his traditions, they have defined a "human good" that not only excludes women but depends upon this exclusion. Thus it is by no means always the case that the ruling ideas are universal in form, so that, if taken literally, they have radical implications. Certainly, most of them were never intended to apply to women, any more than they were meant to apply to animals or plants. *Man* and *mankind*, those ostensibly generic words, have turned out to be far from generic when it comes to claiming rights and privileges.* Frequently, still, false gender neutrality serves the same purpose of disguising the exclusion of women, and even radical social critics have usually failed to question the hierarchy of gender.

Finally, social critics, to be effective, have to be articulate, and to be heard. But those to whom caste, class, race, or gender structures deny education are

---

*One clear example of this has been raised by the issue of abortion. The rights basic to our political culture have been understood to include both the right to life and the right to control one's own body. Because liberal rights were framed as the rights of men, only relatively recently has the problem that arises when one (potential) person's life is inside another person's body been confronted head-on. There is bitter opposition between those who assert that women, like men, have the right to control their own bodies and those who assert that, from the moment of conception, fetuses, like human beings, have the right to life. We have no currently "shared understandings" on abortion, partly because *both* basic liberal rights cannot be universalized to fetuses as well as to women.

far less likely to acquire the tools needed to express themselves in ways that would be publicly recognized were they to interpret shared meanings literally and turn them into social criticism.* Even those who have the tools are likely to be made objects of derision when they make the case that those whom the dominant culture relegates to an inferior role should be treated as equal. This was certainly the case with most of those throughout history who dared suggest that accepted principles about rights and equality be extended to women. Abigail Adams, Mary Wollstonecraft, and John Stuart Mill, to name a few examples, were all ridiculed for such suggestions.

Contrary to Walzer's theory of shared understandings, in fact, oppressors and oppressed—when the voice of the latter can be heard at all—often disagree fundamentally. Oppressors often claim that they, aristocrats or Brahmins or men, are fully human in ways that serfs or untouchables or women are not, and that while the rulers institutionalize equal justice among themselves, it is both just and in the common interest for them to require the other categories of people to perform functions supportive of the fully human existence of those capable of it. But what if the serfs or untouchables or women somehow do become convinced (against all the odds) that they too are fully human and that whatever principles of justice apply among their oppressors should rightfully be applied to them too? With disagreements this basic, rather than a meaningful debate being joined, there would seem to be two irreconcilable accounts of what is just. There would be no shared meanings on the most fundamental of questions.

Contemporary views about gender are a clear example of such disagreement; it is clear that there are *no shared understandings* on this subject in our society, even among women. The problem is rendered even more complex if there are fundamental disagreements not only between the oppressors and the oppressed but even within the ranks of the oppressed. As studies of feminism and antifeminism have shown, women are deeply divided on the subject of gender and sex roles, with antifeminist women not rejecting them as unjust but rather regarding the continued economic dependence of women and the dominance of the world outside the home by men as natural and inevitable,

---

*It is worth noting that of the eleven social critics whom Walzer discusses in *The Company of Critics*, the great majority were born in the middle to upper ranks of their societies, almost all were well educated, and ten were male. The only woman among them, Simone de Beauvoir, was, as Walzer points out, able to be an insightful and effective critic of the situation of women partly because she herself to a large extent avoided it. This same fact, however, not only made her unable to value women's lives or characteristics or to criticize the world of men, but also rendered her ineffective in finding any solution to women's oppression except for those who, like her, could "escape" into the world of men (*The Company of Critics*, chap. 9, esp. pp. 155, 158–62). She suggests no way for women in general to fulfill themselves in what she regards as truly human ways.

given women's special reproductive functions.[87] Feminists tend to attribute such attitudes at least in part to the influence of patriarchal ideology; clearly, religion is an important factor. Such an antifeminist posture becomes increasingly difficult to maintain once feminist reforms are instituted. For then, female proponents of it are faced with the problem of how to reverse political change while maintaining what they believe to be their proper, politically powerless role. Even among feminists, there has grown a rift between those who see the gender system itself as the problem and look forward to an androgynous society, and those who, celebrating women's unique nature and traditional roles, consider the problem to be not the *existence* of these roles but the *devaluation* of women's qualities and activities by a male-dominated culture.[88] Gynocentric feminism faces a similar problem to that faced by antifeminism: How *can* women's work, concerns, and perspectives come to be properly valued, unless women seek and attain power in the predominant, male realm?

These opposite poles of opinion about the very nature of sexual difference and its appropriate social repercussions seem to provide no shared intellectual structure in which to debate questions of distributions—if such debate can take place, as Walzer says it must, among "ordinary people, with a firm sense of their own identity."[89] Divisions between conservative and radical standpoints on such issues may be so deep that they provide little foundation from which the different parties, situated as they *actually* are, can come to any conclusions about what is just. Walzer's theory of justice provides no criterion for adjudicating between such widely disparate viewpoints, aside from an implausible appeal to some deeper, latent understandings that all supposedly hold, beneath their disagreements.

Unlike Walzer's shared meanings criterion, his "separate spheres" criterion for justice *can* successfully oppose pervasive inequality and domination, and has potential for feminist criticism. It leads Walzer to challenge, at least briefly, the entire social system of gender. Thus the paradox of his theory of justice is strikingly exemplified by the theory's feminist implications. Insofar as the reduction of male dominance requires a thoroughgoing feminism that undermines the very roots of our gendered institutions, it is in considerable tension with the relativist requirement that a just society be one that abides by its shared understandings. And insofar as the latter criterion is applied, the feminist implications of the theory lose their force, on account of deeply rooted attitudes about sex difference that have been inherited from our past and continue to pervade many aspects of our culture.

Traditions, Shared Understandings, and the Problem of Domination

We have seen that the traditions, like the "shared meanings" of communities and cultures, have been based far more on some points of view than on others. The free, the educated, the wealthy, and men, as the preceding discussion makes clear, are much more likely to shape them than are the unfree, the uneducated, the poor, and women. Contemporary theorists who appeal to tradition are no different from their predecessors in their inability to deal with this problem. But whereas those in the past, such as Edmund Burke, reveled in the hierarchy and subordination of traditions, their contemporary heirs tend to disguise it. Thus Edward Shils, for example, in summing up his argument for "tradition as an intrinsic value," says:

> The fact that certain beliefs, institutions, and practices existed indicates that *they served those who lived in accordance with them.* . . . They did not arrive arbitrarily at their beliefs; the institutions in which they lived were *not forced upon them from the outside.* These institutions had to make sense to them, if they took them seriously. These traditions were not so crippling that human beings could not live under them. Nor did they prevent the human race from accomplishing great things. Rather the opposite! . . . They should be dealt with more respectfully, perhaps even reverently [emphasis added].[90]

As we have seen, this view of traditions "serv[ing] those who lived in accordance with them" pervades MacIntyre's recent work. Only occasionally does he confront the fact that it is a mythical view, and he never responds satisfactorily to it. Given the class and gender structure of the societies in which the traditions he finds most rational and just developed, it would seem that we have absolutely no way of knowing whether the values celebrated by their warrior or leisured male elites were shared by any of the underclasses whom they successfully repressed. Even if the latter had any way of doing so, are they likely to have dared voice any dissent from the precepts held by those on whom they depended for their livelihoods and sometimes their lives? Even if they had dared, how likely is it that they could have formulated alternative views in such monolithically hierarchical societies?

In a couple of passages in *Whose Justice?* MacIntyre's blinders against the problem of domination seem to be lifted, but he fails to perceive the significance of these passages for his entire argument about traditions. In the context of discussing Aristotle's exclusion of women from the good life, he suggests that the "error" may have arisen from "a kind of fallacious reasoning

69

typical of ideologies of irrational domination"—that of justifying unjustified domination by appealing to characteristics in the dominated that are in fact the result of their subordinate status.[91] However, he does not take this point sufficiently seriously to realize that it undermines a great deal of what is argued or assumed in the traditions he defends, all of which are, as he from time to time admits, based on the notion of a hierarchical social order, usually justified as "natural."

In one other period, and with regard to another major issue, MacIntyre is clearly able to see through the claims of theoretical standards that operated in defense of the interests of a particular social group—the propertied classes of eighteenth-century England.[92] He argues strongly, citing the work of historian Roy Porter, that lacking the means to rule over the propertyless by force, they had to gain their consent by "bluster and swank. . . . The fraternizing game, however nauseating, however phony, had to be played."[93] Here, MacIntyre has no trouble acknowledging that "the dominant standards" of the social order were such that

> some individuals will find themselves omitted from the reciprocity of benefit, some who participate will be cheated, and the less power that individuals or groups have to supply satisfaction or to inflict pain, the less the consideration which need be given to pleasing them. Thus sanctions will be required to curb the rebellious and the deviant. And in eighteenth-century England the rules of justice provided just such sanctions.[94]*

Any reciprocity is clearly illusory. All that counts is one's ownership or nonownership of property: "to be propertyless is to be eligible only to be a victim of the system, whether a victim of its oppression or of its charity."[95] Moreover, he adds, there cannot be any appeal to a standard expressed in principles whose truth would be independent of the attitudes and judgments of the participants in the order. Such an appeal would be seen as intellectually confusing, and those who made it would be marked as "deviants, outsiders whose motivations are not in harmony with and are at least potentially disruptive of the established order of exchanges."[96] What MacIntyre is not able or willing to see, as he exposes this example of theory as ideology, is that the same problem applies to all the traditions on which he relies for "our" conceptions of

---

*Cf. *Whose Justice?*, p. 390, where MacIntyre accuses some sociologists of knowledge of the error of giving "accounts of philosophical thought and enquiry which make these dependent upon, or even nothing but, masks worn by antecedently definable social, political, or economic interests of particular groups." Since he clearly believes that philosophies sometimes *do* constitute such masks, how are we to tell when they do and when they do not? MacIntyre does not provide an answer.

justice and practical rationality, and that women, and other oppressed groups, have been their victims.

MacIntyre is likewise unable or unwilling to see that the major theorists of contemporary liberalism, for whom he has such disdain, have confronted, as he has not, the problem of domination that resides in any tradition-based theory of justice. He concludes that there is no "neutral conception of rationality," which those who disagree radically about justice will be able to use to decide who is in the right. But contemporary liberal theories of justice have come up with far better accounts of the reasoning that must underlie a theory of justice than anything MacIntyre has presented us with. Though they pursue different methods of argument they, unlike him, insist that principles of justice must be acceptable to every member of the society to which they are to apply. MacIntyre entirely distorts contemporary liberalism when he says: "the preferences of some are accorded weight by others only insofar as the satisfaction of those preferences will lead to the satisfaction of their own preferences. Only those who have something to give get. The disadvantaged in a liberal society are those without the means to bargain." One is first struck, on reading this, with the internal inconsistency of MacIntyre's attack on modern liberalism. For earlier in *Whose Justice?* he had attacked liberal theorists of justice for insisting that we divest ourselves of our allegiances, our particularities of social relationships, our responsibilities, and our interests, in order to evaluate rationally contending accounts of justice.[97] As he seemed to realize there, Rawls's original position is designed just to *avoid* ceding bargaining power to the advantaged, which MacIntyre later accuses liberal institutions and relationships of doing. The irony is that it is in such accounts of practical reason and justice as Aristotle's and Aquinas's that there is *no* attempt to avoid the disempowerment of the oppressed, in spite of all their talk about "the good life for a human being." And that is why the traditions have been so easily able to justify the unjust treatment of such groups as slaves, the propertyless, and women.

Near the end of *After Virtue*, MacIntyre states:

> To ask "What is the good for me?" is to ask how best I might live out [the] unity [of my life] and bring it to completion. To ask "What is the good for man?" is to ask what *all answers* to the former question must have in common. . . . It is the systematic asking of these two questions and the attempt to answer them in deed as well as in word which provide the moral life with its unity [emphasis added].[98]

The problem with this account of his theory of the good is that it fraudulently eradicates the problem of dominance that pervades his tradition-constituted theory of justice. For certainly neither the Homeric nor the Aristotelian tradition, nor the other traditions he recounts in *Whose Justice?* were concerned with *all* the answers to the question "What is the good for me?" In his tradition-based theories, the disadvantaged are neither encouraged to ask the question nor listened to if they answer it. The facile wording of the passage just quoted obscures the important fact that "What is the good for me?" may have a very different answer when it is considered alone than when it is considered along with everyone else's answers to the same question.[99] As we have seen, in *Whose Justice?* MacIntyre is more straightforward about the subjectivist standpoint for his moral theorizing. It is "Who am I and how do I understand myself?" that constitutes that standpoint for each of us. The second question—What is the good for all?—seems to have fallen by the wayside on the road to Thomism.

By contrast, as we shall see in chapter 5, the great brilliance of Rawls's original position as a stance from which basic principles of justice are to be determined is that it forces the moral subject into thinking, "What is the good for each and every one of the human beings whose society will be governed by these principles?" It shows us that not knowing whether one will be talented or untalented, born into a loving family or abandoned at birth, black or white, advantaged or disadvantaged, male or female, deeply religious or an atheist, can hardly fail to make a difference to one's thinking about how society is to be justly and reasonably organized. Both MacIntyre and Walzer object that Rawls's theory lacks force because we are never *in* the original position. But their alternative, contextually based theories, building on the prevailing ideologies of male elites, lack moral force because their neglect of domination leaves the rest of us deprived of a voice in the construction of morality.

The traditions of "our" patriarchal past have been of major significance in the perpetuation of the gendered social structures and practices that have resulted in continuing and serious injustices to women. Theories of justice that depend on traditions or on shared meanings—even if their intent is to be critical—cannot deal adequately with the problem of domination. The analysis of MacIntyre's turning for valid notions of justice and rationality to "our" traditions, especially to some of the most misogynist and elitist among them, indicates that reliance on traditions simply cannot be sustained in the face of feminist challenges. Walzer's "shared meanings" method of social criticism, too, has been shown to prejudice the conclusions toward maintaining the power of those who historically have been dominant, and therefore to result in either incoherence or less than radical principles on subjects of central importance such as gender. As I shall argue in chapter 6, Walzer's other method of thinking about justice is far more conducive to challenging the injustices of gender. Meanwhile, in the next chapter, I turn from traditionalism to a contrasting strand in contemporary thought, though one that is equally opposed to conventional liberalism—laissez-faire individualism, or libertarianism—and ask: Can it include women? And can it address gender?

4

Libertarianism: Matriarchy, Slavery, and Dystopia

Libertarianism takes to extremes some of the basic tenets of classic liberal theorists such as John Locke and Benjamin Constant. Libertarians claim that, in the interests of individual liberty, the activities of government must be minimized. (A few anarchist libertarians, indeed, consider that there is no justification for any government at all.) The rights of the individual to conduct his own life and to retain the fruits of his labor are sacrosanct. Government's purpose is merely to protect individuals from one another and against the invasion of foreigners; it must not invade the assets, the homes, or the ways of life of its citizens except insofar as is necessary for this purpose. Libertarians are not conservatives, except in the fiscal sense. Since what they advocate as the best political system—a minimal state—has never been put into effect, they can hardly be understood to be arguing that it should be conserved. In recent times, however, libertarians, sometimes to their chagrin, have found themselves identified with the conservative right, with whom they are at odds on at least as many issues as they are in agreement. This inconsistent combination of political beliefs—laissez-faire minimal statism and the conservatism of the so-called Moral Majority that advocates government enforcement of morality—has of course enjoyed a considerable ascendancy during the Reagan years.

I do not attempt to engage here in a thorough critique of libertarianism from all points of view. Instead I ask, What becomes of libertarian arguments when we apply them to all the adult members of society, women as well as men? Focusing mainly on the work of the most influential of contemporary academic libertarians, Robert Nozick, I conclude that his theory is reduced to absurdity when women are taken into account. Instead of the minimal state that he argues for in *Anarchy, State and Utopia*,[1] what results is a bizarre combination of matriarchy and slavery that all would probably agree is better described as *dystopia*. I then briefly examine the question of whether a libertarianism less exclusively based on private property rights than Nozick's might include women, concluding that such a theory too is likely to run into self-contradiction. As I shall show, libertarianism in any form tacitly assumes, beyond the reach of its principles, a realm of private life in which the reproductive and nurturant needs of human beings are taken care of. It also assumes that work performed in this realm is not work in the same sense, or deserving of the same rewards, as that done outside this sphere. Behind the individualist facade of libertarianism, the family is assumed but ignored.

The rebirth of feminism has raised fundamental and sometimes difficult issues concerning the basic rights of individuals. Arguments for women's rights to control their own bodies have raised the dilemma, previously obscured or ignored by both liberal and libertarian theories of rights, that results from the fact that the potential lives of some are radically dependent upon (because contained within) the bodies of others.[2] Abortion is not the only moral issue raised by this fact. It is also relevant to the claim of paternity rights concerning fetuses (including those of so-called surrogate mothers), the right of a pregnant woman to take drugs, and the issue of whether a dying woman who is pregnant should be subjected to a Caesarean section against her will. All of these and other related issues have reached the courts in recent years.[3] In addition, reformers' arguments about just allocations of property and income after divorce have raised the fundamental question of what is and what is not to be regarded as productive labor, deserving of monetary reward. And the struggle over comparable worth has raised the added complexity of how different types of productivity, commonly divided along sex lines, *within* the realm of wage work are to be measured against one another so that they can be justly compensated. Libertarian theorists have not been accustomed to addressing such questions. Like almost all political theorists, whether explicitly

75

or implicitly, they have assumed as their subject matter the male heads of families. But what happens when we question this assumption?

In his influential *Anarchy, State and Utopia*, Nozick argues that even the least interventionist of modern states have far overreached their legitimate powers. When we recognize the just entitlements of individuals, he claims, we can legitimize only a minimal state, whose functions are narrowly confined to the protection of persons and their property and the enforcement of contracts. Redistributive states, and the theories that claim to justify their interference in the lives of their citizens, are fundamentally misguided. They ignore the fact that the things distributed are products of human labor, not manna from heaven; and they do not recognize that individuals' particular talents and abilities are fundamental parts of themselves, the fruits of which cannot be appropriated without violation of their essential rights.

Nozick writes, as is typical of most contemporary theorists of justice, without regard to the fact that human beings are of two sexes. He moves back and forth between the supposedly generic use of *he* and *man* to the use of gender-neutral terms such as *individuals* and *persons*. As is often the case, this combination of usages seems harmless on the face of it, but is not. In fact, it obscures the total neglect of women and their sex-specific productive capacities.* As I shall argue here, when one considers the fact that women, and only women, have the natural capacity to produce *people*, it becomes apparent that Nozick's entitlement theory of justice—based as it is on the notion that one owns what one produces—leads to absurd and inconsistent conclusions.† Such conclusions can be avoided only by abandoning the most basic tenets of Nozick's libertarianism, that is, only by taking account of human needs and other human qualities in addition to the capacity to produce. But to do this would lead to a very different theory of rights, and to very different conclusions about the legitimate state, than those Nozick arrives at.

---

*In discussing Nozick's ideas in this chapter, I will use his style of language. *Not* to do so would be committing an act of false gender neutrality, on my part.

†The argument that follows focuses on the drastic consequences for Nozick's theory of justice of taking women's reproductive labor into account. By following this line of argument, I do not mean to discount in any way the many other good reasons there are to reject Nozick's reasoning and conclusions. Some of the best arguments against his entitlement theory of justice are to be found in parts 3 and 4 of Jeffrey Paul, ed., *Reading Nozick* (Totowa, N.J.: Rowman and Littlefield, 1981), esp. those by Samuel Scheffler, Thomas Nagel, and Onora O'Neill. See also "Nozick's Entitlement Theory of Justice," in *Social Choice and Justice*, vol. 1 of *Collected Papers of Kenneth J. Arrow* (Cambridge: Belknap Press of Harvard University Press, 1983).

Libertarianism

The Entitlement Theory of Justice

As Nozick acknowledges, the validity of his entitlement theory of just hold-ings is of critical importance to his argument that only a minimal state can be legitimate. "If the set of holdings is properly generated," he says, "there is no argument for a more extensive state based upon distributive justice."[4] Nozick claims that individuals' entitlements to things they own take precedence over any other rights, even the right to basic subsistence. He says, "At most, a right to life would be a right to have or strive for whatever one needs to live, pro-vided that having it does not violate anyone else's [entitlement] rights. . . . [O]ne *first* needs a theory of property rights before one can apply any sup-posed right to life."[5] Thus the major conclusions of *Anarchy, State and Utopia*—that only the minimal state is justified, that taxation of people's earnings is "on a par with forced labor,"[6] and that the welfare rights that many liberals have argued for are completely baseless—are built on Nozick's theory of just entitlements to property.

How, then, does one become entitled to anything? According to Nozick, a distribution (or "holding," as he prefers to call it) is properly generated if it is the result of the legitimate transfer of legitimately acquired holdings. Since things must be justly acquired before they can be justly transferred, at the heart of the entitlement theory is the principle of acquisition, by which previ-ously unowned things come to be held. Given the central place of this princi-ple in his theory, it is surprising that, while citing its "complicated truth," Nozick declines either to formulate it clearly or to argue for it.[7] Apart from several bald statements of the principle, all that he provides directly on the subject of just acquisition is a few pages of exposition and questioning of Locke's arguments about it. Throughout the book, in fact, Nozick's refer-ences to Locke are reminiscent of the medieval scholastics' references to Aristotle: rather than serving as a useful starting point, Locke is presented as the authority to whom we are expected to defer on the subject of property. Apart from this, we are left to glean what we can about the principle of acqui-sition from Nozick's *use* of it in his attack on redistributive theories of justice, such as those of John Rawls and Bernard Williams.[8]

Against such theories, Nozick contends that the justice of any distribution must be historical. It is only the legitimacy of the process that counts, not the resulting facts; it all "depends upon how the distribution came about."[9] He objects to "end-result" theories of justice in part because they ignore the fact that the things whose distribution is at issue are not objects that come from nowhere, to be assigned by some central agency to individuals who come forward to receive them. In his entitlement view, by contrast, production and distribution are intrinsically connected. The crux of his principle of acquisition is as follows:

> Whoever makes something, having bought or contracted for all other held resources used in the process (transferring some of his holdings for these cooperating factors), is entitled to it. The situation is *not* one of something's getting made, and there being an open question of who is to get it. Things come into the world already attached to people having entitlements over them.[10]*

Nozick never directly provides arguments for this principle. Indeed, in discussing Locke's very similar view, he raises, and by no means fully answers, a number of problems that arise in relation to central aspects of it.[11] Nevertheless, he vehemently defends the principle against what he refers to as "patterned" theories of just holdings, which specify that "a distribution is to vary along with some natural dimension . . . or dimensions," such as moral merit or usefulness to society.[12] He clearly rejects Rawls's argument that, since personal advantages such as talents and abilities are "arbitrary from a moral point of view," the distribution that results from the free employment of such abilities has no claim to be just. "Why shouldn't holdings partially depend upon natural endowments?" Nozick asks, and he proceeds to reject a number of arguments for the position that differences arising from the exercise of such individual attributes should be minimized.[13] He claims that to regard natural talents as common or collective assets, as Rawls does, is to draw such a clear distinction "between men and their talents, assets, abilities, and special traits" that it is "an open question . . . [w]hether any coherent conception of a person remains."[14] To so collectivize personal assets, Nozick alleges, is to fail to recognize the distinction among persons, in much the same way that Rawls had himself found objectionable in utilitarianism. By contrast, Nozick regards differences in abilities as justifying different entitlements to the resulting products. His position is well summarized in the following statement:

> It is not true . . . that a person earns Y . . . only if he's earned (or otherwise *deserves*) whatever he used (including natural assets) in the process of earning Y. Some of the things he uses he may just *have*, not illegitimately. It needn't be that the foundations underlying desert are themselves deserved, *all the way down.*

---

*The qualifier in parentheses turns out to be superfluous, since Nozick makes it clear elsewhere that persons are as much entitled to things *given* to them by their rightful owners as to things they buy, barter, or produce. See, for example, pp. 167–68.

On this basis he concludes that "whether or not people's natural assets are arbitrary from a moral point of view, they are entitled to them, and to what flows from them."[15]

Based on these conclusions, Nozick condemns states that redistribute resources through taxation, whether to ensure the basic welfare of those unable to provide it for themselves or to promote equality of opportunity. Such states violate their citizens' just entitlements to their holdings. Goals such as ensuring basic welfare or increasing equality of opportunity can be legitimately pursued *only* by means of attempts to persuade the well-off to aid voluntarily their less well endowed or less fortunate fellow citizens. But what if, within such a system, restricted to voluntary exchange and charitable giving, some persons are left operating under such constraints as to render their choices nonvoluntary? He confronts this potential criticism by asserting: "A person's choice among differing degrees of unpalatable alternatives is not rendered nonvoluntary by the fact that others voluntarily chose and acted within their rights in a way that did not provide him with a more palatable alternative."[16] Such a person's situation, according to Nozick, is unfortunate, but not unjust.

Reproduction and the Entitlement Theory

Nozick's entitlement theory is clearly predicated on the belief, though he never *argues* for it, that each person owns himself. Without this initial assumption, his Lockean theory of acquisition would make no sense. He states that people have the right to control their own bodies, and he cites as a paradigm case of entitlement people's rights to the parts of their own bodies.[17] Objecting to redistributive principles, which he regards as justifying forced labor, he says that they "involve a shift from the classical liberals' notion of self-ownership to a notion of (partial) property rights in *other* people."[18]

The assumption that each person owns himself, however, can work only so long as one neglects two facts. First, persons are not only producers but also the *products* of human labor and human capacities. Anyone who subscribes to Nozick's principle of acquisition must explain how and why it is that persons come to own themselves, rather than being owned, as other things are, by whoever made them. Second, the natural ability to produce people is extremely unequally distributed among human beings. Only women have the natural ability to make people, and all human beings are necessarily, at birth (at least at the present stage of technological development), the products of specifically female capacities and female labor.* When this one simple fact of human life is taken seriously, I will argue, it renders Nozick's entire theory contradictory to the point of absurdity at its pivotal point—the principle of just acquisition. Instead of a utopian minimal state, Nozick's individuals are left in a condition of matriarchy, slavery, and dystopia.

In a strange and highly inconclusive passage near the end of the book, Nozick briefly addresses the fact that persons are products of human labor as well as being producers. He asks whether a Lockean theory of acquisition implies that "parents" own their children, since they make them.[19] (This passage is a prime example of what can be achieved by the practice, used by both Locke and Nozick, of generally using the allegedly generic masculine form of language but having the option of resorting to neutral terms for specific purposes. Locke and Nozick conveniently depart from their more typical male terminology in saying that "parents" make their children. If they said, more consistently with their customary usage, that fathers make their children, the falseness of the claim would be too obvious to be overlooked.) Nozick points out that, although Locke's labor theory of property ownership would seem to entail parents' owning their children, Locke had tried to evade this conclusion. But Nozick, for good reasons, rejects the various ways that Locke tried to deny that children are the property of their parents. It cannot be, as Locke suggests, that a person must comprehend and have full control over the production of a thing in order to become the owner of it, since this would preclude ownership of innumerable other products—such as trees one has planted and nurtured—that Locke would not want excluded from the category of property. Equally unsuccessful, in Nozick's view, is Locke's suggestion that, since God makes us all, parents cannot claim to be the real makers of their children. For this too, as Nozick says, would apply to "many other things that Locke thinks can be owned . . . and perhaps . . . to everything."[20] Nozick also points out that Locke does not claim that something in the nature of persons precludes their *being owned*; after all, he postulates that they *are* owned, by God, and precisely *because* he made them.[21]

---

*In the argument that follows, the only aspects of reproductive labor that I am concerned with are those that occur during pregnancy and birth, resulting in a newborn infant. Obviously, this is but a small part of reproductive labor. As I make clear in other parts of this book, I believe that in a just society, the rest of reproductive labor should be shared equally between the sexes. The fact that in contemporary society it is not at all equally shared makes it impossible to sustain even less extreme forms of libertarianism than Nozick's, as I shall argue briefly toward the end of this chapter.

Libertarianism

As I shall argue, Nozick is no more able than Locke to explain away the implication of his principle of acquisition that people are owned at birth by those who make them. However, he fails entirely to confront this rather significant problem, inherent though it is in the most fundamental principle of his theory. Instead, having presented the problem (though veiled somewhat by the gender-neutral language he employs) and shown how Locke had failed to resolve it, he digresses into a short and seemingly irrelevant discussion of the responsibility of parents to care for their children—Why should ownership lead to *responsibility* here, whereas it leads to entitlement to use or dispose of at will in other cases?—and then abruptly changes the subject. In fact, Locke's problem is not as serious as Nozick's. Though Locke does say that people are owned by God, and although he justifies the enslavement of people in retaliation for their aggression, he explicitly denies that people can ever sell themselves into slavery (*Second Treatise*, paragraph 23). Nozick, as I shall indicate shortly, explicitly allows that they *can*. He mentions, though he does not pursue, two possible means of solution: to argue that indeed "something intrinsic to persons bars those who make them from owning them," and to claim that there is something about the production theory of ownership that "excludes the process whereby parents make their children as yielding ownership."[22] But Nozick cannot, consistently with the rest of his theory of rights, successfully pursue either of these claims to a satisfactory conclusion.

If persons can be owned by *anyone* other than themselves, it would seem to follow from Nozick's principle of just acquisition that they are owned (originally, at least) by those who make them. Thus a major part of the question is whether persons can be owned at all. About this, Nozick is unambiguous: he has no qualms about personal slavery. Raising the question of "whether a free system will allow [an individual] to sell himself into slavery," he responds "I believe that it would."[23] It might be objected, however, that allowing persons to sell themselves into slavery does not imply that they can already be the property of another at birth. After the statement about slavery, Nozick adds, "some things individuals may choose for themselves, no one may choose for another."

We must look at what Nozick's theory as a whole implies about this issue. On the one hand, as I suggested, it would seem to be a central assumption of his theory that persons, originally at least, own themselves. For if individuals are born as the property of another, how can they have "rights . . . [s]o strong and far-reaching . . . that they raise the question of what, if anything, the state and its officials may do."[24] And how can anyone acquire a just Nozickian title

81

to property if he does not own his own labor or his own body? On the other hand, persons do in fact start their lives as the product of a woman's natural capacities and labor. I will suggest two reasons why Nozick's theory, in spite of its apparent dedication to self-ownership, cannot avoid the conclusion that women's entitlement rights to those they produce must take priority over persons' rights to themselves at birth.

The first reason is Nozick's consistent preference for legitimately acquired property rights over all other claims, including basic need and the right to life. It is difficult to see how a theorist who claims that a starving person has no right to food that is owned by another person, even if that other person has food to throw away,[25] could relax his stringent adherence to property rights in order to give an infant, who is after all the product of someone else's body and labor, the right of self-ownership, in contravention of the principle of acquisition. As Nozick writes: "No one has a right to something whose realization requires certain uses of things and activities that other people have rights and entitlements over."[26] If I am (already) my mother's property, I cannot claim a conflicting right to own myself.

The second, closely related reason is that Nozick gives clear priority to those who affect others over those they affect. He sums this up in the epigrammatic form: "From each as they choose, to each as they are chosen." Thus, for example, he argues that those who claim that the inequalities caused by inheritance or gifts are unjust are ignoring the rights of the donors to dispose of their resources as they wish. Such claims are wrongly focused on "recipient justice." In general, according to Nozick, "others have no right to a say in those decisions which importantly affect them that someone else . . . has the right to make."[27] Employing this mode of reasoning, he would be hard-pressed to label as unjust a situation in which one mother generously decides to give her child the gift of self-ownership while another chooses to keep hers as a slave for life. The rights of entitled donors must have priority over the expectations of potential donees, such that—regardless of the inequality of the results—the latter cannot claim that injustice has been done to them.

It is equally difficult to see how one might successfully employ Nozick's second potential escape route from the dilemma that persons seem to be the property of those who produce them. Much more obviously (and literally) than most other produced things, they "come into the world already attached to people." If, as Nozick claims, it is such attachment that entails entitlement, here is a clear case of it! Indeed, there is nothing about a woman's production of an infant that does not easily fulfill the conditions of the principle of acquisition as Nozick specifies them. "Whoever makes something," he says, "having bought or contracted for all other held resources used in the process . . . , is entitled to it."[28] Pregnancy and birth seem to constitute a paradigm of such processes. Once she is freely given a sperm (as usually happens) or buys one (as is becoming no longer very unusual)—in either case amounting to legitimacy in transfer—a fertile woman can make a baby with no other resources than her own body and its nourishment. This is surely what normally happens; given human sexual impulses, one has to come up with farfetched scenarios to imagine a woman's resorting to fraud or force to obtain the one resource her body cannot contribute to the process.* (In a Nozickian world, she would presumably be free to purchase any needed medical care that she could afford, at market rates.)

This example of production, in fact, is unique in *not* involving the complications of most other cases. A human infant originates from a minute quantity of abundantly available and otherwise useless resources. Thus, there can be little dispute over how much of the product comes from the added value of the labor and how much from the original resources. Reproduction pushes to its limits the notion that "it is necessary truth that no object can be made from nothing."[29] Clearly (though the extent of modern medical intervention sometimes obscures the fact), it is the complex capacities of the female reproductive system and its labor that achieve the transformation of two cells into an infant. Moreover, Nozick is in no position to object to women's owning the children they give birth to on the grounds that such production is in some cases relatively effortless or unintentional. For he defends the property rights of the naturally talented to the full fruits of their talent (see, for example, his Wilt Chamberlain example), and of those who "stumble upon" something to what they have found, however valuable.[30] Since he so firmly upholds in all other cases the principle that persons are fully entitled to whatever results from their natural talents and capacities, he would seem to have no way of avoiding the conclusion that only women own the children they produce.

Two other possible objections to this conclusion might be employed by an

*Cases of what is misleadingly called surrogate mothering are among the exceptions to the norm. In such cases, the "use" by the biological mother of the biological father's sperm is conditional upon the terms of the contract entered into about the future custody of the child. (Whether such contracts should be legally enforced is outside of the scope of this discussion; I think not, but I can think of no reason why they should be outlawed in a society based on Nozick's theory.) Other cases of artificial insemination are far simpler; the mother buys or is given the sperm and, according to Nozick's reasoning, the child who results from the combination of it with her own resources belongs to her. Marriage, it might reasonably be argued, involves a prior commitment that children are to be regarded as equally the mother's and the father's. But in a Nozickian world, what motivation would women have to marry, when by doing so they would be losing their sole entitlement to any children they might bear?

advocate of Nozick's theory, though neither turns out to be convincing. The first arises from the Lockean proviso that, in acquiring property, one must leave "enough, and as good . . . in common for others."[31] If mothers own all children at birth, doesn't this monopoly violate the ownership rights of men and infertile women, not to mention the rights of children to self-ownership? Not according to Nozick's interpretation of the proviso. For he argues that the rights of the nonowners are violated only if they are left worse off than they would be in a "baseline" situation in which the owners did not exist.[32] And this is clearly not so in the case of reproduction, for if there were no fertile women there would be no children to be owned by anyone. In a Nozickian world, where children, like any other product of human capacities and labor, would be commodities, those unable to bear children would presumably be free to offer as high a price for them as the market demanded. Similarly, all would be free to bargain with their mothers about the price of self-ownership. Just as, according to Nozick, a medical researcher who discovers a new cure may justly refuse to sell except on his own terms, childbearing women, by refusing to share the ownership of children except on whatever terms they choose, are not depriving others of anything they could acquire without the women's special talents. To paraphrase what Nozick says about the discoverer of the drug, these women do not "worsen the situation of others; if [they] did not [produce children] no one else would have, and the others would remain without [them]."[33] Since the children themselves, of course, would not exist in the baseline situation, they can make no claims.

Finally, Nozick cannot (consistently) appeal to the notion that reproduction is different from those other forms of production that lead to ownership, in that it has a different kind of purpose or internal goal. For he argues explicitly, against Bernard Williams's appeal to such a notion, that the producer alone is entitled to determine the purpose of his activity.[34] Thus he would appear to have no valid objection to a woman's producing a child for whatever purpose she chooses: to keep it in a cage to amuse her, perhaps, as some people keep birds, or even to kill it and eat it, if she were so inclined. But isn't this, surely, to carry the *reductio ad absurdum* of Nozick's theory that I am engaged in *too* far? Doesn't this farfetched, repulsive example involve gross violation of the moral side constraints that Nozick claims protect persons and their liberties from the assaults of others?

No, it seems not. For Nozick, perhaps because of his zeal to leave the strong free from obligation to the vulnerable, specifies the characteristics in virtue of which persons are protected by moral side constraints in such a way

84

as to leave infants, small children, and many of the developmentally disabled completely unprotected by them. First, he presents a "traditional" list of characteristics that he supposes, in some combination or other, constitute the reasons for the moral side constraints on how persons may treat one another. But almost none of them characterizes an infant. An infant is, of course, "sentient," but is decidedly *not* "self-conscious; rational (capable of using abstract concepts, not tied to responses to immediate stimuli); possessing free will; . . . a moral agent capable of governing its behavior by moral principles and capable of engaging in mutual limitation of conduct. . . ." Not satisfied with these characteristics, whether taken separately or in combination, Nozick turns to an even more demanding criterion: the ability of a being "to have or strive for meaningful life," "to regulate and guide its life in accordance with some overall conception it chooses to accept."[35] Clearly, no infant, very small child, or person with serious developmental disabilities has *this* capacity. Most infants are capable, if given appropriate and adequate physical and psychological nurturance, of *developing* such a capacity; but at the time of birth, it is uncertain whether such nurturance will be forthcoming. Moreover, an infant in a Nozickian society has no *right* to it, or even to a bare subsistence. We must presume that, like other persons misguided enough to claim such rights, "if his goal requires the use of means which others have rights over, he must enlist their voluntary cooperation. . . . [H]e must put together, with the co-operation of others, a feasible package."[36*] An infant, being for a long time necessarily dependent on the goodwill of others before attaining the capacities that Nozick regards as the basis for a person's having moral side constraints to protect him from violation of his rights, *cannot be regarded by him as having any such inviolable rights*. He has no grounds, therefore, for arguing against a mother's right to dispose of her infant as she chooses.

The Paradox of Nozick's Entitlement Theory

There seems to be no doubt that, by all the canons of Nozick's entitlement theory of justice, children are the property of those who make them. What-

---

*The only political theorist who explicitly *applies* something like this notion to the situation of infancy is Thomas Hobbes, who argues that infants must be understood to have consented to their parents' sovereignty over them in exchange for being nurtured rather then abandoned at birth. (Hobbes, *Leviathan*, chap. 20.)

ever else persons may be, and long before they qualify for Nozickian side con-straints, they are, according to his principles of just acquisition, first and fore-most the property of their mothers. It is difficult even to imagine all the ab-surdities of a society premised on such a principle—a society in which persons, including mothers themselves, could not gain self-ownership unless and until their own mothers either gave or sold them their freedom! Surely this would be a "matriarchy" of a sort no more appealing to feminists than to antifeminists. The immediate problem of this analysis for Nozick, however, is that it leaves the core of his theory—the principle of acquisition—mired in self-contradiction. If persons do not even "own" themselves, in the sense of being entitled to their own persons, bodies, natural talents, abilities, and so on, then there would appear to be no basis for anyone's owning anything else. Nozick's theory of entitlement is clearly premised on the notion that each person owns himself. But as I have shown, when we consider women's repro-ductive capacities and labor, the notion of self-ownership that is so central to the principle of acquisition turns out to be completely undermined by that very principle.

Nozick is clear about how broad he thinks the scope of a theory of justice should be. He says, "surely a regular, ordinary, everyday part [of the social structure], possessing no very unusual features, should turn out to be just when it satisfies the fundamental principles of justice; otherwise, special ex-planations must be offered."[37] As I have shown, any special explanations that might be offered to exempt reproduction from the implications of Nozick's entitlement theory of justice turn out to be inconsistent with his own princi-ples. We have discovered an important and everyday example of an individu-al's producing something, using nothing but her own abilities and resources legitimately transferred to her, in which it is clearly absurd to regard that prod-uct as her property. As I have shown, Nozick can provide no reason that is consistent with the rest of his theory for distinguishing women's reproductive abilities and labor from other kinds of abilities and labor; yet applying his prin-ciple of acquisition to this case leads into a morass of incoherence and self-contradiction. There would appear to be no alternative to rejecting the gen-eral principle that persons are entitled to whatever they produce, regardless of the needs of anybody else. Nozick has no recourse, then, other than to retreat from his entire entitlement theory of rights and the minimal state he builds on it, and to return to a more "patterned" derivation of justice that takes into account needs, deserts, and other human capacities as well as productivity.

*   *   *

Libertarianism

We have seen that Nozick's version of libertarianism leads to self-contradictory conclusions when women are included among its subjects. Even if they did not contradict themselves, these conclusions would surely not be accepted by anybody as the basis for any kind of society, let alone a just one. Like a number of other contemporary theorists, Nozick is able to reach the conclusions he does without confronting the absurdities we have examined only because of his neglect of women and his implicit assumption that the gender-structured family exists—crucial to, but outside of, the scope of his theory. His argument occasionally mentions wives (in order to illustrate points having nothing in particular to do with women or wifehood) and children. In his final discussion of the utopian framework of voluntaristic communities that he endorses, he mentions family obligations as an obstacle to the individual's ability to shift from one community to another. He also admits that children "present yet more difficult problems. In some way it must be ensured that they are *informed* of the range of alternatives in the world."[38] But of course in any real world, children need a lot more than this if they are to become those moral agents, capable of living meaningful lives, that Nozick requires as subjects of his theory. They need years and years of attentive care, at least some of which needs to be provided by persons who love them and know them very well—in most cases, their parents. Nozick's theory is able to ignore this fact of life, and childhood in general, only by assuming that women, in families, continue to do their work of nurturing and socializing the young and of providing a sphere of intimate relations. As we are finding to be so often the case, the family and a large part of the lives of most women, especially, are assumed by the theory but are not part of it in the important sense of having its conclusions applied to them.

Nozick's extreme property rights–based libertarianism fails to be able to take women into account. When we apply the theory to women as well as men, as we have seen, we are led into a self-contradictory, "matriarchal" mire. Ayn Rand's libertarianism, which has been so influential, directly and indirectly, on recent politics in the United States, also seems susceptible to the critique I have made here. Though less systematically presented than Nozick's, Rand's theory is very similar in its emphasis on the inviolability of property rights in what one produces.[39] But what of versions of libertarianism that are less exclusively based on the primacy of property rights? Such theories are founded in part on either an individualistic variant of Aristotelianism, in which each person's rational aim is to promote his own flourishing as a human being, or on the greater efficiency of an unregulated private property economy over any alternative. Although, unlike Nozick, some such theorists support some minimal governmental welfare system to keep indigent people at subsistence level, some do not, and all are opposed to any further governmental regulation or redistribution.[40] Fundamentally, they believe that society is best and most morally arranged when it leaves each to produce what he can by the use of his own talents, and to enjoy the produce of such labor and luck combined.

Many arguments have been made against such theories. But one basic problem has received little emphasis, because both the libertarians and their critics make the same unwarranted assumption that the family and its gender structure, and sex roles in society at large, exist outside the scope of their arguments. Libertarian theories are founded on the notion that persons are fundamentally self-interested; some, such as Rand's, are openly hostile to altruism. Yet, ironically, they take for granted that whole vast sphere of life in which persons (mostly women) take care of others, often at considerable cost to their own advancement as individuals. They are therefore able to ignore the crucial fact that much of human labor, energy, and skill is *not* devoted to the production of things that can then belong to their producers. It is devoted to the reproduction of human beings themselves.

Some sixty years ago, George Bernard Shaw pointed out wittily, as a basic flaw in any labor theory of property rights, that "the clearest case in the world of a person producing something herself by her own painful, prolonged and risky labor is that of a woman who produces a baby; but then she cannot live on the baby: the baby lives greedily on her."[41] But Shaw's voice has long been drowned out by those who prefer to forget this very real problem with such theories of property rights and with the minimal state that they argue follows from them. As we shall see in chapter 7, it is the combination of this continued neglect and devaluation of human *re*productive work with the persistent division of labor between the sexes and the increasing instability of marriage that is causing the growing poverty of women and children that is one of the greatest crises faced by our society today.

5

Justice as Fairness: For Whom?

John Rawls's A *Theory of Justice* has had the most powerful influence of any work of contemporary moral and political theory.[1] The scope of Rawls's influence is indicated by the fact that all the theorists I have discussed so far make an issue of their respective disagreements with his method and, in most cases, with his conclusions.[2] Now, I turn to Rawls's theory of justice as fairness, to examine not only what it explicitly says and does not say, but also what it *implies*, on the subjects of gender, women, and the family.

There is strikingly little indication, throughout most of A *Theory of Justice*, that the modern liberal society to which the principles of justice are to be applied is deeply and pervasively gender-structured. Thus an ambiguity runs throughout the work, which is continually noticeable to anyone reading it from a feminist perspective. On the one hand, as I shall argue, a consistent and wholehearted application of Rawls's liberal principles of justice can lead us to challenge fundamentally the gender system of our society. On the other hand, in his own account of his theory, this challenge is barely hinted at, much less developed. After critiquing Rawls's theory for its neglect of gender, I shall ask two related questions: What effects does a feminist reading of

89

Rawls have on some of his fundamental ideas (particularly those most attacked by critics); and what undeveloped potential does the theory have for
feminist critique, and in particular for our attempts to answer the question,
Can justice co-exist with gender?

Central to Rawls's theory of justice is a construct, or heuristic device, that
is both his most important single contribution to moral and political theory
and the focus of most of the controversy his theory still attracts, nearly twenty
years after its publication. Rawls argues that the principles of justice that
should regulate the basic institutions of society are those that would be arrived
at by persons reasoning in what is termed "the original position." His specifi-
cations for the original position are that "the parties" who deliberate there are
rational and mutually disinterested, and that while no limits are placed on the
general information available to them, a "veil of ignorance" conceals from
them all knowledge of their individual characteristics and their social position. Though the theory is presented as a contract theory, it is so only in an
odd and metaphoric sense, since "no one knows his situation in society nor
his natural assets, and therefore no one is in a position to tailor principles to
his advantage." Thus they have "no basis for bargaining in the usual sense."
This is how, Rawls explains, "the arbitrariness of the world . . . [is] corrected
for," in order that the principles arrived at will be fair. Indeed, since no one
knows who he is, all think identically and the standpoint of any one party represents that of all. Thus the principles of justice are arrived at unanimously.[3]
Later in this chapter, I shall address some of the criticisms that have been
made of Rawls's original position and of the nature of those who deliberate
there. I shall show that his theory can be read in a way that either obviates
these objections or answers them satisfactorily. But first, let us see how the
theory treats women, gender, and the family.

Justice for All?

Rawls, like almost all political theorists until very recently, employs in *A
Theory of Justice* supposedly generic male terms of reference.[4] *Men, mankind, he*, and *his* are interspersed with gender-neutral terms of reference such
as *individual* and *moral person*. Examples of intergenerational concern are
worded in terms of "fathers" and "sons," and the difference principle is said to

correspond to "the principle of fraternity."[5] This linguistic usage would perhaps be less significant if it were not for the fact that Rawls self-consciously subscribes to a long tradition of moral and political philosophy that has used in its arguments either such "generic" male terms or more inclusive terms of reference ("human beings," "persons," "all rational beings as such"), only to exclude women from the scope of its conclusions. Kant is a clear example.[6] But when Rawls refers to the generality and universality of Kant's ethics, and when he compares the principles chosen in his own original position to those regulative of Kant's kingdom of ends, "acting from [which] expresses our nature as free and equal rational persons,"[7] he does not mention the fact that women were not included among those persons to whom Kant meant his moral theory to apply. Again, in a brief discussion of Freud's account of moral development, Rawls presents Freud's theory of the formation of the male superego in largely gender-neutral terms, without mentioning the fact that Freud considered women's moral development to be sadly deficient, on account of their incomplete resolution of the Oedipus complex.[8] Thus there is a blindness to the sexism of the tradition in which Rawls is a participant, which tends to render his terms of reference more ambiguous than they might otherwise be. A feminist reader finds it difficult not to keep asking, Does this theory of justice apply to women?

This question is not answered in the important passages listing the characteristics that persons in the original position are not to know about themselves, in order to formulate impartial principles of justice. In a subsequent article, Rawls has made it clear that sex *is* one of those morally irrelevant contingencies that are hidden by the veil of ignorance.[9] But throughout *A Theory of Justice*, while the list of things unknown by a person in the original position includes "his place in society, his class position or social status, . . . his fortune in the distribution of natural assets and abilities, his intelligence and strength, and the like, . . . his conception of the good, the particulars of his rational plan of life, even the special features of his psychology,"[10] "his" sex is not mentioned. Since the parties also "know the general facts about human society,"[11] presumably including the fact that it is gender-structured both by custom and still in some respects by law, one might think that whether or not they knew their sex might matter enough to be mentioned. Perhaps Rawls meant to cover it by his phrase "and the like," but it is also possible that he did not consider it significant.

The ambiguity is exacerbated by the statement that those free and equal moral persons in the original position who formulate the principles of justice are to be thought of not as "single individuals" but as "heads of families" or "representatives of families."[12] Rawls says that it is not necessary to think of the parties as heads of families, but that he will generally do so. The reason he does this, he explains, is to ensure that each person in the original position cares about the well-being of some persons in the next generation. These "ties of sentiment" between generations, which Rawls regards as important for the establishment of intergenerational justice—his just savings principle—, would otherwise constitute a problem because of the general assumption that the parties in the original position are mutually disinterested. In spite of the ties of sentiment *within* families, then, "as representatives of families their interests are opposed as the circumstances of justice imply."[13]

The head of a family need not necessarily, of course, be a man. Certainly in the United States, at least, there has been a striking growth in the proportion of female-headed households during the last several decades. But the very fact that, in common usage, the term "female-headed household" is used *only* in reference to households without resident adult males implies the assumption that any present male takes precedence over a female as the household or family head. Rawls does nothing to contest this impression when he says of those in the original position that "imagining themselves to be fathers, say, they are to ascertain how much they should set aside for their sons by noting what they would believe themselves entitled to claim of their fathers."[14] He makes the "heads of families" assumption only in order to address the problem of justice between generations, and presumably does not intend it to be a sexist assumption. Nevertheless, he is thereby effectively trapped into the public/domestic dichotomy and, with it, the conventional mode of thinking that life within the family and relations between the sexes are not properly regarded as part of the subject matter of a theory of social justice.

Let me here point out that Rawls, for good reason, states at the outset of his theory that the family *is* part of the subject matter of a theory of social justice. "For us" he says, "the primary subject of justice is the basic structure of society, or more exactly, the way in which the major social institutions distribute fundamental rights and duties and determine the division of advantages from social cooperation." The political constitution and the principal economic and social arrangements are basic because "taken together as one scheme, [they] define men's rights and duties and influence their life prospects, what they can expect to be and how well they can hope to do. The basic structure is the primary subject of justice *because its effects are so profound and present from the start*" (emphasis added).[15] Rawls specifies "the monogamous family" as an example of such major social institutions, together with the political constitution, the legal protection of essential freedoms, competitive markets, and private property.[16] Although this initial inclusion of the family as a basic social institution to which the principles of justice should apply is surprising in the light of the history of liberal thought, with its dichotomy between domestic and public spheres, it is necessary, given Rawls's stated criteria for inclusion in the basic structure. It would scarcely be possible to deny that different family structures, and different distributions of rights and duties within families, affect men's "life prospects, what they can expect to be and how well they can hope to do," and even more difficult to deny their effects on the life prospects of women. There is no doubt, then, that in Rawls's initial definition of the sphere of social justice, the family is included and the public/domestic dichotomy momentarily cast in doubt. However, the family is to a large extent ignored, though assumed, in the rest of the theory.[*]

The Barely Visible Family

In part 1 of A *Theory of Justice*, Rawls derives and defends the two principles of justice—the principle of equal basic liberty, and the "difference principle" combined with the requirement of fair equality of opportunity. These principles are intended to apply to the basic structure of society. They are "to govern the assignment of rights and duties and to regulate the distribution of social and economic advantages."[17] Whenever the basic institutions have within them differences in authority, in responsibility, or in the distribution of resources such as wealth or leisure, the second principle requires that these differences must be to the greatest benefit of the least advantaged and must be attached to positions accessible to all under conditions of fair equality of opportunity.

In part 2, Rawls discusses at some length the application of his principles of justice to almost all the institutions of the basic social structure that are set out at the beginning of the book. The legal protection of liberty of thought and conscience is defended, as are democratic constitutional institutions and procedures; competitive markets feature prominently in the discussion of the just

---

[*]It is noteworthy that in a subsequent paper on the subject of why the basic structure is the primary subject of justice, Rawls does *not* mention the family as part of the basic structure. See "The Basic Structure As Subject," *American Philosophical Quarterly* 14, no. 2 (1977): 159.

distribution of income; the issue of the private or public ownership of the means of production is explicitly left open, since Rawls argues that his principles of justice might be compatible with certain versions of either.[18] But throughout all these discussions, the issue of whether the monogamous family, in either its traditional or any other form, is a just social institution, is never raised. When Rawls announces that "the sketch of the system of institutions that satisfy the two principles of justice is now complete,"[19] he has paid no attention at all to the internal justice of the family. In fact, apart from passing references, the family appears in A *Theory of Justice* in only three contexts: as the link between generations necessary for the just savings principle; as an obstacle to fair equality of opportunity (on account of the inequalities among families); and as the first school of moral development. It is in the third of these contexts that Rawls first specifically mentions the family as a just institution—not, however, to *consider* whether the family "in some form" is a just institution but to *assume* it.[20]

Clearly, however, by Rawls's own reasoning about the social justice of major social institutions, this assumption is unwarranted. The serious significance of this for the theory as a whole will be addressed shortly. The central tenet of the theory, after all, is that justice as fairness characterizes institutions whose members could hypothetically have agreed to their structure and rules from a position in which they did not know which place in the structure they were to occupy. The argument of the book is designed to show that the two principles of justice are those that individuals in such a hypothetical situation would agree upon. But since those in the original position are the heads or representatives of families, they are not in a position to determine questions of justice within families. As Jane English has pointed out, "By making the parties in the original position heads of families rather than individuals, Rawls makes the family opaque to claims of justice."[21] As far as children are concerned, Rawls makes an argument from paternalism for their temporary inequality and restricted liberty.[22] (This, while it may suffice in basically sound, benevolent families, is of no use or comfort in abusive or neglectful situations, where Rawls's principles would seem to require that children be protected through the intervention of outside authorities.) But wives (or whichever adult member[s] of a family are *not* its "head") go completely unrepresented in the original position. If families are just, as Rawls later assumes, then they must become just in some different way (unspecified by him) from other institutions, for it is impossible to see how the viewpoint of their less advantaged members ever gets to be heard.

94

Justice as Fairness: For Whom?

There are two occasions when Rawls seems either to depart from his assumption that those in the original position are "family heads" or to assume that a "head of a family" is equally likely to be a woman as a man. In the assignment of the basic rights of citizenship, he argues, favoring men over women is "justified by the difference principle . . . only if it is to the advantage of women and acceptable from their standpoint." Later he seems to imply that the injustice and irrationality of racist doctrines are also characteristic of sexist ones.[23] But in spite of these passages, which appear to challenge formal sex discrimination, the discussions of institutions in part 2 implicitly rely, in a number of respects, on the assumption that the parties formulating just institutions are (male) heads of (fairly traditional) families, and are therefore not concerned with issues of just distribution within the family or between the sexes. Thus the "heads of families" assumption, far from being neutral or innocent, has the effect of banishing a large sphere of human life—and a particularly large sphere of most women's lives—from the scope of the theory.

During the discussion of the distribution of wealth, for example, it seems to be assumed that all the parties in the original position expect, once the veil of ignorance is removed, to be participants in the paid labor market. Distributive shares are discussed in terms of household income, but reference to "individuals" is interspersed into this discussion as if there were no difference between the advantage or welfare of a household and that of an individual.[24] This confusion obscures the fact that wages are paid to employed members of the labor force, but that in societies characterized by gender (all current societies) a much larger proportion of women's than men's labor is unpaid and is often not even acknowledged as labor. It also obscures the fact that the resulting disparities in the earnings of men and women, and the economic dependence of women on men, are likely to affect power relations within the household, as well as access to leisure, prestige, political power, and so on, among its adult members. Any discussion of justice *within* the family would have to address these issues. (In the last two chapters of this book, I shall examine current gendered family structure and practices in the light of standards of justice, including Rawls's, and, finding them wanting, suggest some ways in which the family, and marriage in particular, might be reformed so as to become more just.)

Later, in Rawls's discussion of the obligations of citizens, his assumption that justice is agreed on by heads of families in the original position seems to prevent him from considering another issue of crucial importance: women's exemption from the draft. He concludes that military conscription is justifiable in the case of defense against an unjust attack on liberty, so long as institutions "try to make sure that the risks of suffering from these imposed misfortunes are more or less evenly shared by all members of society over the course of their life, and that there is no avoidable *class* bias in selecting those who are called for duty" (emphasis added).[25] The complete exemption of women from this major interference with the basic liberties of equal citizenship is not even mentioned.

In spite of two explicit rejections of the justice of formal sex discrimination in part 1, then, Rawls seems in part 2 to be heavily influenced by his "family heads" assumption. He does not consider as part of the basic structure of society the greater economic dependence of women and the sexual division of labor within the typical family, or any of the broader social ramifications of this basic gender structure. Moreover, in part 3, where he takes as a given the justice of the family "in some form," he does not discuss any alternative forms. Rather, he sounds very much as though he is thinking in terms of traditional, gendered family structure and roles. The family, he says, is "a small association, normally characterized by a definite hierarchy, in which each member has certain rights and duties." The family's role as moral teacher is achieved partly through parental expectations of the "virtues of a good son or a good daughter." In the family and in other associations such as schools, neighborhoods, and peer groups, Rawls continues, one learns various moral virtues and ideals, leading to those adopted in the various statuses, occupations, and family positions of later life. "The content of these ideals is given by the various conceptions of a good wife and husband, a good friend and citizen, and so on."[26] Given these unusual departures from the supposedly generic male terms of reference used throughout the book, it seems likely that Rawls means to imply that the goodness of daughters is distinct from the goodness of sons, and that of wives from that of husbands. A fairly traditional gender system seems to be assumed.

Rawls not only assumes that "the basic structure of a well-ordered society includes the family *in some form*" (emphasis added); he adds that "in a broader inquiry the institution of the family might be questioned, and other arrangements might indeed prove to be preferable."[27] But why should it require a broader inquiry than the colossal task in which A *Theory of Justice* is engaged, to raise questions about the institution and the form of the family? Surely Rawls is right in initially naming it as one of those basic social institutions that most affect the life chances of individuals and should therefore be part of the primary subject of justice. The family is not a private association like a church or a university, which vary considerably in the type and degree of commitment each expects from its members, and which one can join and leave voluntarily. For although one has some choice (albeit a highly constrained one) about marrying into a gender-structured family, one has no choice at all about being born into one. Rawls's failure to subject the structure of the family to his principles of justice is particularly serious in the light of his belief that a theory of justice must take account of "how [individuals] get to be what they are" and "cannot take their final aims and interests, their attitudes to themselves and their life, as given."[28] For the gendered family, and female parenting in particular, are clearly critical determinants in the different ways the two sexes are socialized—how men and women "get to be what they are."

If Rawls were to assume throughout the construction of his theory that all human adults are participants in what goes on behind the veil of ignorance, he would have no option but to require that the family, as a major social institution affecting the life chances of individuals, be constructed in accordance with the two principles of justice. I shall begin to develop this positive potential of Rawls's theory in the final section of this chapter, and shall take it further in the concluding chapter of the book. But first I turn to a major problem for the theory that results from its neglect of the issue of justice within the family: its placing in jeopardy Rawls's account of how one develops a sense of justice.

Gender, the Family, and the Development of a Sense of Justice

Apart from being briefly mentioned as the link between generations necessary for Rawls's just savings principle, and as an obstacle to fair equality of opportunity, the family appears in Rawls's theory in only one context—albeit one of considerable importance: as the earliest school of moral development. Rawls argues, in a much-neglected section of part 3 of A *Theory of Justice*, that a just, well-ordered society will be stable only if its members continue to develop a sense of justice, "a strong and normally effective desire to act as the principles of justice require."[29] He turns his attention specifically to childhood moral development, aiming to indicate the major steps by which a sense of justice is acquired.

It is in this context that Rawls *assumes* that families are just. Moreover, these supposedly just families play a fundamental role in his account of moral development. First, the love of parents for their children, which comes to be reciprocated, is important in his account of the development of a sense of self-worth. By loving the child and being "worthy objects of his admiration . . . they arouse in him a sense of his own value and the desire to become the sort of person that they are." Rawls argues that healthy moral development in early life depends upon love, trust, affection, example, and guidance.[30]

At a later stage in moral development, which he calls "the morality of association," Rawls perceives the family, though he describes it in gendered and hierarchical terms, as the first of many associations in which, by moving through a sequence of roles and positions, our moral understanding increases. The crucial aspect of the sense of fairness that is learned during this stage is the capacity—which, as I shall argue, is essential for being able to think *as if* in the original position—to take up the different points of view of others and to learn "from their speech, conduct, and countenance" to see things from their perspectives. We learn to perceive, from what they say and do, what other people's ends, plans, and motives are. Without this experience, Rawls says, "we cannot put ourselves into another's place and find out what we would do in his position," which we need to be able to do in order "to regulate our own conduct in the appropriate way by reference to it." Building on attachments formed in the family, participation in different roles in the various associations of society leads to the development of a person's "capacity for fellow feeling" and to "ties of friendship and mutual trust." Just as in the first stage "certain natural attitudes develop toward the parents, so here ties of friendship and confidence grow up among associates. In each case certain natural attitudes underlie the corresponding moral feelings: a lack of these feelings would manifest the absence of these attitudes."[31]

This whole account of moral development is strikingly unlike the arid, rationalist account given by Kant, whose ideas are so influential in many respects on Rawls's thinking about justice. For Kant, who claimed that justice must be grounded in reason alone, any feelings that do not follow from independently established moral principles are morally suspect—"mere inclinations."[32] By contrast, Rawls clearly recognizes the importance of feelings, first nurtured within supposedly just families, in the development of the capacity for moral thinking. In accounting for his third and final stage of moral development, where persons are supposed to become attached to the principles of justice themselves, Rawls says that "the sense of justice is continuous with the love of mankind." At the same time, he acknowledges our particularly strong feelings about those to whom we are closely attached, and says that this is rightly reflected in our moral judgments: even though "our moral sentiments display an independence from the accidental circumstances of our world, . . . our natural attachments to particular persons and groups still have an appropriate place." He indicates clearly that empathy, or imagining oneself in the circumstances of others, plays a major role in moral development. It is not surprising that he turns away from Kant, and toward moral philosophers such as Adam Smith, Elizabeth Anscombe, Philippa Foot, and Bernard Williams in developing his ideas about the moral emotions or sentiments.[33]

Rawls's summary of his three psychological laws of moral development emphasizes the fundamental importance of loving parenting for the development of a sense of justice. The three laws, Rawls says, are

> not merely principles of association or of reinforcement. . . . [but] assert that the active sentiments of love and friendship, and even the sense of justice, arise from the manifest intention of other persons to act for our good. Because we recognize that they wish us well, we care for their well-being in return.[34]

Each of the laws of moral development, as set out by Rawls, depends upon the one before it, and the first assumption of the first law is: "given that family institutions are just, ..." Thus Rawls frankly and for good reason acknowledges that the whole of moral development rests at base upon the loving ministrations of those who raise small children from the earliest stages, and on the moral character—in particular, the *justice*—of the environment in which this takes place. At the foundation of the development of the sense of justice, then, are an activity and a sphere of life that, though by no means necessarily so, have throughout history been predominantly the activity and the sphere of women.

Rawls does not explain the basis of his assumption that family institutions are just. If gendered families are *not* just, but are, rather, a relic of caste or feudal societies in which roles, responsibilities, and resources are distributed not in accordance with the two principles of justice but in accordance with innate differences that are imbued with enormous social significance, then Rawls's whole structure of moral development would seem to be built on shaky ground. Unless the households in which children are first nurtured, and see their first examples of human interaction, are based on equality and reciprocity rather than on dependence and domination—and the latter is too often the case—how can whatever love they receive from their parents make up for the injustice they see before them in the relationship between these same parents? How, in hierarchical families in which sex roles are rigidly assigned, are we to learn, as Rawls's theory of moral development requires us, to "put ourselves into another's place and find out what we would do in his position"? Unless they are parented equally by adults of both sexes, how will children of both sexes come to develop a sufficiently similar and well-rounded moral psychology to enable them to engage in the kind of deliberation about justice that is exemplified in the original position? If both parents do not *share* in nurturing activities, are they both likely to maintain in adult life the capacity for empathy that underlies a sense of justice?[35] And finally, unless the household is connected by a continuum of just associations to the larger communities within which people are supposed to develop fellow feelings for each other, how will they grow up with the capacity for enlarged sympathies such as are clearly required for the practice of justice? Rawls's neglect of justice within the family is clearly in tension with the requirements of his own theory of moral development. Family justice must be of central importance for social justice.

I have begun to suggest a feminist reading of Rawls, drawing on his theory of moral development and its emphasis on the moral feelings that originate in the family. This reading can, I think, contribute to the strengthening of Rawls's theory against some of the criticisms that have been made of it.[36] For, in contrast with his account of moral development, much of his argument about how persons in the original position arrive at the principles of justice is expressed in terms of mutual disinterest and rationality—the language of rational choice. This, I contend, leaves what he says unnecessarily open to three criticisms: it involves unacceptably egoistic and individualistic assumptions about human nature; taking an "outside" perspective, it is of little or no relevance to actual people thinking about justice; and its aim to create universalistic and impartial principles leads to the neglect of "otherness" or difference.[37] I think all three criticisms are mistaken, but they result at least in part from Rawls's tendency to use the language of rational choice.

In my view, the original position and what happens there are described far better in other terms. As Rawls himself says, the combination of conditions he imposes on them "forces each person in the original position to take the good of others into account."[38] The parties can be presented as the "rational, mutually disinterested" agents characteristic of rational choice theory only because they do not know *which* self they will turn out to be. The veil of ignorance is such a demanding stipulation that it converts what would, without it, be self-interest into equal concern for others, including others who are very different from ourselves. Those in the original position cannot think from the position of *nobody*, as is suggested by those critics who then conclude that Rawls's theory depends upon a "disembodied" concept of the self. They must, rather, think from the perspective of *everybody*, in the sense of *each in turn*. To do this requires, at the very least, both strong empathy and a preparedness to listen carefully to the very different points of view of others. As I have suggested, these capacities seem more likely to be widely distributed in a society of just families, with no expectations about or reinforcements of gender.

Rawls's Theory of Justice as a Tool for Feminist Criticism

The significance of Rawls's central, brilliant idea, the original position, is that it forces one to question and consider traditions, customs, and institutions from all points of view, and ensures that the principles of justice will be acceptable to everyone, regardless of what position "he" ends up in. The critical force of the original position becomes evident when one considers that some of the most creative critiques of Rawls's theory have resulted from more radical or broad interpretations of the original position than his own.[39] The theory, in principle, avoids both the problem of domination that is inherent in theories of justice based on traditions or shared understandings and the partiality of libertarian theory to those who are talented or fortunate. For feminist readers, however, the problem of the theory as stated by Rawls himself is encapsulated in that ambiguous "he." As I have shown, while Rawls briefly rules out formal, legal discrimination on the grounds of sex (as on other grounds that he regards as "morally irrelevant"), he fails entirely to address the justice of the gender system, which, with its roots in the sex roles of the family and its branches extending into virtually every corner of our lives, is one of the fundamental structures of our society. If, however, we read Rawls in such a way as to take seriously both the notion that those behind the veil of ignorance do not know what sex they are and the requirement that the family and the gender system, as basic social institutions, are to be subject to scrutiny, constructive feminist criticism of these contemporary institutions follows. So, also, do hidden difficulties for the application of a Rawlsian theory of justice in a gendered society.

I shall explain each of these points in turn. But first, both the critical perspective and the incipient problems of a feminist reading of Rawls can perhaps be illuminated by a description of a cartoon I saw a few years ago. Three elderly, robed male justices are depicted, looking down with astonishment at their very pregnant bellies. One says to the others, without further elaboration: "Perhaps we'd better reconsider that decision." This illustration graphically demonstrates the importance, in thinking about justice, of a concept like Rawls's original position, which makes us adopt the positions of others—especially positions that we ourselves could never be in. It also suggests that those thinking in such a way might well conclude that more than formal legal equality of the sexes is required if justice is to be done. As we have seen in recent years, it is quite possible to enact and uphold "gender-neutral" laws concerning pregnancy, abortion, childbirth leave, and so on, that in effect discriminate against women. The United States Supreme Court decided in 1976, for example, that "an exclusion of pregnancy from a disability-benefits plan providing general coverage is not a gender-based discrimination at all."[40] One of the virtues of the cartoon is its suggestion that one's thinking on such matters is likely to be affected by the knowledge that one might become "a pregnant person." The illustration also points out the limits of what is possible, in terms of thinking ourselves into the original position, as long as we live in a gender-structured society. While the elderly male justices can, in a sense, imagine themselves as pregnant, what is a much more difficult question is whether, in order to construct principles of justice, they can imagine themselves as women. This raises the question of whether, in fact, sex *is* a morally irrelevant and contingent characteristic in a society structured by gender.

Let us first assume that sex is contingent in this way, though I shall later question this assumption. Let us suppose that it is possible, as Rawls clearly considers it to be, to hypothesize the moral thinking of representative human beings, as ignorant of their sex as of all the other things hidden by the veil of ignorance. It seems clear that, while Rawls does not do this, we must consistently take the relevant positions of both sexes into account in formulating and applying principles of justice. In particular, those in the original position must take special account of the perspective of women, since their knowledge of "the general facts about human society" must include the knowledge that women have been and continue to be the less advantaged sex in a great number of respects. In considering the basic institutions of society, they are more likely to pay special attention to the family than virtually to ignore it. Not only is it potentially the first school of social justice, but its customary unequal assignment of responsibilities and privileges to the two sexes and its socialization of children into sex roles make it, in its current form, an institution of crucial importance for the perpetuation of sex inequality.

In innumerable ways, the principles of justice that Rawls arrives at are inconsistent with a gender-structured society and with traditional family roles. The critical impact of a feminist application of Rawls's theory comes chiefly from his second principle, which requires that inequalities be both "to the greatest benefit of the least advantaged" and "attached to offices and positions open to all."[41] This means that if any roles or positions analogous to our current sex roles—including those of husband and wife, mother and father—were to survive the demands of the first requirement, the second requirement would prohibit any linkage between these roles and sex. Gender, with its ascriptive designation of positions and expectations of behavior in accordance with the inborn characteristic of sex, could no longer form a legitimate part of the social structure, whether inside or outside the family. Three illustrations will help to link this conclusion with specific major requirements that Rawls makes of a just or well-ordered society.

First, after the basic political liberties, one of the most essential liberties is "the important liberty of free choice of occupation."[42] It is not difficult to see that this liberty is compromised by the assumption and customary expectation, central to our gender system, that women take far greater responsibility for housework and child care, whether or not they also work for wages outside the home. In fact, both the assignment of these responsibilities to women—resulting in their asymmetric economic dependence on men—and the related responsibility of husbands to support their wives compromise the liberty of choice of occupation of both sexes. But the customary roles of the two sexes inhibit women's choices over the course of a lifetime far more severely than those of men; it is far easier in practice to switch from being a wage worker to occupying a domestic role than to do the reverse. While Rawls has no objection to some aspects of the division of labor, he asserts that, in a well-ordered society, "no one need be servilely dependent on others and made to choose between monotonous and routine occupations which are deadening to human thought and sensibility" and that work will be "meaningful for all."[43] These conditions are far more likely to be met in a society that does not assign family responsibilities in a way that makes women into a marginal sec-

103

tor of the paid work force and renders likely their economic dependence upon men. Rawls's principles of justice, then, would seem to require a radical rethinking not only of the division of labor within families but also of all the nonfamily institutions that assume it.

Second, the abolition of gender seems essential for the fulfillment of Rawls's criterion for political justice. For he argues that not only would equal formal political liberties be espoused by those in the original position, but that any inequalities in the *worth* of these liberties (for example, the effects on them of factors like poverty and ignorance) must be justified by the difference principle. Indeed, "the constitutional process should preserve the equal representation of the original position to the degree that this is practicable."[44] While Rawls discusses this requirement in the context of class differences, stating that those who devote themselves to politics should be "drawn more or less equally from all sectors of society,"[45] it is just as clearly and importantly applicable to sex differences. The equal political representation of women and men, especially if they are parents, is clearly inconsistent with our gender system. The paltry number of women in high political office is an obvious indication of this. Since 1789, over 10,000 men have served in the United States House of Representatives, but only 107 women; some 1,140 men have been senators, compared with 15 women. Only one recent appointee, Sandra Day O'Connor, has ever served on the Supreme Court. These levels of representation of any other class constituting more than a majority of the population would surely be perceived as a sign that something is grievously wrong with the political system. But as British politician Shirley Williams recently said, until there is "a revolution in shared responsibilities for the family, in child care and in child rearing," there will not be "more than a very small number of women . . . opting for a job as demanding as politics."[46]

Finally, Rawls argues that the rational moral persons in the original position would place a great deal of emphasis on the securing of self-respect or self-esteem. They "would wish to avoid at almost any cost the social conditions that undermine self-respect," which is "perhaps the most important" of all the primary goods.[47] In the interests of this primary value, if those in the original position did not know whether they were to be men or women, they would surely be concerned to establish a thoroughgoing social and economic equality between the sexes that would protect either sex from the need to pander to or servilely provide for the pleasures of the other. They would emphasize the importance of girls' and boys' growing up with an equal sense of

104

respect for themselves and equal expectations of self-definition and development. They would be highly motivated, too, to find a means of regulating pornography that did not seriously compromise freedom of speech. In general, they would be unlikely to tolerate basic social institutions that asymmetrically either forced or gave strong incentives to members of one sex to serve as sex objects for the other.

There is, then, implicit in Rawls's theory of justice a potential critique of gender-structured social institutions, which can be developed by taking seriously the fact that those formulating the principles of justice do not know their sex. At the beginning of my brief account of this feminist critique, however, I made an assumption that I said would later be questioned—that a person's sex is, as Rawls at times indicates, a contingent and morally irrelevant characteristic, such that human beings really can hypothesize ignorance of this fact about them. First, I shall explain why, unless this assumption is a reasonable one, there are likely to be further feminist ramifications for a Rawlsian theory of justice, in addition to those I have just sketched out. I shall then argue that the assumption is very probably not plausible in any society that is structured along the lines of gender. I reach the conclusions not only that our current gender structure is incompatible with the attainment of social justice, but also that the disappearance of gender is a prerequisite for the *complete* development of a nonsexist, fully human theory of justice.

Although Rawls is clearly aware of the effects on individuals of their different places in the social system, he regards it as possible to hypothesize free and rational moral persons in the original position who, temporarily freed from the contingencies of actual characteristics and social circumstances, will adopt the viewpoint of the "representative" human being. He is under no illusions about the difficulty of this task: it requires a "great shift in perspective" from the way we think about fairness in everyday life. But with the help of the veil of ignorance, he believes that we can "take up a point of view that everyone can adopt on an equal footing," so that "we share a common standpoint along with others and do not make our judgments from a personal slant." The result of this rational impartiality or objectivity, Rawls argues, is that, all being convinced by the same arguments, agreement about the basic principles of justice will be unanimous. He does not mean that those in the original position will agree about *all* moral or social issues—"ethical differences are bound to remain"—but that complete agreement will be reached on all basic principles, or "essential understandings." A critical assumption of this argument for unanimity, however, is that all the parties have similar motivations and psychologies (for example, he assumes mutually disinterested rationality and an absence of envy) and have experienced similar patterns of moral development, and are thus presumed capable of a sense of justice. Rawls regards these assumptions as the kind of "weak stipulations" on which a general theory can safely be founded.[48]

The coherence of Rawls's hypothetical original position, with its unanimity of representative human beings, however, is placed in doubt if the kinds of human beings we actually become in society differ not only in respect to interests, superficial opinions, prejudices, and points of view that we can discard for the purpose of formulating principles of justice, but also in their basic psychologies, conceptions of the self in relation to others, and experiences of moral development. A number of feminist theorists have argued in recent years that, in a gender-structured society, the different life experiences of females and males from the start in fact affect their respective psychologies, modes of thinking, and patterns of moral development in significant ways.[49] Special attention has been paid to the effects on the psychological and moral development of both sexes of the fact, fundamental to our gendered society, that children of both sexes are reared primarily by women. It has been argued that the experience of individuation—of separating oneself from the nurturer with whom one is originally psychologically fused—is a very different experience for girls than for boys, leaving the members of each sex with a different perception of themselves and of their relations with others. (This thesis, developed by Nancy Chodorow on the basis of psychoanalytic object-relations theory, will be explained in more detail in chapter 6.) In addition, it has been argued that the experience of *being* primary nurturers (and of growing up with this expectation) also affects the psychological and moral perspective of women, as does the experience of growing up in a society in which members of one's sex are in many ways subordinate to the other sex. Feminist theorists have scrutinized and analyzed the different experiences we encounter as we develop, from our actual lived lives to our absorption of their ideological underpinnings, and have filled out in valuable ways Simone de Beauvoir's claim that "one is not born, but rather becomes, a woman."[50]

What seems already to be indicated by these studies, despite their incompleteness so far, is that *in a gender-structured society* there is such a thing as the distinct standpoint of women, and that this standpoint cannot be adequately taken into account by male philosophers doing the theoretical equivalent of the elderly male justices depicted in the cartoon. The formative influence of female parenting on small children, especially, seems to suggest that sex difference is even more likely to affect one's thinking about justice in a gendered society than, for example, racial difference in a society in which race has social significance, or class difference in a class society. The notion of the standpoint of women, while not without its own problems, suggests that a fully human moral or political theory can be developed only with the full participation of both sexes. At the very least, this will require that women take their place with men in the dialogue in approximately equal numbers and in positions of comparable influence. In a society structured along the lines of gender, this cannot happen.

In itself, moreover, it is insufficient for the development of a fully human theory of justice. For if principles of justice are to be adopted unanimously by representative human beings ignorant of their particular characteristics and positions in society, they must be persons whose psychological and moral development is in all essentials identical. This means that the social factors influencing the differences presently found between the sexes—from female parenting to all the manifestations of female subordination and dependence—would have to be replaced by genderless institutions and customs. Only children who are equally mothered and fathered can develop fully the psychological and moral capacities that currently seem to be unevenly distributed between the sexes. Only when men participate equally in what have been principally women's realms of meeting the daily material and psychological needs of those close to them, and when women participate equally in what have been principally men's realms of larger scale production, government, and intellectual and artistic life, will members of both sexes be able to develop a more complete *human* personality than has hitherto been possible. Whereas Rawls and most other philosophers have assumed that human psychology, rationality, moral development, and other capacities are completely represented by the males of the species, this assumption itself has now been exposed as part of the male-dominated ideology of our gendered society.

What effect might consideration of the standpoint of women in gendered society have on Rawls's theory of justice? It would place in doubt some assumptions and conclusions, while reinforcing others. For example, the discussion of rational plans of life and primary goods might be focused more on relationships and less exclusively on the complex activities that he values most highly, if it were to take account of, rather than to take for granted, the traditionally more female contributions to human life.[51] Rawls says that self-respect or self-esteem is "perhaps the most important primary good," and that "the parties in the original position would wish to avoid at almost any cost the social conditions that undermine [it]."[52] Good early physical and especially psychological nurturance in a favorable setting is essential for a child to develop self-respect or self-esteem. Yet there is no discussion of this in Rawls's consideration of the primary goods. Since the basis of self-respect is formed in very early childhood, just family structures and practices in which it is fostered and in which parenting itself is esteemed, and high-quality, subsidized child care facilities to supplement them, would surely be fundamental requirements of a just society. On the other hand, as I indicated earlier, those aspects of Rawls's theory, such as the difference principle, that require a considerable capacity to identify with others, can be strengthened by reference to conceptions of relations between self and others that seem in gendered society to be more predominantly female, but that would in a gender-free society be more or less evenly shared by members of both sexes.

The arguments of this chapter have led to mixed conclusions about the potential usefulness of Rawls's theory of justice from a feminist viewpoint, and about its adaptability to a genderless society. Rawls himself neglects gender and, despite his initial statement about the place of the family in the basic structure, does not consider whether or in what form the family is a just institution. It seems significant, too, that whereas at the beginning of A *Theory of Justice* he explicitly distinguishes the institutions of the basic structure (*including* the family) from other "private associations" and "various informal conventions and customs of everyday life," in his most recent work he distinctly reinforces the impression that the family belongs with those "private" and therefore nonpolitical associations, for which he suggests the principles of justice are less appropriate or relevant.[53] He does this, moreover, despite the fact that his own theory of moral development rests centrally on the early experience of persons within a family environment that is both loving and just. Thus the theory as it stands contains an internal paradox. Because of his assumptions about gender, he has not applied the principles of justice to the realm of human nurturance, a realm that is essential to the achievement and the maintenance of justice.

On the other hand, I have argued that the feminist *potential* of Rawls's method of thinking and his conclusions is considerable. The original position, with the veil of ignorance hiding from its participants their sex as well as their other particular characteristics, talents, circumstances, and aims, is a powerful concept for challenging the gender structure. Once we dispense with the traditional liberal assumptions about public versus domestic, political versus nonpolitical spheres of life, we can use Rawls's theory as a tool with which to think about how to achieve justice between the sexes both within the family and in society at large.

6

Justice from Sphere to Sphere: Challenging the Public/Domestic Dichotomy

As we have learned in the last three chapters, major contemporary Anglo-American theories of justice are to a great extent about men with wives at home. This is less immediately obvious than with theorists in the past, especially in the case of those who use falsely gender-neutral language, but it becomes clear as soon as we try to extend their arguments to women. The basic tenets of extreme libertarianism unravel into self-contradiction and absurdity. Concepts of rationality, justice, and the human good that are supposedly based on "our" traditions are exposed as male-centric. Theories that rely on "shared understandings" also reveal their tendencies to reinforce patriarchy by neglecting to examine the effects of past and present domination on these understandings. When we have inserted reproductive capacities and work into libertarian equations about ownership, when we have asked, *Whose* traditions? and *Which* shared understandings? we have found that these theories depend upon sometimes well hidden and sometimes less well hidden patriarchal assumptions.

With the theory of justice as fairness we encountered a way of thinking that, with the elimination of its "heads of families" premise, has real potential

110

for challenging gender. But in order to take up this challenge, we must expose and elucidate the problems of a dichotomy that has been accepted as fundamental to liberal thought so far: that between the "public" world of political life and the marketplace and the "private" domestic world of family life and personal relations. In this chapter, I shall argue that a fully humanist theory of justice cannot be achieved without thorough examination and critique of the public/domestic dichotomy. The findings of the last two decades of feminist scholarship in a number of disciplines prove invaluable to this undertaking. As Carole Pateman has said, "the dichotomy between the public and the private . . . is, ultimately, what the feminist movement is about."[1]

Later in this chapter, I shall expose the weaknesses of this ideological division. In four major respects, I shall argue, the personal *is* political, and the public/domestic dichotomy is a misleading construct, which obscures the cyclical pattern of inequalities between men and women. First, power—which has always been understood as paradigmatically political—is of central importance in family life. Second, the domestic sphere is itself created by political decisions, and the very notion that the state can choose whether or not to intervene in family life makes no sense. Third, the family is undeniably political because it is the place where we *become* our gendered selves. And fourth, the division of labor within the gender-structured family raises both practical and psychological barriers against women in all the other spheres of life. Before we get to these arguments, however, I shall first look at some ideas of two contemporary theorists—Michael Walzer and Roberto Unger—that contribute to the critique. Neither draws out at all fully the feminist implications of his arguments. But both, in what they say and in what they do not say, provide helpful starting points from which to critique the public/domestic dichotomy and the notion of the "nonpolitical" family.

Justice in Its Separate Spheres

Michael Walzer's *Spheres of Justice* is unusual among mainstream contemporary theories of justice in that it pays any attention at all to women and gender.[2] From its largely nonsexist language to its insistence that the family constitutes a significant "sphere of justice" and its specific references to power imbalances between the sexes and discrimination, Walzer's theory stands out in contrast to most moral and political philosophers' continued indifference to feminist issues. Viewing the book through the prism of gender, however, accentuates both its strengths and its weaknesses. I have already focused on its weaknesses, arguing against the reliance on "shared understandings" as a criterion for justice (see chapter 3). Not only do we have no such shared understandings about gender; when meanings *appear* to be shared, they are often the outcome of the domination of some groups over others, the latter being silenced or rendered "incoherent" by the more powerful. Now I turn to the theory's strengths. Walzer's theoretical framework—separate spheres having to allow for different inequalities to exist side by side only insofar as a situation that he calls "dominance" is not created—has considerable force as a tool for social, and particularly for feminist, criticism.

Walzer argues that justice does not require the equal distribution of each social good within its respective sphere. What is just within each sphere depends on what that particular sphere is all about. In addition, the "complex equality" that he advocates requires that these spheres of justice be kept autonomous, in the sense that the inequality that exists within each must not be allowed to translate itself into inequalities within the others, creating what he calls "dominance."[3] The influence of money, for example, should be very strictly limited in the sphere of electoral politics. His critique of dominance leads to the adoption of the principle that "no social good x should be distributed to men and women who possess some other good y merely because they possess y and without regard to the meaning of x." Social justice consists in the distribution of "different goods to different companies of men and women for different reasons and in accordance with different procedures."[4]

This conception of justice as depending on the autonomy of the various spheres of distribution is presented by Walzer as "a critical principle—indeed, . . . a radical principle."[5] A number of his own specific applications of the principle—notably, to the issue of worker ownership and control of all but small-scale enterprises[6]—confirm this characterization. It is not surprising that the implications of his principle are radical, for in actual societies, as Walzer says, the standards for distribution that the criterion establishes

> are often violated, the goods usurped, the spheres invaded, by powerful men and women.
> In fact, the violations are systematic. . . . For all the complexity of their distributive arrangements, most societies are organized on what we might think of as a social version of the gold standard: one good or one set of goods is dominant and determinative of value in all the spheres of distribution. And that good or set of goods

is commonly monopolized, its value upheld by the strength and cohesion of its owners.[7]

Walzer himself briefly acknowledges that the gender structure violates his requirements for a society that is just according to the standard of separate spheres or complex equality. I shall take up this issue, and take it further than he does. Gender, I shall argue, is a prime and socially all-pervasive case of dominance, and therefore a serious threat to complex equality. Given that many people in our society think the gender structure is just and appropriate—or do not even consider it alterable—the implications of Walzer's comments on it undermine his "shared meanings" criterion for social justice. Although they do not seem to be widely shared beliefs in our society, the feminist implications of the separate spheres criterion for justice point decisively to the need for social change. They suggest what many feminists have been arguing (which will also be confirmed by the data presented in chapter 7): the unequal distribution of rights, benefits, responsibilities, and powers within the family is closely related to inequalities in the many other spheres of social and political life. There is a cyclical process at work, reinforcing the dominance of men over women, from home to work to what is conventionally referred to as the "political" arena, and thence back home again.

In his own working out and discussion of the application of his theory, Walzer is some of the time clearly aware of the feminist implications of his case for complex equality. At the beginning of his chapter on recognition, for example, he states that the argument that is to follow applies only in part to women. He points out that the extent to which women are still designated and defined by their position within the family is symbolized by the continued use of the titles *Miss* and *Mrs.* "The absence of a universal title," he says, "suggests the continued exclusion of women, or of many women, from the social universe, the sphere of recognition as it is currently constituted."[8] What is acknowledged here is the tip of an iceberg that is ignored in most of the other chapters. For the exclusion, or the inclusion on very different terms, of women is equally true of almost all of the other spheres of justice discussed in the book. Political power and office, hard work, money and commodities, security—Are any of these things evenly distributed between the sexes? In each case, the assignment of women to the functional role of actual or potential wife and mother and, as primary parent, to basic or at least periodic dependence upon a man, has a great deal to do with the fact that women, in general, benefit less from the benefits and are burdened more by the burdens in the distribution of most social goods than are men. While Walzer occasionally extends the feminist perspective he displays in the argument about recognition, and develops it briefly in a section entitled "The Woman Question," he frequently overlooks its implications.

Introducing his discussion of the oppression of women, Walzer asserts that "the real domination of women has less to do with their familial place than with their exclusion from all other places." While the family disfavors women by imposing sex roles upon many activities "to which sex is entirely irrelevant," he argues that liberation from this "political and economic misogyny" begins outside the family. Social goods must be distributed in accordance with their own relevant reasons, not determined by women's familial roles. The market must set "no internal bar to the participation of women." However, as he seems to imply, the liberation from misogyny cannot take place entirely outside the family: "The family itself must be reformed so that its power no longer reaches into the sphere of office" (or any of the other spheres of distribution, we might add).[9] On a number of occasions, Walzer criticizes the operation of the gender system outside the family. But in spite of the fact that his separate spheres criterion would seem to demand it, he pays almost no attention to the continued operation of the gender structure within the family.

It would be wrong to attribute this to a belief that justice is not an appropriate moral virtue within the family. For although Walzer perceives the family as "a sphere of special relationships," he also asserts plainly that "the sphere of personal relations, domestic life, reproduction, and child rearing remains . . . the focus of enormously important distributions."[10] And where there are distributions, whether of responsibilities, rights, favors, goods, or power, there is potential for justice and injustice. He does not, however, give this important sphere of differential distribution the attention it warrants. In the chapter called "Hard Work," he discusses many kinds of (undesirable but necessary) *paid* work at some length, but pays virtually no attention to all the unpaid work, much of it "hard" by his definition, that is done for no pay by women at home. He makes only brief reference to the immensely time-consuming activity of child care, which is certainly necessary and, under some conditions, can also be undesirable. If his general argument were not in so many respects egalitarian, one might suppose that he accepted, as a less egalitarian thinker might, paid domestic labor for those who could afford it as the solution for the family responsibilities of wives and/or mothers who chose to work, to seek recognition, political power or office, and so on, in the outside world. But this, besides being economically out of the question for many, would not be a solution acceptable to Walzer, since he regards a family with live-in servants as "inevitably . . . a little tyranny," and considers domestic service of any sort to be "degraded" work. In a just society, he considers that the market will raise the wages of unskilled workers much closer to those of skilled ones than at present, with the desirable result that workers will be much less likely to be willing to take on such degraded work.[11] For good reason, then, Walzer does not accept the low-paid and low-status domestic labor of disadvantaged women—in our society, almost always women of color, often in search of legal immigrant status—as a solution to the problem of more advantaged women. He would not echo the sentiments of an upper-middle-class American man who once asked me, What *would* suburban American women do without Jamaica?

Besides wanting a society just enough to end paid domestic labor, Walzer disapproves of day care. The communal care of young children, he says, is "likely to result in a great loss of love," except in a small, close-knit society such as the kibbutz. This opinion is echoed in a passage in which he talks of children who are "abandoned to bureaucratic rearing."[12] How, then, does he propose that the work currently done almost entirely by women within the household would be done in a society that regards the family, and relations between the sexes in particular, as a sphere in which the standards of justice should apply? Walzer's answers to this question are important, of course, to any feminist reader, and they are highly unusual for a mainstream theorist of justice. But they are so rapidly whisked over, in a clause and a footnote, that they are easily missed. The chapter on hard work is almost all about hard *wage* work, which, as he points out, is done largely by women. But he does conclude there that the only answer to all hard work, and particularly to "dirty" work, in a society of equals is that "at least in some partial and symbolic sense, we will all have to do it." Otherwise, those who do it will be degraded by it, because of the exemption of others, and will never be equal members of the political community. "What is required, then, is a kind of domestic *corvée*, not only in households—*though it is especially important there*—but also in communes, factories, offices, and schools"[13] (emphasis added). Thus in a society of equals, "at least in some partial and symbolic sense," Walzer affirms that housework will be shared, regardless of sex. And while child care is a different matter, since it does not meet his negative definition of hard work (at least, for those whose circumstances are fortunate), Walzer suggests the same solution. Parenthetically, in a footnote, he asks "(why can't the parents share in social *re*production?)."[14]*

While I disagree strongly with Walzer's dismissal of the value of day care,† I agree that these solutions—if the sharing is real and complete rather than "partial and symbolic"—represent one way in which the injustices inherent in the traditional gender-structured family can be done away with. Unless and until the unpaid and largely unrecognized work of the household is shared equally by its adult members, women will not have equal opportunities with men either within the family or in any of the other spheres of distribution— from politics to free time, from recognition to security to money. This sharing is necessary if Walzer's separate spheres criterion for justice is to be fully met: if a society of equal men and women is to distribute its social goods in such a way that what happens within the family is not to dominate over and invade all the other spheres. The family can be perceived as a separate sphere *only* insofar as equality between the sexes reigns within it. On the other hand, this solution constitutes a radical break not only from prevailing patterns of behavior but also from widely, though not completely, shared understandings in our society about the social meanings, institutions, and implications of sexual difference. It is a feminist solution, constituting no less than the demolition of gender in its most entrenched bastion, the family, with likely reverberations throughout all social spheres. Walzer can claim that his briefly indicated solution to sexual inequality is just by his shared meanings criterion only by showing that deep or latent in our shared current understandings lies the justification for the abolition of gender.

According to the separate spheres criterion, the family and personal life can be regarded as just *only if and insofar as* it contains no inequalities, at least among its adult members, that translate into inequalities in other spheres. But to hold the family to this standard is clearly a challenge to the public/domestic dichotomy, according to which marriage and the family are supposedly self-regulating, beyond the range of state intervention. If privacy

---

*The importance of shared child rearing for justice between the sexes is not primarily due to its being undesirable work, for in favorable circumstances it can be immensely pleasurable and challenging. Two reasons why shared child rearing is a prerequisite for justice between the sexes are (1) it is immensely time-consuming, and prevents those who do it single-handedly from the pursuit of many other social goods, such as education, earnings, or political office, and (2) it is likely to reduce sex stereotyping in children, as I shall argue further in chapter 8.

†Even a "mass society" does not have to provide "mass" day care. It can provide small-scale, loving day care for all if it cares enough and is prepared to subsidize the full costs for parents unable to afford it. Good day care, besides being a positive experience for the child, also helps to solve two other problems. Without it, the shared parenting solution is of no help to single parents; and good, subsidized day care can help to alleviate the obstacle that the inequality of family circumstances poses for equality of opportunity.

itself is to carry the same value for all of us, women and men, then the families in which we enjoy it must make us all feel secure and equal. But, given the history of gender, we know that equality between the sexes, whether in the family or anywhere else, is unlikely simply to happen. Only legal, political, and social changes can bring it about.

Unveiling the Myth of the Benign Family

Another area of nonfeminist political theory where there is potential for rethinking the dichotomy of public and domestic and for assessing family life by standards of justice is within the critical legal studies movement.* There has in recent years developed a powerful and growing body of feminist work within or influenced by that movement, some of which I shall turn to later in this chapter. But some of its other theorists, too, in their critiques of current law, legal practice, and legal thought, make arguments that can contribute to the rethinking and the restructuring that are needed if we are to have a society that can overcome the injustices still suffered by women and children. This feminist potential is in large part due to the fact that the critical legal studies movement is—like its ancestor, legal realism—concerned with the *actual* inequalities and power differentials that do so much to cancel out the formal equalities of the law.

The fundamental aims of Roberto Unger's political and legal theory are to expose, and to work toward eradicating, the tension between the liberal dedication to formal equality of rights and the actual relations of dominance and dependency that characterize modern liberal-capitalist societies. In *Knowledge and Politics*, Unger theorizes from an explicitly communitarian point of view.[15] A radical, however, he differs from reactionary communitarians such as MacIntyre in that he does not look to past traditions for the foundations of his preferred community. Nor does he think, as Walzer does, that the basis of the egalitarian community he hopes to build is already here, latent in our shared meanings. He hopes that by developing from the human capacity for love its political equivalent—sympathy—and by transforming workplaces into the "communities of life" or "organic groups" in which such sympathy can develop, we will be able to approach the elimination of the dualisms of liberalism, especially that of individual and community. Uniquely self-critical

---

*Critical legal studies is a movement of the left within the academic legal community that disputes the claims to objectivity of legal practice and theory, stressing their inevitably political character.

among communitarians, Unger, toward the end of his book, lays out the problems inherent in such a theory so frankly and convincingly that he seems to undermine his own theory.[16]*

Unger's progress toward the conceptualization of a new vision of social structures is impeded by his neglect of gender and its impact on liberal thought and practices. Throughout his analysis of liberalism and his critique of all its dualisms, he does not fully confront the central dualism between public and domestic, or the gendered structure of society on which both this and other dualisms heavily depend.[17] Rather, he himself *succumbs* to dualistic thinking; he puts forward the view that the realm in which human experience approaches the ideal that life has to offer—the private realm of art, religion, and personal love—is an "extraordinary" realm that is *not part of everyday life*. He says these things "represent the good in a merely abstract way, a way separated from everyday life and set up in opposition to it."[18] Unger's own separation of the "everyday" world of work and market from the "extraordinary" realm of love rests to a great extent on the assumption that the "selves" his theory addresses and is concerned with are male selves in a gender-structured society.

Not only is this assumption totally unacceptable if Unger's theory is to apply to all of us, but it is dysfunctional in the context of his own theoretical and practical political aims. He does not see that the kind of love and the kind of work that are located within the family have great potential for his own radical politics. Most of the time he ignores the realm of family life. When he briefly mentions it, it is "split," on the one hand, into an idealized vision, distinguished from the self-interested realm of the "everyday" by being governed by love, and, on the other hand, into an illiberal regime of "substantive justice" with no concern for fairness to its individual members.[19] Two things are noticeably absent. One is a critique of existing family structures and practices, which for a theorist so preoccupied with personal relations of dominance and dependence is truly remarkable. When Unger says, discussing the democratic groups he sees as the essential basis for political community, that "men whose everyday experience is one of submission or of predominance cannot be expected to think and to act as equals when they pass upon the affairs of the group,"[20] his insight *demands* that the gender structure of family life be transformed. The critique of the family that is missing here has since

---

*The section entitled "The Dilemmas of Communitarian Politics" is the only place I know of in communitarian thought where its problems, including the problem of domination, are at all fully confronted.

been provided by feminist legal theorists influenced by the critical legal studies movement.

The second absence is an appreciation of the positive potential of a different kind of family for developing the kind of equal, caring individuals that Unger's social ideal requires us to be. He quite neglects the moral possibilities of a transformed family—a place where reason and emotion are equally called for, where all people care for others on a day-to-day basis and, through doing so, can learn to reconcile their own ambitions and desires with those of others and to see things from the points of view of others who may differ from themselves in important respects. The fact that the family "as it exists in the modern state" does not hold out much promise for his communitarian ideals should not deter a theorist as radical as Unger.[21] For if one can transform the workplace and the market in all the ways he suggests, decentralizing and democratizing them, why not pay similar attention to the ways in which the family might be transformed? If life in such groups is to change the character of social relations and individual experience, the gendered and inegalitarian structure of the family cannot be ignored. If Unger paid more attention to the experience of actual people of both sexes and all ages in their personal relations, he might not need to be so pessimistic about what he sees as the gap between the "extraordinary" and the "everyday."[22]

Similarly, Unger's radical rethinking of contract in his more recent work looks, at best, at only half of the picture that needs to be re-examined. In his 1983 article "The Critical Legal Studies Movement," he looks hard and critically at the extent to which the prevailing mode of contract thinking rationalizes dominance and dependence in the world of paid work and commerce, but he pays very little attention to the family.[23] Only hinting at a critique of it, he fails to see that before we have any chance of attaining the kind of "superliberal" community he now looks toward—in which asymmetric personal dependency and domination will be abolished—we must subject marriage to at least as thorough a questioning, in the light of contract theory, as that to which he subjects extrafamilial property relations and paid work. If the institution in which we are primarily socialized is pervaded by domination, what hope is there for freeing from domination the society into which we are being socialized?

In his recent, "superliberal" theory, Unger both critiques liberalism and expands on some of its implications. He confronts the vision of social relations that, he says, is used to explain and to justify the current legal systems of the rich liberal-capitalist North Atlantic societies. This vision consists of a triptych, in which a democratic ideal for the state and citizenship is displayed side by side with a picture of the private communities of family and friendship, and with a contrasting picture of contract and impersonal hierarchy in "the everyday realm of work and exchange."[24] Drawing on *The Merchant of Venice* to explain by analogy what he calls this "crude" view of social relations, he likens the second and third of these spheres, the family and the market, to Belmont—where people are held together by mutual affection—and Venice—where people are motivated by self-interest and regulated by contracts. The charm of Belmont, where "citizens can flee occasionally," Unger adds, serves to make the calculating relations of Venice seem tolerable.[25] He looks toward the elimination, so far as it is possible, of the rigid divisions of social life that are justified by the Belmont/Venice mythology.

But even in this recent work, in which he expresses a somewhat critical view of existing family structure and some concern about gender inequality, Unger still makes mistakes similar to those he is criticizing. Although he regards the mythical contrast of the realm of contract with that of altruistic community as "dangerous" and recognizes that it idealizes the family, this recent theory suffers from the same failure of vision that pervades his earlier work: it maintains the illusion that the realm of personal relations, particularly the family, is not a part of everyday life. This is clearly evident from his statement about the Belmont/Venice analogy that "the most remarkable feature of this vision is its exclusion of the more morally ambitious models of human connection [democracy and the private community of family and friendship] from the prosaic activities and institutions that absorb *most people most of the time*."[26] Thus he draws the analogy in order to critique and to work for transformation of the self-seeking Venice sphere. However, presumably because his male-centric focus obscures from him the fact that many people *are* absorbed much of the time in the activities of family life, he is far less inclined to pursue the need for radical change of the supposedly altruistically based family sphere represented by Belmont.

One of the major tools that Unger employs in his critique of current liberal social and economic institutions is a transformed way of thinking about contract.[27] Contract, as Unger explains, consists of two principles and two counterprinciples. The principles are: freedom *to* contract (whether and with whom to contract), and freedom *of* contract (the choice of terms). The corresponding counterprinciples are: that the freedom to choose the contract partner "not be allowed to work in ways that subvert the communal aspects of social life," and the nonenforcement of unfair contracts.[28] Typically, within liberal legal theory, the principles have been emphasized as the norms and the counterprinciples have been downplayed or regarded as applicable only in somewhat exceptional cases. Unger argues, persuasively, that if one focuses instead on the counterprinciples, one concludes that a far more egalitarian and democratic ordering of social life is called for.

There is potential in this radical rethinking of contract doctrine for taking a very critical look at current family law—especially its pivotal aspects, marriage and divorce law. But while Unger hints at such a critical perspective, he does not pursue it. What he does do, however, is to *open up* a critical perspective on the public/domestic dichotomy. He critiques the traditional liberal mode of contrasting what he calls the "Venetian" world of contract with the "Belmontine" world of private community. This myth holds that the private world of marital relations is akin to the world of friendship, and that their "peculiar communal quality" is in danger of being destroyed by the intrusion of contract law.[29] It views the application of contract law to relations within the family as inappropriate, for two reasons. The first reason is that trust, not negotiation and agreement, is supposed to be the basis of family life, and "the language of formal entitlement" would endanger its unity. The second reason, which, as he says, is usually left implicit, is the inequality of power within the family. The family "constitutes a certain structure of power . . . [which] calls upon its members to accept the legitimacy of gross inequalities in the distribution of trust," since the maintenance of the family is held to depend on the authority of its head. As Unger points out, classical contract theory stands opposed to "such a frankly personalistic and asymmetrical exercise of power."[30] It preaches equality in distrust, not inequality in trust.

Unger presents this vision of the family—"a structure of power, ennobled by sentiment"—as "the dominant conception." But it is, though briefly presented, a far franker admission of inequality within families than is generally acknowledged in discussions of family law by nonfeminist theorists. Unger recognizes that the paradoxical effect of the idealization of the family in liberal thought is to ignore the fact that "mutual responsibility may do better, legally and factually, in the pitiless world of deals than in the supposedly communal haven of family life."[31] Given his assertion at the outset of the essay that the ultimate stakes in politics are direct relations between people, one might expect him to pursue this promising line of thought. It points in the direction of a serious critique of marriage and the family, including a critique of some of the myths about why contractual thinking is inappropriate within the family. Although Unger regards the mythical contrast of contract to community as "dangerous," however, his challenge of it is confined almost entirely to its "contract" dimension, which he, along with the mythmakers, finds confined to the marketplace. The problem with the essay from a feminist point of view is that, having pointed out the irony that "the communal ideal" is *in fact* identified with the "personalistic authority and dependence that often characterize family life," Unger pays no further attention to it.[32]

If the inequalities that he attributes to liberal capitalism need to be confronted, then surely it is even more necessary that he challenge the division of labor between the sexes, centered in family life, which is a peculiarly *pre*liberal anomaly in modern society. The gender structure, based as it is on an accident of birth, is far closer to feudalism or to a caste system than to most institutions fostered by or tolerated within liberal societies. While Unger focuses attention on the inequality of property ownership, which "threatens to reduce some individuals to direct dependence upon others,"[33] he fails to challenge the extent of direct personal economic dependence that results directly from the division of labor within the average family. If, as he says, the aim of the critical legal studies movement is to push liberal preconceptions to their conclusions, then surely one of its initial tasks must be to confront the preliberal relic that is gender.

If we wish to complete the unveiling of the mythology that separates life into the two contrasting spheres of Belmont and Venice, and if we acknowledge the crucial connections between personal relations in the macro- and the micro-institutions of society, we must explicitly pursue the critique of the family. It is first essential to take a frank look at the institution of marriage in liberal society, and to destroy the mythical notion of it as a realm to which contractual thinking is inappropriate. While the law has, indeed, been reluctant to enforce contracts between married persons, marriage itself has long been regarded as a contract, though it is a very peculiar one: it is a contract that does not conform with the *principles* (let alone the counterprinciples) of liberal contract doctrine.[34] It is a preformed status contract, which restricts the parties' freedom to choose their partners (for example, there must be only one partner, and of the opposite sex) and of which they are not free to choose the terms.

The courts' refusal to enforce explicit contracts between husband and wife has been by no means completely attributable to reluctance to intrude into a private community supposedly built upon trust.[35] It has been due at least as much to the fact that the courts have regarded the terms of marriage as already established. When, for example, they have refused to enforce intramarital agreements in which wives have agreed to forgo support for other consideration, and in which husbands have agreed to pay their wives for work done in a family business, they have done so on the grounds that the wife's right to support, in the former case, and her obligation to provide services for her husband, in the latter, are fixed by the marriage contract itself. Likewise, when courts have showed reluctance to enforce the terms of the preformed contract itself—for example, refusing to establish a level of adequate support that a wife must receive—it has been on the grounds that, so long as husband and wife cohabit, it is up to him as the family head to determine such matters.[36] Another respect in which marriage is an anomalous contract is that the parties to it are not required to be familiar with the terms of the relationship into which they are entering—or of its dissolution. Thus it could hardly be called a "fully articulated act of will," such as contracts are usually required to be.[37]

Such anomalies are revealing in terms of family law doctrine, and important as reinforcements of the customs of patriarchal society. By now, however, at least as significant as the courts' reinforcement of sex roles within marriage are these long-standing customs themselves, reinforced by socialization patterns, and the greater actual power of husbands in the marital relationship. As I will explain at greater length in chapter 7, these factors create a cycle in which the division of labor between the sexes (with wives performing a far greater share of the unpaid labor of the family, and tending to subordinate their outside work lives to the needs of their husbands and children) reinforces and increases over time the asymmetric power relation between them. Gender-structured marriage is a clear case of socially created and reinforced inequality. In order to think about how to transform personal relations within marriage, it is essential to be fully aware of the present repercussions of the fact that for many centuries marriage has been the paradigmatic contract between unequals, operating so as to accentuate and deepen the initial inequality.

By not addressing the fact that marriage *is* a contract, Unger obscures the fact that it violates the principles, let alone the counterprinciples, of contract doctrine. And by not directly confronting the issue of sex roles within marriage, he also fails to question the Belmont/Venice myth's reliance on the family to make the market tolerable, "because its citizens can flee occasionally to Belmont and appeal from Venetian justice to Belmontine mercy."[38] This promise of solace is of small comfort to most women with families, whose opportunities within the world of wage work or business are much constrained by what is required of them at home, where they do not "occasionally flee," but spend a great deal of their time and energy. As in *Knowledge and*

Politics, such lacunae seem explicable only in terms of a male-centeredness that pervades Unger's view of the world.

Unger also fails to point out the egalitarian transformation of family relations that might result from applying the *counterprinciples*—which he emphasizes in the case of commercial contracts—to marriage. To a feminist reader, the potential applicability of much of this critique of contract to the sphere of marriage and divorce is immediately apparent, but Unger barely hints at it. Though he strongly challenges "the stark opposition of community as selfless devotion and contract as unsentimental money-making," he does not pay attention to the need for family law to be transformed.[39] But if, in a better society, there is to be "a subtle and continuous shading of contract and community" from the public (contract) side, is there not as great a need for this subtle shading to proceed from the side of domestic community as well? If unrestrained self-interest is not a satisfactory assumption on the one hand, is "selfless devotion" any more satisfactory an assumption on the other? This line of thought has been perceptively developed by some of the feminists influenced by the critical legal studies movement, especially Clare Dalton, Martha Minow, and Frances Olsen.[40] The re-examination of contract can have implications for the institution of the family that are just as radical as those Unger draws out of it for the institutional basis of economic life.

Both Walzer's and Unger's theories begin to point toward a challenging of both the public/domestic dichotomy and the gender structure, though neither takes the challenge very far. More important, both theorists' egalitarian visions for society require and can benefit from a radical questioning of and proposal to restructure the current distributions of power and responsibilities, rights and roles, between the sexes. Feminist theorists—political, legal, sociopsychological, and historical—have developed this challenge.

The Personal as Political

"The personal is political" is the central message of feminist critiques of the public/domestic dichotomy. It is the core idea of most contemporary feminism. Though many of those who fought in the nineteenth and early twentieth centuries for suffrage and for the abolition of the oppressive legal status of wives were well aware of the connections between women's political and personal dominations by men, few pre-1960s feminists questioned women's special role in the family. While arguing for equal rights, such as the vote or access to education, most accepted the prevailing assumption that women's close association with and responsibility for the care of the family was natural and inevitable.

The earliest claims that the personal is political came from those radical feminists of the 1960s and 1970s who argued that, since the family was at the root of women's oppression, it must be "smashed."[41] The anti-family nature of some early radical feminism has been exaggerated and exploited both by antifeminists and by those who have been termed "conservative" or "backlash" feminists. They have focused on it in order to attack all, or all but their own version, of feminism.[42] But most contemporary feminists, while critiquing the gender-structured family, have not attacked all varieties of family. Many advocate that "family" be defined so as to include any intimately connected and committed group, specifically endorsing homosexual marriage; most, certainly, refuse to accept that the choice must be between accepting women's double burden and abolishing the family. We refuse to give up on the institution of the family, and refuse to accept the division of labor between the sexes as natural and unchangeable. More and more, as the extent to which gender is a social construction has become understood, feminists have come to recognize how variable are the potential forms and practices of family groups. The family is in no way inevitably tied to its gender structure, but until this notion is successfully challenged, and nontraditional groupings and divisions of labor are not only recognized but encouraged, there can be no hope of equality for women in either the domestic or the public sphere.

Thus feminists have turned their attention to the politics of what had previously been regarded—and, as I have shown, still is seen by most political theorists—as paradigmatically *non*political. That the personal sphere of sexuality, of housework, of child care and family life *is* political became the underpinning of most feminist thought. Feminists of different political leanings and in a variety of academic disciplines have revealed and analyzed the multiple interconnections between women's domestic roles and their inequality and segregation in the workplace, and between their socialization in gendered families and the psychological aspects of their oppression. We have strongly and persistently challenged the long-standing underlying assumption of almost all political theories: that the sphere of family and personal life is so separate and distinct from the rest of social life that such theories can justifiably assume but ignore it.

As my argument so far has made clear, however, these feminist arguments have not been acknowledged by most contemporary political theorists writing about justice. In discussing some of the central feminist arguments about the essentially political nature of personal life and of the family in particular, I shall establish that domestic life needs to be just and to have its justice reinforced by the state and its legal system. In the circumstances of the division of labor that is practiced within the vast majority of households in the United States today, women are rendered vulnerable by marriage and especially by motherhood, and there is great scope for unchecked injustice to flourish.

The interconnections between the domestic and the nondomestic aspects of our lives are deep and pervasive. Given the power structures of both, women's lives are far more detrimentally affected by these interconnections than are men's. Consider two recent front-page stories that appeared on subsequent days in the *New York Times*. The first was about a tiny elite among women: those who work as lawyers for the country's top law firms.[43] If these women have children with whom they want to spend any time, they find themselves off the partnership track and instead, with no prospects of advancement, on the "mommy track." "Nine-to-five" is considered part-time work in the ethos of such firms, and one mother reports that, in spite of her twelve-hour workdays and frequent work on weekends, she has "no chance" of making partner.[44] The article fails to mention that these women's children have fathers, or that most of the men who work for the same prestigious law firms also have children, except to report that male lawyers who take parental leave are seen as "wimp-like." The sexual division of labor in the family, even in these cases where the women are extremely well qualified, successful, and potentially influential, is simply assumed.[45]*

The next day's *Times* reported on a case of major significance for abortion rights, decided by a Federal Appeals Court in Minnesota.[47] The all-

---

*Felice Schwartz, too, in a recent controversial article at first assumes the traditional division of parenting labor between the sexes, even when both parents are high-powered professionals. She justifies this by saying that "the one immutable, enduring difference between men and women is maternity," in which she includes everything from the anticipation of motherhood through the psychological adjustment to having a child to child rearing. But a few lines later, seemingly in total contradiction with this, she acknowledges that "today, in the developed world, the only role still uniquely gender related is childbearing." She adds that though "men and women are still socialized to perform their traditional roles . . . certainly both men and women are capable of the full range of behavior." Thus what starts out as immutable becomes by the next paragraph almost entirely alterable. The *reasons* that, as Schwartz reports, "some 90% of executive men but only 35% of executive women have children by the age of 40" and that her article focuses on executives who are mothers rather than all those who are parents, can be discerned only if one tries to understand the interrelation of the public and the domestic spheres.[46]

male panel of judges ruled 7 to 3 that the state may require a woman under eighteen years who wishes to obtain an abortion to notify *both* her parents—even in cases of divorce, separation, or desertion—or to get special approval from a state judge. The significance of this article is amplified when it is juxtaposed with the previous one. For it shows us how it is that those who rise to the top in the highly politically influential profession of law are among those who have had the least experience of all in raising children. There is a high incidence of recruitment of judges from those who have risen to partnership in the most prestigious law firms. Other judges are often drawn from the equally highly competitive field of academic law, which also places its greatest demands (those of the tenure hurdle) on lawyers during the child-rearing years, and therefore discriminates against those who participate in parenting. Those who are chosen, therefore, would seem to be those least well informed to make decisions about abortion, especially in cases involving relations between teenage girls and their parents. Here we find a systematically built-in absence of mothers (and presumably of "wimp-like" participating fathers, too) from high-level political decisions concerning some of the most vulnerable persons in society—women, disproportionately poor and black, who become pregnant in their teens, and their future children. It is not hard to see here the ties between the supposedly distinct public and domestic spheres.

This is but one example of what feminists mean by saying that "the personal is political," sometimes adding the corollary "the political is personal." It is because of this claim, of course, that the family became and has remained central to the politics of feminism and to feminist theory. Contemporary feminism poses a significant challenge to the long-standing and still-surviving assumption of political theories that the sphere of family and personal life is sharply distinct from the rest of social and political life, that the state can and should restrain itself from intrusion into the domestic sphere, and that political theories can therefore legitimately ignore it. In contrast, both challenging and aiming to restructure the public/domestic dichotomy are fundamental to the feminist enterprise.

I must point out here what many feminists who challenge the traditional dichotomy of public and domestic do *not* claim, especially because it is a claim that some do make.[48] Challenging the dichotomy does not necessarily mean denying the usefulness of a concept of privacy or the value of privacy itself in human life. Nor does it mean denying that there are *any* reasonable distinctions to be made between the public and domestic spheres. It does not

127

mean, to many feminists, including myself, a simple or a total *identification* of the personal and the political. Carol Pateman, Linda Nicholson, and Mary O'Brien, for example, all distance themselves from the literal interpretation that some radical feminists give to "the personal is political," and I agree with them in not accepting a complete overlapping or identification of the two. Anita Allen's recent book, *Uneasy Access*, is a feminist argument based on women's often unfulfilled need for personal privacy.[49] Both the concept of privacy and the existence of a personal sphere of life in which the state's authority is very limited are essential. However, such a sphere can be just and secure only if its members are equals, and if those who must be temporarily regarded as unequal—children—are protected from abuse. "How political *is* the personal?" and "*In what ways* is the personal political and is the political personal?" are important questions within feminist argument.[50] My discussion in chapter 7 about the politics of marriage contributes to this argument. Here, I shall lay out four major flaws in the dichotomy between "private" domestic life and "public" life in the marketplace or politics, as it is currently drawn or assumed in theories of justice. These constitute, in other words, four respects in which the personal is political.

First, what happens in domestic and personal life is not immune from the dynamic of *power*, which has typically been seen as the distinguishing feature of the political. Power within the family, whether that of husband over wife or of parent over child, has often not been recognized as such, either because it has been regarded as natural or because it is assumed that, in the family, altruism and the harmony of interests make power an insignificant factor. This seems to be tacitly assumed by most contemporary theorists of justice, given their neglect of intrafamilial relations. But the notion that power in its crassest form, physical violence, is not a factor in family life is a myth that has been exposed during the last century and increasingly exposed in the last two decades. As has now become well known, wife abuse, though still seriously underreported, is not an uncommon phenomenon. According to a 1976 national survey, it is estimated that between 1.8 and 5.7 million women in the United States are beaten each year in their homes. A recent government study of marital violence in Kentucky found that 4 percent of women living with a male partner had been kicked or bitten, struck with a fist or an object, beaten up, or either threatened or attacked with a knife or gun during the previous year. Nine percent reported this degree of physical abuse at some time in the past from the man they lived with, and some estimates of actual incidence are far higher. Thirty percent of all female murder victims in 1986

128

were killed by their husbands or boyfriends, compared with 6 percent of male victims killed by wives or girlfriends.[51]

People are far more tolerant of physical abuse of a woman by a man when they believe she is his wife or girlfriend than otherwise. This is probably due in part to the fact that violence used to be a legally sanctioned part of male dominance in the patriarchal family. The privacy that early liberal theorists claimed for the "individuals" they wrote about was the power of patriarchs; it was taken for granted that husbands and fathers should have power over their wives and children, including the right to "chastise" them physically. Until recently, though in principle no longer legally sanctioned, violence within families was in practice ignored; the police and the courts were loath to "intervene" in ostensibly "private" familial disputes. In the late nineteenth and early twentieth centuries, child abuse was "discovered." And in the 1970s and 1980s, partly as a result of the feminist and children's rights movements that originated in the 1960s, wife abuse has been "discovered" and child abuse "rediscovered." Family violence is now much less sanctioned or ignored than in the past; it is becoming recognized as a serious problem that society must act on. There is now no doubt that family violence, as it affects both wives and children, is closely connected with differentials of power and dependency between the sexes. It is certainly impossible to claim, in the face of current evidence, that the family is private and nonpolitical because power is an insignificant factor in it. In addition to physical force, there are subtler, though no less important, modes of power that operate within families, some of which will be discussed in the next chapter. As feminists have pointed out, in many respects the notion that state intervention in the family should be minimized has often served to reinforce the power of its economically or physically more powerful members. The privacy of home can be a dangerous place, especially for women and children.[52]

The second problem with the public/domestic dichotomy is that, as feminist historians and lawyers have shown, to the extent that a more private, domestic sphere does exist, its very existence, the limits that define it, and the types of behavior that are acceptable and not acceptable within it all result from political decisions.[53] If there *were* a clear sphere from which the state refrained from intruding, that sphere would have to be defined, and its definition would be a political issue. But in fact, the state has not just "kept out of" family life. In innumerable ways, the state determines and enforces the terms of marriage. For hundreds of years, the common law deprived women of their legal personhood upon marriage. It enforced the rights of husbands to their wives' property and even to their wives' bodies, and made it virtually impossible for women to divorce or even to live separately from their husbands. Long after married women gained rights over their own property and the possibility of divorce, as we have seen, marriage has remained a peculiar contract, a preformed status contract whose terms have been enforced in innumerable ways. Courts have refused to allow wives to trade or forgo their rights to support, but have also refused to "intrude" into the family to enforce any specific level of support; few jurisdictions recognize marital rape; and married women have been "compelled, by law, to perform housework without pay [and] the obligation cannot be altered."[54] In addition, until the "divorce revolution" of the last two decades, the terms of divorce strongly reinforced traditional sex roles within marriage, by means of rewards and punishments. As Lenore Weitzman wrote in 1985, "the common law assumption that the husband was the head of the family remained firmly embodied in statute and case law until the last decade."[55]

There is a whole other dimension, too, to the state's pervasive regulation of family life. Historically, the law closed off to women most means of making a living wage. Until very recently, women have been legally denied rights routinely exercised by men in the spheres of work, marketplace, and politics, on the grounds that the exercise of such rights would interfere with the performance of their domestic responsibilities. All of this obviously reinforced the patriarchal structure of marriage, but the myth of the separation of the public and the domestic, of the political from the personal, was sustained throughout. Even now that most of the explicit legal disabilities of women have been done away with, the state has a direct hand in regulating family life in such crucial areas as marriage, divorce, and child custody. Who can marry whom, who is legally the child of whom, on what grounds marriages can be dissolved, and whether both spouses or only one must consent to their dissolution, are all directly determined by legislation. In turn, such laws themselves and how they are applied can have a critical impact on how people live their domestic lives, and thence a cyclical effect on their entire lives.

As Frances Olsen has pointed out with great clarity and perceptiveness, the very notion that the state has the option to intervene or not to intervene in the family is not only mythical but meaningless. In many ways "the state is responsible for the background rules that affect people's domestic behaviors." The law does not on the one hand legitimize any and all kinds of behavior within the family—murder being the most obvious example. But neither does it regulate the behavior of family members toward each other in the same way that it regulates the behavior of strangers; for example, parents can "ground" their children as a means of discipline, or enlist the state's help in restraining children who run away. Children cannot sue their parents (as others could) for kidnapping them on such occasions and, as Olsen says, "the staunchest opponents of state intervention in the family will insist that the state reinforce parents' authority over their children." "Because the state is deeply implicated in the formation and functioning of families," she argues, "it is nonsense to talk about whether the state does or does not intervene in the family."[56] On the vital question of divorce, for example, would "nonintervention" mean allowing divorce, or not allowing it? Making a divorce difficult or easy to acquire? The issue is not whether, but *how* the state intervenes. The myth that state intervention in the family is an option allows those who support the status quo to call it "nonintervention" and to label policies that would alter it—such as the provision of shelters for battered wives— "intervention." This language takes the focus off more pertinent questions such as whether the policy in question is equitable or prevents harm to the vulnerable.[57] Chapter 8 suggests some ways in which the state and its laws, which cannot avoid playing a crucial role in marriage and the family, might do so in ways that are more just and equitable than they do at present.

The third reason it is invalid to assume a clear dichotomy between a nonpolitical sphere of family life and a public or political sphere is that domestic life is where most of our early socialization takes place. Feminist scholarship has contributed much to our understanding of how we *become* our gendered selves. Psychoanalytic and other psychologically based theories have explained how gender is reproduced specifically through gendered parenting. One of the earliest of such theories of development (though still highly influential, on account of its persuasiveness) is that of Nancy Chodorow. She argues, building on object-relations theory, that a child's experience of individuation—separating from the caregiver with whom he or she is at first psychologically fused—is a very different experience for those of the same sex as the nurturer than it is for those of the other sex.[58] In a gender-structured society like ours, where primary nurturers are almost always mothers (and, if not, other females), this makes for a sexually differentiated developmental path for girls and for boys. The psychological task of identification with the same-sexed parent is very different for girls, for whom the mother (or female surrogate) is usually present, than for boys, for whom the parent to identify with is often absent for long periods of the day, engaged in tasks the child has no concrete knowledge of. Chodorow argues that, as a result, the

131

personality characteristics in girls and women that make them more psychologically connected with others, more likely to choose nurturing and to be regarded as especially suited for it—and those in men that lead them to a greater need and capacity for individuation and orientation toward achieving "public" status—can be explained by the assignation of primary parenting within the existing gender structure. Thus mothering itself is "reproduced" in girls. Once we admit the idea that significant differences between women and men are *created* by the existing division of labor within the family, it becomes increasingly obvious just how political an institution the family is.

Moreover, the connections between domestic life and the rest of life are accentuated by the fact that the complete answer to the question of why women are primary parents cannot be arrived at by looking solely at the family and at the psychology of gender development. A large part of the answer is to be found in the sex segregation of the workplace, where the great majority of women are still concentrated in low-paid, dead-end occupations. This fact makes it economically "rational" in most two-parent families for the mother to be the primary child rearer, which continues the cycle of gender.

A fourth respect in which "the personal is political" and the public/domestic dichotomy breaks down is that the division of labor within most families raises psychological as well as practical barriers against women in all other spheres. In liberal democratic politics, as well as in most workplace situations, speech and argument are often recognized as crucial components of full participation. Michael Walzer, for example, writes: "Democracy is . . . *the political way* of allocating power. . . . What counts is argument among the citizens. Democracy puts a premium on speech, persuasion, rhetorical skill. Ideally, the citizen who makes the most persuasive argument . . . gets his way."[59] Women, however, are often handicapped by being deprived of any authority in their speech. As one recent feminist analysis has diagnosed the problem, it is not "that women have not learned how to be in authority," but rather "that authority currently is conceptualized so that female voices are excluded from it."[60] This results, to a large extent, from the fact that women's public and private personae are inextricably linked in the minds of many men and is exacerbated by the fact that women are often represented in token numbers, both in influential positions in the workplace and on authoritative political bodies. One example of this is the sex bias in the nation's courtrooms, which has been increasingly well documented during the last few years. It affects judicial attitudes toward women as defendants, plaintiffs, victims, and lawyers, with consequent effects on sentencing, treatment of domestic-violence and rape victims, alimony and child support awards, and damages awards.[61] Sometimes women in the public sphere are simply not seen or heard. Sometimes we are seen and heard only insofar as we make ourselves seem as much as possible like men. Sometimes we are silenced by being demeaned or sexually harassed. And sometimes what we say is silenced or distorted because we have projected onto us the personae of particularly important women (especially their mothers) in the intrapsychic lives of men.

All of these handicaps, which women carry with them from the sexual division of labor at home to the outside spheres of life, certainly do not make it easy for us to make transitions back and forth between them. Because of the past and present division of labor between the sexes, for women especially, the public and the domestic are in many ways *not* distinct, separate realms at all. The perception of a sharp dichotomy between them depends on the view of society from a traditional male perspective that tacitly assumes different natures and roles for men and women. It cannot, therefore, be maintained in a truly humanist theory of justice—one that will, for the first time, include all of us. As the next chapter will show further, specifically in the context of contemporary life in the United States, what have been presented as separate spheres are in fact closely linked parts in a cycle of inequality between the sexes.

7

Vulnerability by Marriage

As the preceding chapters made clear, major contemporary theories of social justice pay little or no attention to the multiple inequalities between the sexes that exist in our society, or to the social construct of gender that gives rise to them. Neither mainstream theorists of social justice nor their critics (with rare exceptions) have paid much attention to the internal inequalities of the family. They have considered the family relevant for one or more of only three reasons. Some have seen the family as an impediment to equal opportunity. But the focus of such discussion has been on class differentials among families, not on sex differentials within them. While the concern that the family limits equality of opportunity is legitimate and serious, theorists who raise it have neglected the issue of gender and therefore ignored important aspects of the problem. Those who discuss the family without paying attention to the inequalities between the sexes are blind to the fact that the gendered family radically limits the equality of opportunity of women and girls of all classes—as well as that of poor and working-class children of both sexes. Nor do they see that the vulnerability of women that results from the patriarchal structure and practices of the family *exacerbates* the problem that the inequality of families poses for children's equality of opportunity. As I shall argue in this chapter, with the increasing prevalence of families headed by a single female, children suffer more and more from the economic vulnerability of women.

Second and third, theorists of justice and their critics have tended either to idealize the family as a social institution for which justice is not an appropriate virtue, or, more rarely, to see it as an important locus for the development of a sense of justice. I have disagreed strongly with those who, focusing on an idealized vision of the family, perceive it as governed by virtues nobler than justice and therefore not needing to be subjected to the tests of justice to which we subject other fundamental social institutions. While I strongly support the *hope* that families will live up to nobler virtues, such as generosity, I contend that in the real world, justice is a virtue of fundamental importance for families, as for other basic social institutions. An important sphere of distribution of many social goods, from the material to the intangible, the family has a history of distributing these goods in far from just ways. It is also, as some who have overlooked its internal justice have acknowledged, a sphere of life that is absolutely crucial to moral development. If justice cannot at least begin to be learned from our day-to-day experience within the family, it seems futile to expect that it can be developed anywhere else. Without just families, how can we expect to have a just society? In particular, if the relationship between a child's parents does not conform to basic standards of justice, how can we expect that child to grow up with a sense of justice?

It is not easy to think about marriage and the family in terms of justice. For one thing, we do not readily associate justice with intimacy, which is one reason some theorists idealize the family. For another, some of the issues that theories of justice are most concerned with, such as differences in standards of living, do not obviously apply among members of a family. Though it is certainly not the case in some countries, in the United States the members of a family, so long as they live together, usually share the same standard of living. As we shall see, however, the question of who earns the family's income, or how the earning of this income is shared, has a great deal to do with the distribution of power and influence within the family, including decisions on how to spend this income. It also affects the distribution of other benefits, including basic security. Here, I present and analyze the facts of contemporary gender-structured marriage in the light of theories about power and vulnerability and the issues of justice they inevitably raise. I argue that marriage and the family, as currently practiced in our society, are unjust institutions. They constitute the pivot of a societal system of gender that renders women vulnerable to dependency, exploitation, and abuse. When we look seriously at the distribution between husbands and wives of such critical social goods as work (paid and unpaid), power, prestige, self-esteem, opportunities for self-development, and both physical and economic security, we find socially constructed inequalities between them, right down the list.

The argument I shall make in this chapter depends to a large extent on contemporary empirical data, but also reflects the insights of two theorists, moral philosopher Robert Goodin and economist Albert O. Hirschman. Neither has used his argument to make a case about the injustice of the gender-structured family, but both establish convincing arguments about power and vulnerability that will be invaluable as we look at the data about contemporary marriage.

Goodin's recent book *Protecting the Vulnerable* discusses the significance of socially caused vulnerability for issues of justice. He argues that, over and above the general moral obligations that we owe to persons in general, "we bear special responsibilities for protecting those who are particularly vulnerable to us."[1] His major aim is to justify the obligations that welfare states place on citizens to contribute to the welfare of their more vulnerable fellow citizens. But his arguments can be employed to shed light on a number of other important social issues and institutions, including marriage and the family. Goodin's theory is particularly applicable to marriage because of its concern not only with the protection of the vulnerable but also with the moral status of vulnerability itself. Obviously, as he acknowledges, some cases of vulnerability have a large natural component—the vulnerability of infants, for example, although societies differ in how they allocate responsibility for protecting infants. Some instances of vulnerability that may at first appear "natural," such as those caused by illness, are in fact to a greater or lesser extent due to existing social arrangements.[2] And "some of the most important dependencies and vulnerabilities seem to be *almost wholly social in character*" (emphasis added).[3] Because asymmetric vulnerabilities create social obligations, which may fail to be fulfilled, and because they open up opportunities for exploitation, Goodin argues that insofar as they are alterable they are morally unacceptable and should be minimized. In this, he cites and follows the example of John Stuart Mill, who complained about the "great error of reformers and philanthropists [who] . . . nibble at the consequences of unjust power, instead of redressing the injustice itself."[4] As Goodin concludes, in the case of those vulnerabilities that are "created, shaped, or sustained by current social arrangements . . . [w]hile we should always strive to protect the vulnerable, we should also strive to reduce the latter sort of vulnerabilities insofar as they render the vulnerable liable to exploitation."[5]

One of the tests Goodin employs to distinguish such unacceptable relations of asymmetrical vulnerability from acceptable relations of mutual vulnerability or interdependence is to examine the respective capacities of the two parties to withdraw from the relationship. Even if there is some degree of inequality in a relationship, Goodin says, "as long as the subordinate party can withdraw without severe cost, the superordinate cannot exploit him."[6] As I shall argue, the differing respective potentials for satisfactory withdrawal from the relationship is one of the major elements making marriage, in its typical contemporary manifestations in the United States, a morally unacceptable relationship of vulnerability.

The idea that the mutuality or asymmetry of a relationship can be measured by the relative capacities of the parties to withdraw from it has been developed extensively by Albert O. Hirschman, in two books written many years apart. In his 1970 book entitled *Exit, Voice and Loyalty*, Hirschman makes a convincing connection between the influence of voice by members within groups or institutions and the feasibility of their exit from them. There is a complex relation, he argues, between voice and exit. On the one hand, if the exit option is readily available, this will "tend to *atrophy the development of the art of voice.*" Thus, for example, dissatisfied customers who can easily purchase equivalent goods from another firm are unlikely to expend their energies voicing complaints. On the other hand, the nonexistence or low feasibility of the exit option can impede the effectiveness of voice, since the *threat* of exit, whether explicit or implicit, is an important means of making one's voice influential. Thus "voice is not only handicapped when exit is possible, but also, though in a quite different way, when it is not." Because of this, for members' influence to be most effective, "there should be the possibility of exit, but exit should not be too easy or too attractive."[7] Hirschman concludes that institutions that deter exit by exacting a very high price for it, thereby rendering implausible the threat of exit, also repress the use and effectiveness of voice. Thus both potential modes of influence for combating deterioration are rendered ineffective.

Because the subjects of Hirschman's attention in *Exit, Voice and Loyalty* are groups with many members, his concern is with the power of the members vis-à-vis the institution, rather than with the power of the members relative to one another. But in the case of a two-member institution, such as marriage, special dynamics result from the fact that exit by one partner does not just weaken the institution, but rather results in its dissolution. Whether or not the other party wishes to exit, he or she is effectively expelled by the decision of the other to exit. Because of this, the *relative* potential of the exit option for the two parties is crucial for the relationship's power structure. Hirschman had made this argument, in the context of international relations, in a book published twenty-five years earlier, *National Power and the Structure of Foreign Trade*.[8] There he showed how state A can increase its power and influence by developing trading relations with state B, which is more dependent on the continuance of the trading relationship than A is. While both states gain something from the trade, the gain is far more significant in the one case than in the other. Thus the less dependent state's greater potential for exiting unharmed from the relationship gives it power or influence that can be used (through explicit or implicit threat of withdrawal) to make the more dependent state comply with its wishes. In addition, because of the extent of its dependence on trade with A, state B may alter its economic behavior in such a way that it becomes even more dependent on its trade with A.[9] Power (which may or may not remain latent) is likely to result from dependencies that are entered into voluntarily by parties whose initial resources and options differ, and in such circumstances the asymmetric dependency may well increase in the course of the relationship.

How do these principles apply to marriage? Few people would disagree with the statement that marriage involves, in some respects, especially emotionally, *mutual* vulnerability and dependence. It is, clearly, also a relationship in which some aspects of unequal vulnerability are not determined along sex lines. For example, spouses may vary in the extent of their love for and emotional dependence on each other; it is certainly not the case that wives always love their husbands more than they are loved by them, or vice versa. Nevertheless, as we shall see, in crucial respects gender-structured marriage *involves women in a cycle of socially caused and distinctly asymmetric vulnerability*. The division of labor within marriage (except in rare cases) makes wives far more likely than husbands to be exploited both within the marital relationship and in the world of work outside the home. To a great extent and in numerous ways, contemporary women in our society are *made* vulnerable by marriage itself. They are first set up for vulnerability during their developing years by their personal (and socially reinforced) expectations that they will be the primary caretakers of children, and that in fulfilling this role they will need to try to attract and to keep the economic support of a man, to whose work life they will be expected to give priority. They are rendered vulnerable by the actual division of labor within almost all current marriages. They are disadvantaged at work by the fact that the world of wage work, including the professions, is still largely structured around the assumption that "workers" have wives at home. They are rendered far more vulnerable if they become the primary caretakers of children, and their vulnerability peaks if their marriages dissolve and they become single parents.

Part of the reason that many nonfeminist social theorists have failed to recognize this pattern is that they confuse the socially caused (and therefore avoidable) vulnerability of women with the largely natural (and therefore largely unavoidable) vulnerability of children. This goes along with the usually unargued and certainly unfounded assumption that women are inevitably the primary caretakers of children. But as I shall show, women are made vulnerable, both economically and socially, by the interconnected traditions of female responsibility for rearing children and female subordination and dependence, of which both the history and the contemporary practices of marriage form a significant part.

It may be argued that it makes no sense to claim that something as ill-defined and variable as "modern marriage" is unjust, since marriages and families take so many forms, and not all marriages result in the dependence and vulnerability of their female members. There is some validity to this objection, and I shall try to counter it by making qualifications and pointing out exceptions to some of the general points I shall make. Part of the peculiarity of contemporary marriage comes from its very lack of definition. The fact that society seems no longer to have any consensual view of the norms and expectations of marriage is particularly apparent from the gulf that exists between the continued *perception* of most men and women that it is still the primary responsibility of husbands to "provide for" their wives by participating in wage work and of wives to perform a range of unpaid "services" for their husbands, and the *fact* that most women, including mothers of small children, are both in the labor force *and* performing the vast majority of household duties. In addition, the persistent perception of the male as provider is irreconcilable with both the prevalence of separation and divorce and the fact that, more and more, women and children are *not* being provided for after divorce. Between the expectations and the frequent outcome lies an abyss that not only is unjust in itself but radically affects the ways in which people behave within marriage. There is no way to alleviate the continuing inequality of women without more clearly defining and also reforming marriage. It seems evident, both from the disagreements between traditionalists and feminists and from the discrepancy between people's expectations of marriage and what in fact often happens to those who enter into it that there exists no clear current consensus in this society about what marriage is or should be.

Marriage has a long history, and we live in its shadow. It is a clear case of Marx's notion that we make our history "under circumstances directly encountered, given and transmitted from the past."[10] Certainly, gender is central to the way most people think about marriage. A recent, detailed study of thousands of couples, of different types—married and unmarried, heterosexual, gay and lesbian—confirms the importance of gender to our concept of marriage. Philip Blumstein and Pepper Schwartz's findings in *American Couples* demonstrate how not only current family law but the traditional expectations of marriage influence the attitudes, expectations, and behavior of married couples. By contrast, the lack of expectations about gender, and the lack of history of the institution of marriage, allow gay and lesbian couples more freedom in ordering their lives together and more chance to do so in an egalitarian manner. As the study concludes: "First, while the heterosexual model offers more stability and certainty, it inhibits change, innovation, and *choice* regarding roles and tasks. Second, the heterosexual model, which provides so much efficiency, is predicated on the man's being the dominant partner." The unmarried couples interviewed did not, in general, assume so readily that one partner would be the primary economic provider or that they would pool their income and assets. Homosexual couples, because of the absence of both marriage and the "gender factor," made even fewer such assumptions than did cohabiting heterosexual couples. They were almost unanimous, for example, in refusing to assign to either partner the role of homemaker. By contrast, many of the married respondents still enthusiastically subscribed to the traditional female/male separation of household work from wage work. While the authors also found the more egalitarian, two-paycheck marriage "emerging," they conclude that "the force of the previous tradition still guides the behavior of most modern marriages."[11]

It is important to recollect, in this context, how recently white married women in the United States have begun to work outside the home in significant numbers. Black women have always worked, first as slaves, then mostly—until very recently—as domestic servants. But in 1860, only 15 percent of all women were in the paid labor force and, right up to World War II, wage work for married women was strongly disapproved of. In 1890, only 5 percent of married women were in the labor force, and by 1960 the rate of

140

married women's labor force participation had still reached only 30 percent. Moreover, wage work has a history of extreme segregation by sex that is closely related to the traditional female role within marriage. The largest category of women workers were domestic servants as late as 1950, since which time clerical workers have outnumbered them. Service (mostly no longer domestic) is still very predominantly female work. Even the female-dominated professions, such as nursing, grade-school teaching, and library work, have been "pink-collar labor ghettos [which] have historically discouraged high work ambitions that might detract from the pull of home and children." Like saleswomen and clerical workers, these female professionals "tend to arrive early in their 'careers' at a point above which they cannot expect to rise."[12] In sum, married women's wage work has a history of being exceptional, and women's wage work in general has been—as much of it still is—highly segregated and badly paid.

The traditional idea of sex-differentiated marital responsibility, with its provider-husband and domestic-wife roles, continues to be a strong influence on what men and women think and how they behave. Husbands, at least, tend to feel this way even when their wives *do* work outside the home; and when there is disagreement about whether the wife should work, it is more often the case that she wants to but that he does not want to "let" her. Thirty-four percent of the husbands and 25 percent of the wives surveyed by Blumstein and Schwartz did not think that couples should share the responsibility for earning a living. These percentages rise sharply when children are involved: 64 percent of husbands and 60 percent of wives did not think that the wife should be employed if a couple has small children.[13] Given the emphasis our society places on economic success, belief in the male provider role strongly reinforces the domination of men within marriage. Although, as we shall see, many wives actually work longer hours (counting paid and unpaid work) than their husbands, the fact that a husband's work is predominantly paid gives him not only status and prestige, both within and outside the marriage, but also a greater sense of entitlement. As a consequence, wives experiencing divorce, especially if they have been housewives and mothers throughout marriage, are likely to devalue their own contributions to the marriage and to discount their right to share its assets. "Many divorcing women still see the money their husbands have earned as 'his money.'"[14] In ongoing marriages too, it is not uncommon for husbands to use the fact that they are the primary breadwinners to enforce their views or wishes.[15]

Vulnerability by Anticipation of Marriage

In many respects, marriage is an institution whose tradition weighs upon those who enter into it. The cycle of women's vulnerability begins early, with their anticipation of marriage. Almost all women and men marry, but marriage has earlier and far greater impact on the lives and life choices of women than on those of men.* Socialization and the culture in general place more emphasis on marriage for girls than for boys and, although people have recently become less negative about remaining single, young women are more likely than young men to regard "having a good marriage and family life" as extremely important to them.[17] This fact, together with their expectation of being the parent primarily responsible for children, clearly affects women's decisions about the extent and field of education and training they will pursue, and their degree of purposiveness about careers. It is important to note that vulnerability by anticipation of marriage affects at least as adversely the futures of many women who do *not* marry as it affects those who do. This is particularly significant among disadvantaged groups, particularly poor urban black women, whose actual chances of marrying and being economically supported by a man are small (largely because of the high unemployment rate among the available men), but who are further burdened by growing up surrounded by a culture that still identifies femininity with this expectation.

Even though the proportion of young women who plan to be housewives exclusively has declined considerably,[18] women's choices about work are significantly affected from an early age by their expectations about the effects of family life on their work and of work on their family life. As is well known, the participation of women in the labor force, especially women with small children, has continued to rise.† But, although a small minority of women are rapidly increasing the previously tiny percentages of women in the elite professions, the vast majority of women who work outside the home are still in low-paying jobs with little or no prospect of advancement. This fact is clearly related to girls' awareness of the complexity they are likely to face in combining work with family life.[20] As the authors of one study conclude: "the occu-

---

*For the past century, nearly 90 percent of women have married by the age of thirty and between 80 percent and 90 percent have become mothers by the age of forty. In 1986, only 4.7 percent of women and 5.7 percent of men aged 45-54 in the U.S. had never married.[16]

†The labor force participation rate of U.S. women has risen steadily for three decades, from 35 percent (of those aged sixteen or more) in 1960 to 57 percent in 1986. Roughly 70 percent of women between the ages of twenty and thirty-four were employed in 1983, including (in 1983 and 1986) more than 50 percent of married women with children under the age of six.[19]

142

pational aspirations and expectations of adolescents are highly differentiated by sex . . . [and this] differentiation follows the pattern of sexual segregation which exists in the occupational structure." They found not only that the high school girls in their large-scale study were much less likely than the boys to aspire to the most prestigious occupations, but that the girls who had such aspirations displayed a much lower degree of confidence than the boys about being able to attain their goals.[21]

As the women Kathleen Gerson recently studied looked back on their girlhood considerations about the future, virtually all of them saw themselves as confronting a choice: *either* domesticity and motherhood *or* career.[22]* Given the pervasiveness of sex-role socialization (including the mixed or negative messages that girls are often given about their future work lives), the actual obstacles that our social structures place in the way of working mothers, and the far greater responsibility, both psychological and practical, that is placed on mothers than on fathers for their children's welfare, it is not surprising that these women perceived a conflict between their own work interests and the interests of any children they might have.[23] While many reacted against their own mothers' domestic lives, very few were able to imagine successfully combining motherhood with a career. And those who did generally avoided confronting the dilemmas they would have to face.[24] But most grew up with the belief that "a woman can have either a career or children, but not both."[25] Not surprisingly, many of them, assuming that they would want to have children, followed educational and work paths that would readily accommodate the demands of being a primary parent. The only way that those who were career-oriented came to believe that they might avoid the difficult choice, and even attempt to combine their work with mothering, was by deciding to be trailblazers, rejecting strongly ingrained beliefs about the incompatibility of the two.

Needless to say, such a choice does not confront boys in their formative years. *They* assume—reasonably enough, given our traditions and present conditions and beliefs—that what is expected of them as husbands and fathers is that, by developing a solid work life, they will provide the primary financial sup-

*Though Gerson's sample includes no women of color, it represents in other respects a wide range of class backgrounds and present situations. Gerson presents a number of surprising findings. One is that more of the women in her sample *changed* their orientation—from domestic to nondomestic or vice versa—than maintained their original orientation. What happened within their marriages and in their work lives was clearly influential here. Another is that many (45%) of her sample started out with nondomestic orientations, at a time when few of their mothers presented role models for this choice (p. 61). As Gerson shows, reaction against mothers' choices and situations was just as likely to influence daughters' choices as was identification with them.

port of the family. Men's situation can have its own strains, since those who feel trapped at work cannot opt for domesticity and gain as much support for this choice as a woman can.[26] For those who become unemployed, the conflict of their experience with society's view of the male as provider can be particularly stressful. But boys do not experience the dilemma about work and family that girls do as they confront the choices that are crucial to their educations, future work lives and opportunities, and economic security.

When women envisage a future strongly influenced by the demands on them as wives and particularly as mothers, they are likely to embark on traditionally female fields of study and/or occupational paths. The typical route for women is still to finish their education with high school and to marry and have children in their early twenties, though a growing minority are continuing their education, establishing themselves in careers, and marrying later.[27] Some of those who are primarily family-oriented foresee their wage work as temporary or intermittent, while some envisage trying to combine some continued work in the marketplace with traditionally female family responsibilities. But whether such women enter clerical, sales, or service work, or train for one of the predominantly female professions such as teaching or nursing, they are heading not only for the relatively more flexible hours or greater replaceability that most of these jobs afford but also for low pay, poor working conditions, and, above all, blocked mobility. In 1987, women who worked year-round at full-time jobs earned a median wage of $15,704—71 percent of the $22,204 earned by full-time working men.[28] The fact that women's educational achievement is becoming equal to men's, through the level of master's degrees, is clearly affecting women's *participation* in the work force.[29] But, though it could also potentially affect their earnings relative to men's, it has done so very little up to now, in part because the professional and service occupations that are more than two-thirds female—such as education, humanities, home economics, library science, and health science—are far worse paid than those that are still more than two-thirds male—such as science and engineering.[30] Occupational sex segregation cancels out women's educational advances: in 1985, the average full-time working white woman with a college degree or higher earned $2,000 less than the average white man who had only a high-school diploma; and the average black woman with some college education earned slightly less than the average white man who had only an elementary school education.[31]

Regardless of educational achievement, women are far more likely than men to work in administrative support jobs, as a secretary, typist, or bookkeeper, for example, which in most cases hold no prospects for advancement. Almost 30 percent of employed women worked in this category in 1985, compared with fewer than 6 percent of men.[32] A study of workplaces during the late 1960s and the 1970s (*after* the 1963 Equal Pay Act and Title VII of the 1964 Civil Rights Act) found the sex segregation of specific jobs and occupational ladders in both manufacturing and nonmanufacturing firms to be so pervasive that more than 90 percent of women would have had to change jobs in order for women to share equally the same job titles as men. Frequently, workplaces had only one or two job titles that included members of both sexes. On top of all this, recent research has shown that large discrepancies exist between male and female wages for the same job title. While female secretaries earned a median wage of $278 per week in 1985, the median for male secretaries was $365; moreover, in twenty-four other narrowly defined occupations in which females earned *less* than they would have as secretaries, males earned *more* in every case than a female secretary. Indeed, some firms designate particular jobs as male and others designate the same jobs as female, and the wage rates differ accordingly. It seems, therefore, that "the wage level for a particular job title in a particular establishment is set *after the employer decides whether those jobs will be filled by women or men*."[33] Barbara Bergmann's detailed study of sex segregation in the workplace leads her to conclude:

> Women are fenced off from a disproportionate share of what we might call "labor-market turf." . . . [Thus] the supply and the demand in the markets for men's and women's labor are powerfully affected by discrimination. . . . The exclusion of women from a big share of all of the jobs in the economy is what creates two labor markets where there should be only one. The discriminatory assignment of jobs to one sex or the other is what sets the level of demand in each market . . . [and] force[s] women to have to sell their labor at a low price.[34]

Thus workplace discrimination *per se* is very significant. In addition, as I have suggested, some of the segregation of wage work by sex is attributable to the individual choices that women and men make in the context of their own socialization and with knowledge of the gender structure of the family in particular. M. Rivka Polatnick has recently summarized the situation:

> Not only during the period of childrearing do women become economically or professionally disadvantaged vis-à-vis men; most women's lives have already been constructed in anticipation of that period. "Helpful advice" from family, friends, and guidance counselors, and discriminatory practices in schools and in the job

market steer women toward jobs and interests compatible with a future in childrearing.[35]

It is no wonder, then, that most women are, even before marriage, in an economic position that sets them up to become more vulnerable during marriage, and most vulnerable of all if their marriage ends and—unprepared as they are—they find themselves in the position of having to provide for themselves and their children.

Vulnerability Within Marriage

Marriage continues the cycle of inequality set in motion by the anticipation of marriage and the related sex segregation of the workplace. Partly because of society's assumptions about gender, but also because women, on entering marriage, tend already to be disadvantaged members of the work force, married women are likely to start out with less leverage in the relationship than their husbands. As I shall show, answers to questions such as whose work life and work needs take priority, and how the unpaid work of the family will be allocated—if they are not simply assumed to be decided along the lines of sex difference, but are live issues in the marriage—are likely to be strongly influenced by the differences in earning power between husbands and wives. In many marriages, partly because of discrimination at work and the wage gap between the sexes, wives (despite initial personal ambitions and even when they are full-time wage workers) come to perceive themselves as benefiting from giving priority to their husbands' careers. Hence they have little incentive to question the traditional division of labor in the household. This in turn limits their own commitment to wage work and their incentive and leverage to challenge the gender structure of the workplace. Experiencing frustration and lack of control at work, those who thus turn toward domesticity, while often resenting the lack of respect our society gives to full-time mothers, may see the benefits of domestic life as greater than the costs.[36]

Thus, the inequalities between the sexes in the workplace and at home reinforce and exacerbate each other. It is not necessary to choose between two alternative, competing explanations of the inequalities between men and women in the workplace—the "human capital" approach, which argues that, because of expectations about their family lives, women *choose* to enter lower-paid and more dead-end occupations and specific jobs,[37] and the workplace discrimination explanation, which blames factors largely outside the control of female employees. When the pivotal importance of gender-structured marriage and the expectation of it are acknowledged, these explanations can be seen, rather, as complementary reasons for women's inequality. A *cycle of power relations and decisions pervades both family and workplace, and the inequalities of each reinforce those that already exist in the other.* Only with the recognition of this truth will we be able to begin to confront the changes that need to occur if women are to have a real opportunity to be equal participants in either sphere.[38]

Human capital theorists, in perceiving women's job market attachment as a matter of voluntary choice, appear to miss or virtually to ignore the fact of unequal power within the family. Like normative theorists who idealize the family, they ignore potential conflicts of interest, and consequently issues of justice and power differentials, *within* families. This means that they view the question of whether a wife works solely in terms of the total aggregate costs and benefits for the family unit as a whole.[39] They assume that if a wife's paid work benefits the family more (in terms, say, of aggregate income and leisure) than her working exclusively within the household, her rational choice, and that of her husband, will be that she should get a job; if the reverse is true, she should not. But this simplistic attention to the family's "aggregate good" ignores the fact that a wife, like a husband, may have an independent interest in her own career advancement or desire for human contact, for example, that may give her an incentive to work even if the family as a whole may on that account find its life more difficult. Further, the human capital approach overlooks the fact that such goods as leisure and influence over the expenditure of income are by no means always equally shared within families. It also fails to recognize that the considerable influence that husbands often exert over their wives' decisions on whether to take paid work may be motivated not by a concern for the aggregate welfare of the household but, at least in part, by their desire to retain the authority and privilege that accrues to them by virtue of being the family's breadwinner.[40] Thus the decisions of married women about their participation in the job market, even when they *are* choices, may not be such simple or voluntary choices as human capital theory seems to imply.

In addition, those who seek to explain women's comparative disadvantage in the labor market by their preference for domestic commitments do not consider whether at least some of the causality may run in the opposite direction. But there is considerable evidence that women's "choices" to become domestically oriented, and even whether to have children, may result at least in part from their frequently blocked situations at work. Kathleen Gerson's study shows that, though they usually did not notice the connection, many of the women in her sample decided to leave wage work and turn to childbearing and domesticity coincidentally with becoming frustrated with the dead-end nature of their jobs. Conversely, she found that some women who had initially thought of themselves as domestically oriented, and who had in many cases chosen traditionally female occupations, reversed these orientations when unusual and unexpected opportunities for work advancement opened up to them.[41]

Even if these problems with the human capital approach did not exist, we would still be faced with the fact that the theory can explain, at most, half of the wage differential between the sexes. In the case of the differential between white men and black women, 70 percent of it is unexplained. At *any* given level of skill, experience, and education, men earn considerably more than women. The basic problem with the human capital approach is that, like much of neoclassical economic theory, it pays too little attention to the multiple constraints placed on people's choices. It pays too little attention to differentials of power between the sexes both in the workplace and in the family. It thus ignores the fact that women's commitment and attachment to the workplace are strongly influenced by a number of factors that are largely beyond their control. As we have seen, a woman's typically less advantaged position in the work force and lower pay may lead her to choices about full-time motherhood and domesticity that she would have been less likely to make had her work life been less dead-ended. They also give her less power in relation to her husband should she want to resist the traditional division of labor in her household and to insist on a more equal sharing of child care and other domestic responsibilities. Those who stress the extent to which both husbands and wives cling to the "male provider/female nurturer" roles as unobjectionable because efficient and economically rational for the family unit need to take a step back and consider the extent to which the continued sex segregation of the work force serves to perpetuate the traditional division of labor within the household, even in the face of women's rising employment.

148

Vulnerability by Marriage

HOUSEWORK AND THE CYCLE OF VULNERABILITY

It is no secret that in almost all families women do far more housework and child care than men do. But the distribution of paid and unpaid work within the family has rarely—outside of feminist circles—been considered a significant issue by theorists of justice. Why should it be? If two friends divide a task so that each takes primary responsibility for a different aspect of it, we would be loath to cry "injustice" unless one were obviously coercing the other. But at least three factors make the division of labor within the household a very different situation, and a clear question of justice. First, the uneven distribution of labor within the family is strongly correlated with an innate characteristic, which appears to make it the kind of issue with which theorists of justice have been most concerned. The virtually automatic allocation to one person of more of the paid labor and to the other of more of the unpaid labor would be regarded as decidedly odd in any relationship other than that of a married or cohabiting heterosexual couple.* One reason for this is that, as we shall see, it has distinct effects on the distribution of power. While the unequal distribution of paid and unpaid work has different repercussions in different types of marriages, it is always of significance. Second, though it is by no means always absolute, the division of labor in a traditional or quasi-traditional marriage is often quite complete and usually long-standing. It lasts in many cases at least through the lengthy years of child rearing, and is by no means confined to the preschool years. Third, partly as a result of this, and of the structure and demands of most paid work, the household division of labor has a lasting impact on the lives of married women, especially those who become mothers. It affects every sphere of their lives, from the dynamics of their marital relationship to their opportunities in the many spheres of life outside the household. The distribution of labor within the family by sex has deep ramifications for its respective members' material, psychological, physical, and intellectual well-being. One cannot even begin to address the issue of why so many women and children live in poverty in our soci-

---

*Blumstein and Schwartz's comparisons of homosexual couples (male and female) with heterosexual couples (cohabiting and married) demonstrate vividly the extent to which the division of labor in the household is affected by sex difference. In all but about 1 percent of contemporary homosexual households, they found that the homemaker/provider division of roles is avoided. Even when one partner is not working, and is in fact doing more of the housework, the tendency is to think of him or her as "temporarily unemployed" or "a student." Lesbians take particular care to distribute household duties equitably. And yet, contrary to what one might expect on the basis of some arguments (including that of economist Gary Becker), such households seem to be managed with considerable efficiency. Blumstein and Schwartz, *American Couples*, pp. 116, 127–31, 148–51.

149

ety, or why women are inadequately represented in the higher echelons of our political and economic institutions, without confronting the division of labor between the sexes within the family. Thus it is not only itself an issue of justice but it is also at the very root of other significant concerns of justice, including equality of opportunity for children of both sexes, but especially for girls, and political justice in the broadest sense.

The justice issues surrounding housework are not simply issues about who does *more* work. However, on average, wives living with their husbands *do* now work slightly more total hours than their husbands do.[42] In addition, this averaging obscures a great variety of distributions of both quantity and type of work within marriages. For the purposes of this discussion, it will be helpful to separate couples into two major categories: those in which the wife is "predominantly houseworking" (either a full-time housewife or employed part-time) and those in which the wife is "predominantly wage-working" (employed full-time or virtually full-time).[43] Within each category, I shall look at issues such as the distribution of work (paid and unpaid), income, power, opportunity to choose one's occupation, self-respect and esteem, and availability of exit. As we shall see, wives in each category experience a somewhat different pattern of injustice and vulnerability. But, except in the case of some of the small number of elite couples who make considerable use of paid help, the typical divisions of labor in the family cannot be regarded as just.

Predominantly Houseworking Wives

When a woman is a full-time housewife—as are about two-fifths of married women in the United States who live with their husbands—she does less total work, on average, than her employed husband: 49.3 hours per week, compared with his 63.2. This is also true of couples in which the wife works part-time (defined as fewer than thirty hours per week, including commuting time), though the average difference per week is reduced to eight hours in this case.[44] This is, of course, partly because housework is less burdensome than it was before the days of labor-saving devices and declining fertility. Not surprisingly, however, during the early years of child rearing, a nonemployed wife (or part-time employed wife) is likely to work about the same total number of hours as her employed husband. But the *quantity* of work performed is only one of a number of important variables that must be considered in order for us to assess the justice or injustice of the division of labor in the family, particularly in relation to the issue of the cycle of women's vulnerability.

In terms of the quality of work, there are considerable disadvantages to the role of housewife.[45] One is that much of the work is boring and/or unpleasant.

Vulnerability by Marriage

Surveys indicate that most people of both sexes do not like to clean, shop for food, or do laundry, which constitute a high proportion of housework. Cooking rates higher, and child care even higher, with both sexes, than other domestic work.[46] In reality, this separation of tasks is strictly hypothetical, at least for mothers, who are usually cleaning, shopping, doing laundry, and cooking at the same time as taking care of children. Many wage workers, too, do largely tedious and repetitive work. But the housewife-mother's work has additional disadvantages. One is that her hours of work are highly unscheduled; unlike virtually any other worker except the holder of a high political office, she can be called on at any time of the day or night, seven days a week. Another is that she cannot, nearly as easily as most other workers, change jobs. Her family comes to depend on *her* to do all the things she does. Finding substitutes is difficult and expensive, even if the housewife is not discouraged or forbidden by her husband to seek paid work. The skills and experience she has gained are not valued by prospective employers. Also, once a woman has taken on the role of housewife, she finds it extremely difficult, for reasons that will be explored, to shift part of this burden back onto her husband. Being a housewife thus both impairs a woman's ability to support herself and constrains her future choices in life.[47]

Many of the disadvantages of being a housewife spring directly or indirectly from the fact that all her work is unpaid work, whereas more than four-fifths of her husband's total work is paid work. This may at first seem a matter of little importance. If wives, so long as they stay married, usually share their husbands' standards of living for the most part, why should it matter who earns the income? It matters a great deal, for many reasons. In the highly money-oriented society we live in, the housewife's work is devalued. In fact, in spite of the fact that a major part of it consists of the nurturance and socialization of the next generation of citizens, it is frequently not even acknowledged as work or as productive, either at the personal or at the policy level. This both affects the predominantly houseworking wife's power and influence within the family and means that her social status depends largely upon her husband's, a situation that she may not consider objectionable so long as the marriage lasts, but that is likely to be very painful for her if it does not.[48]

Also, although married couples usually share material well-being, a housewife's or even a part-time working wife's lack of access to much money of her own can create difficulties that range from the mildly irritating through the humiliating to the devastating, especially if she does not enjoy a good relationship with her husband. Money is the subject of most conflict for married couples, although the issue of housework may be overtaking it.[49] Bergmann reports that in an informal survey, she discovered that about 20 percent of the housewife-mothers of her students were in the position of continually having to appeal to their husbands for money. The psychological effects on an adult of economic dependence can be great. As Virginia Woolf pointed out fifty years ago, any man who has difficulty estimating them should simply imagine himself depending on his wife's income.[50] The dark side of economic dependence is also indicated by the fact that, in the serious predivorce situation of having to fight for their future economic well-being, many wives even of well-to-do men do not have access to enough cash to pay for the uncovering and documentation of their husband's assets.

At its (not so uncommon) worst, the economic dependence of wives can seriously affect their day-to-day physical security. As Linda Gordon has recently concluded: "The basis of wife-beating is male dominance—not superior physical strength or violent temperament . . . but social, economic, political, and psychological power. . . . Wife-beating is the chronic battering of a person of inferior power who for that reason cannot effectively resist."[51] Both wife abuse and child abuse are clearly exacerbated by the economic dependence of women on their husbands or cohabiting male partners. Many women, especially full-time housewives with dependent children, have no way of adequately supporting themselves, and are often in practice unable to leave a situation in which they and/or their children are being seriously abused. In addition to increasing the likelihood of the more obvious forms of abuse—physical and sexual assault—the fear of being abandoned, with its economic and other dire consequences, can lead a housewife to tolerate infidelity, to submit to sexual acts she does not enjoy, or experience psychological abuse including virtual desertion.[52] The fact that a predominantly houseworking wife has no money of her own or a small paycheck is not necessarily significant, but it can be very significant, especially at crucial junctures in the marriage.

Finally, as I shall discuss, the earnings differential between husband and housewife can become devastating in its significance for her and for any dependent children in the event of divorce (which in most states can now occur without her consent). This fact, which significantly affects the relative potential of wives and husbands for exit from the marriage, is likely to influence the distribution of power, and in turn paid and unpaid work, *during* the marriage as well.

152

Vulnerability by Marriage

Predominantly Wage-Working Wives and Housework

Despite the increasing labor force participation of married women, including mothers, "working wives still bear almost all the responsibility for housework." They do less of it than housewives, but "they still do the vast bulk of what needs to be done," and the difference is largely to be accounted for not by the increased participation of men, but by lowered standards, the participation of children, purchased services such as restaurant or frozen meals, and, in elite groups, paid household help. Thus, while the distribution of paid labor between the sexes is shifting quite considerably onto women, that of unpaid labor is not shifting much at all, and "the couple that shares household tasks equally remains rare."[53] The differences in total time spent in all "family work" (housework and child care plus yard work, repairs, and so on) vary considerably from one study to another, but it seems that fully employed husbands do, *at most*, approximately half as much as their fully employed wives, and some studies show a much greater discrepancy.

Bergmann reports that "husbands of wives with full-time jobs averaged about two minutes more housework per day than did husbands in housewife-maintaining families, hardly enough additional time to prepare a soft-boiled egg."[54] Even unemployed husbands do much less housework than wives who work a forty-hour week. Working-class husbands are particularly vocal about not being equal partners in the home, and do little housework. In general, however, a husband's income and job prestige are *inversely* related to his involvement in household chores, unless his wife is employed in a similarly high-paid and prestigious job. Many husbands who profess belief in sharing household tasks equally actually do far less than their wives, when time spent and chores done are assessed. In many cases, egalitarian attitudes make little or no difference to who actually does the work, and often "the idea of shared responsibility turn[s] out to be a myth."[55]

Some scholars are disinclined to perceive these facts as indicating unequal power or exploitation. They prefer to view them as merely embodying adherence to traditional patterns, or to justify them as efficient in terms of the total welfare of the family (the husband's time being too valuable to spend doing housework).[56] There are clear indications, however, that the major reason that husbands and other heterosexual men living with wage-working women are not doing more housework is that *they do not want to, and are able, to a very large extent, to enforce their wills.* How do we know that the unequal allocation of housework is not equally women's choice? First, because most people do not like doing many of the major household chores. Second, because almost half of wage-working wives who do more than 60 percent of the housework say that they would prefer their husbands to do more of it.[57] Third, because husbands with higher salaries and more prestigious jobs than their wives (the vast majority of two-job couples) are in a powerful position to resist their wives' appeal to them to do more at home, and it is husbands with the highest prestige who do the least housework of all. Even when there is little conflict, and husbands and wives seem to agree that the woman should do more of the housework, they are often influenced by the prevailing idea that whoever earns less or has the less prestigious job should do more unpaid labor at home. But since the maldistribution of wages and jobs between the sexes in our society is largely out of women's control, even *seemingly nonconflictual* decisions made on this basis cannot really be considered fully voluntary on the part of wives.[58] Finally, the resistance of most husbands to housework is well documented, as is the fact that the more housework men do, the *more* it becomes a cause of fighting within couples. Examining factors that caused the breakup of some of the couples in their sample, Blumstein and Schwartz say:

> Among both married and cohabiting couples, housework is a source of conflict. . . . [A] *woman cannot be perceived as doing less housework than her partner wants her to do without jeopardizing the relationship*. However, a man, who is unlikely to be doing even half the work, can be perceived as doing less than his fair share without affecting the couple's durability. *It is difficult for women to achieve an equal division of housework and still preserve the relationship*[59] [emphasis added].

As a result, in many of the households in which men and women both work full-time—those for which much paid household help or reliance on other purchased services is not a practical option—the unequal distribution of housework between husbands and wives leads to gross inequities in the amount and type of work done by each. "Drudge wives," as Bergmann has recently termed women in such households, do more total work than their husbands, averaging 71.1 hours a week to the husband's 64.9. But of greater overall significance is the fact that a vastly higher proportion of the wife's than of the husband's work is unpaid. She averages 28.1 hours of unpaid "family" work to 43 hours of paid work, whereas he averages only 9.2 hours of family work to 55.8 hours of paid work.[60] One important effect of unequal sharing of housework and other family work within dual working couples is that the amount of time and energy the wife has left to commit to her wage work is

154

considerably more limited than her husband's. It used to be assumed, in the days when the full traditional division of labor in the family prevailed, that any job requiring responsibility and commitment was incompatible with day-to-day responsibilities for home and children. This was why, or so it was argued, men could not, and should not be expected to, share in these tasks.[61] But now many women, whether forced by economic need or refusing to accept the choice between parenthood and career that men have never had to make, are trying to do both.[62] Their chances of success are significantly affected by the fact that, although they are likely to expend significant amounts of time on their homes and children, they must compete at work, not only with men from families like their own, who do significantly less family work than they do, but also with men whose wives are full-time housewives or work only part-time.

WIVES AND WAGE WORK

While theorists of justice have largely ignored it, women's double burden and its effects have long been recognized by feminists. Largely because of the unequal distribution of housework and child care, married women's opportunities in the work force are considerably more constrained than men's. As Gerson notes, "the simple fact of [women's] working . . . does not by itself entail significant social change." Though women are now less inclined than they were a generation ago to be part-time and sporadic workers, there is a wide gap between the increase in their labor force participation and their labor force attachment and position.[63] Because of their lower level of labor force attachment, their tendency to work part-time and at jobs that in other respects bend to meet the needs of the family, and their propensity to accommodate their own employment to their husbands', women's wages become lower in relation to men's as they get older. Whereas the ratio between an average full-time working woman's earnings and a full-time working man's is 83:100 between the ages of twenty-one to twenty-nine, the wage gap by ages forty-five to sixty-four has increased to 60:100.[64]

The constraints placed on wives as workers are strengthened by the fact that many full-time employers assume, in innumerable ways, that "someone" is at home at least part-time during the day to assume primary responsibility for children. The traditional or quasi-traditional division of labor is clearly assumed in the vast discrepancy between normal full-time working hours and children's school hours and vacations. It is assumed by the high degree of geographical mobility required by many higher-level management positions. It is also implicit in the structure of the professions, in which the greatest demands are placed on workers at the very peak of the child-rearing years. Academia and the law are two clear examples; both tenure and partnership decisions are typically made for a person between the ages of thirty and thirty-five, with obvious discriminatory implications for the professional parent (almost always a woman) who does not have a partner willing to assume the major responsibility for children.

Because the structure of most wage work is inconsistent with the parenting responsibilities chiefly borne by women, far fewer women (especially married women) than men *do* work full-time. Only 27 percent of all wives in families with children worked full-time year-round in 1984, compared with 77 percent of husbands.[65] Some mothers conclude that, given the demands of their work, the only reasonable answer to the needs of their children is to take time out of the workplace altogether. Others work part-time. But the repercussions of either of these choices, given the current structure and attitudes of the workplace, are often serious and long-lasting. The investment in career assets is by far the most valuable property owned by most couples. To the extent that wives work part-time or intermittently, their own career potential atrophies, and they become deeply dependent on their husbands' career assets. Even when a wife maintains her career, her husband's work needs—in terms of time, freedom from other preoccupations, education and training, and geographical mobility—usually take priority. This is often the case even with dual-career couples who are similarly qualified and claim to be committed to an egalitarian ideology.[66] In relation to the outside world of employment, therefore, the notion that husbands and wives are equals is myth. Typically, women as workers are disadvantaged by marriage itself, and the more so the longer the duration of the marriage.[67]

POWER IN THE FAMILY

There are very few studies of power within marriage. Of those few, the one most frequently cited until recently—Robert O. Blood, Jr., and Donald M. Wolfe's 1960 *Husbands and Wives*—though informative, is now outdated and unreliable in the way it interprets its own findings.[68] The study in itself is of considerable interest for the question of power and gender, given its influential character, not only because of what it purports to discover but also because these findings are both distorted and blurred by the authors' initial assumption that a moderate degree of male dominance is the desirable norm within families.* This assumption leads them to define what their own scale indicates to be moderate male dominance as "relative equalitarianism" in family decision making. When reinterpreted in the absence of this sexist normative assumption, we find that what Blood and Wolfe's study of married life in the 1950s discovered was not, as they claimed, that "the American family has changed its authority pattern from one of patriarchal male dominance to one of equalitarian sharing," but rather that male dominance was still the norm, though its extent varied in accordance with a number of factors.[69] The most important of these was the discrepancy in income and wage-work success between the husband and the wife.

As Blood and Wolfe report their findings about what variables affect family power, they are again misleading, due to their implicit assumptions. They conclude that the distribution of power, and its ebb and flow during the course of a marriage, vary with the "resources" that each spouse contributes to the family. But they completely fail to notice that the only resources that affect marital power are those—such as income, success, and prestige—that are valued in the world *outside* the marriage. Resources such as domestic services and childbearing and child-rearing capacities, skills, and labor are not only not positively correlated with marital power but are in fact *negatively* correlated with it. While Blood and Wolfe note that the housewife with preschool children is at the least powerful point in her marriage, and that her power decreases as the number of children rises, they do not question why she should be so powerless at a time when she is contributing so much to the family. Because of their unstated sexist assumptions about what constitutes a "resource," they explain her lack of power in terms of her extreme financial dependence on her husband, and fail to perceive her husband as dependent on *her* for any resources at all.[70]

Only recently, with the publication of Blumstein and Schwartz's *American Couples,* have we had a large-scale and more neutral account of the power picture behind decision making by couples. They asked thousands of couples to respond on a scale of 1 to 9 (with 5 defined as "both equally") to the question: "In general, who has more say about important decisions affecting your

---

*Blood and Wolfe's study is based on interviews with the wives (only) in 731 city (Detroit) and 178 farm families, during the 1950s. The authors' biases are apparent throughout, from their labeling of the less powerful husband "Caspar Milquetoast" to their pronouncement that families ranging from husband-dominance to "extreme equalitarianism" are "appropriate," but that wife-dominance is a "deviant" and "not normal" reversal of marital roles. *Husbands and Wives,* pp. 11, 45.

relationship, you or your partner?" Clearly, what this new study reveals about married couples confirms the major findings that Blood and Wolfe's earlier study discovered but obscured. First, though the number of marriages in which spouses consider that they share decision-making power relatively equally has increased considerably, the tendency in others is still distinctly toward male rather than female dominance.[71] Second, it is still clearly the case that the possession by each spouse of resources valued by the *outside* world, especially income and work status, rather than resources valuable primarily within the family, has a significant effect on the distribution of power in the relationship.

Blumstein and Schwartz preface their findings about couples, money, and power by noting that they are not likely to accord with "cherished American beliefs about fairness and how people acquire influence in romantic relationships." Perhaps this is why, as they point out, although "economic factors tend to be involved in every aspect of a couple's life," standard textbooks on marriage and the family are unlikely to devote more than five pages to this subject. Just as political and moral theorists have been extremely reluctant to admit that questions of justice pertain to family life, a similar tendency to idealize—and to conceal dominance—has apparently characterized sociologists of the family until recently, too. But Blumstein and Schwartz's study establishes quite decisively that "in three out of four of the types of couples . . . studied [all types except lesbian couples], . . . the amount of money a person earns—in comparison with a partner's income—establishes relative power."[72] Given that even the 26 percent of all wives who work full-time earn, on average, only 63 percent as much as the average full-time working husband, and the average wife who works for pay (full- or part-time) earns only 42 percent as much, it is therefore not at all surprising that male dominance is far more common than female dominance in couples who deviate from a relatively egalitarian distribution of power.[73] When women are employed, and especially when their earnings approach those of their husbands, they are more likely to share decision-making power equally with their husbands and to have greater financial autonomy. In marriages in which the husband earned over $8,000 more than the wife (more than half the marriages in the Blumstein and Schwartz sample), the husband was rated as more powerful (as opposed to an equal sharing of power or to the wife's being more powerful) in 33 percent of cases. In marriages in which the incomes of husband and wife were approximately equal, only 18 percent of the husbands were rated as more powerful. The workplace success of wives, then, helps considerably to equalize the balance of power within their marriages and gains them greater respect from their husbands, who often have little respect for housework. Success at work, moreover, can reduce the expectation that a wife will do the vast bulk of family work.[74] Nevertheless, the full-time employment, and even the equal or greater earnings, of wives do not guarantee them equal power in the family, for the male-provider *ideology* is sometimes powerful enough to counteract these factors.[75]

Given these facts about the way power is distributed in the family, and the facts brought out earlier about the typical contentiousness of the issue of housework, it is not difficult to see how the vulnerability of married women in relation to the world of work and their inequality within the family tend to form part of a vicious cycle. Wives are likely to start out at a disadvantage, because of both the force of the traditions of gender and the fact that they are likely to be already earning less than their husbands at the time of marriage. In many cases, the question of who is responsible for the bulk of the unpaid labor of the household is probably not raised at all, but *assumed*, on the basis of these two factors alone. Because of this "nondecision" factor, studies of marital power that ask only about the respective influence of the partners over *decisions* are necessarily incomplete, since they ignore distributions of burdens and benefits that may not be perceived as arising from decisions at all.[76]

However, there *is* often conflict about how much time each partner should devote to wage work and how much to family work. This may include disagreement over the issue of whether the wife should have a job at all, whereas this is almost always taken for granted (a "nondecision") in the case of the husband. Since the partner whose wage work is given priority and who does far less unpaid family work is likely to increase the disparity between his and his spouse's earnings, seniority, and work status, his power in the family will tend to grow accordingly. Hence if, as is likely, he wishes to preserve a traditional or semitraditional division of labor in the family, he is likely to be able to do so. This need not involve constant fighting, with the man always winning; his "man" power and his earning power combined may be so preeminent that the issue is never even raised. Either way, his wife is likely to find it difficult to reallocate the family work so as to make him responsible for more of it so that she can take a job or expend more time and energy on the one she has. In addition, the weight of tradition and of her own sex-role socialization will contribute to her powerlessness to effect change.

Vulnerability by Separation or Divorce

The impact of the unequal distribution of benefits and burdens between husbands and wives is hardest and most directly felt by the increasing numbers of women and children whose families are no longer intact. In 1985, 28 percent of ever-married white women and 49 percent of ever-married black women in the United States were separated, divorced, or widowed.[77] Marital disruption through the death of a spouse, divorce, or separation is consistently rated as the most psychologically stressful life event for men and women alike.[78] But in women's lives, the personal disruption caused by these events is frequently exacerbated by the serious social and economic dislocation that accompanies them.

Every year, divorce disrupts the lives of more than three million men, women, and children in the United States.[79] The annual divorce rate per 1,000 married women increased from 9.2 in 1960 to 22.6 in 1981; it has leveled off and even declined slightly during the 1980s. Half of all marriages contracted in the 1970s are projected to end in divorce, and between 50 and 60 percent of the children born in the early 1980s are likely to experience the breakup of their parents' marriage by the age of eighteen. Rates of separation and divorce are much higher for black than for white women: in 1983 there were 126 divorced white women for every 1,000 married women; for black women, the ratio was 297 to 1,000.[80] In 1985, about 23 percent of children under the age of eighteen lived with only one parent—in about 90 percent of cases, the mother. Contrary to popular prejudice, female-maintained families with children consist in only a fairly small percentage of cases of never-married women raising children alone. They are in the vast majority of cases the result of separation or divorce.[81]

Not only has the rate of divorce increased rapidly but the differential in the economic impact of divorce on men and women has also grown. Divorce and its economic effects contribute significantly to the fact that nearly one-quarter of all children now live in single-parent households, more than half of them, even after transfer payments, below the poverty level. Moreover, partly because of the increased labor force participation of married women, there has been a growing divergence between female-maintained families and two-parent families.[82] These dramatic shifts, with their vast impact on the lives of women and children, must be addressed by any theory of justice that can claim to be about all of us, rather than simply about the male "heads of households" on which theories of justice in the past have focused.

Vulnerability by Marriage

There is now little doubt that, while no-fault divorce does not appear to have caused the increasing rate of divorce, it has considerably affected the economic outcome of divorce for both parties.[83] Many studies have shown that whereas the average economic status of men improves after divorce, that of women and children deteriorates seriously. Nationwide, the per-capita income of divorced women, which was only 62 percent that of divorced men in 1960, decreased to 56 percent by 1980.[84] The most illuminating explanation of this is Lenore Weitzman's recent pathbreaking study, *The Divorce Revolution*. Based on a study of 2,500 randomly selected California court dockets between 1968 and 1977 and lengthy interviews with many lawyers, judges, legal experts, and 228 divorced men and women, the book both documents and explains the differential social and economic impact of current divorce law on men, women, and children. Weitzman presents the striking finding that in the first year after divorce, the average standard of living of divorced men, adjusted for household size, increases by 42 percent while that of divorced women falls by 73 percent. "For most women and children," Weitzman concludes:

> divorce means precipitous downward mobility—both economically and socially. The reduction in income brings residential moves and inferior housing, drastically diminished or nonexistent funds for recreation and leisure, and intense pressures due to inadequate time and money. Financial hardships in turn cause social dislocation and a loss of familiar networks for emotional support and social services, and intensify the psychological stress for women and children alike. On a societal level, divorce increases female and child poverty and creates an ever-widening gap between the economic well-being of divorced men, on the one hand, and their children and former wives on the other.[85]

Weitzman's findings have been treated with disbelief by some, who claim, for example, that California, being a community property state, is atypical, and that these figures could not be projected nationwide without distortion. However, studies done in other states (including common law states and both urban and rural areas) have corroborated Weitzman's central conclusion: that the economic situation of men and that of women and children typically diverge after divorce.[86]

The basic reason for this is that the courts are now treating divorcing men and women more or less as equals. Divorcing men and women are not, of course, equal, both because the two sexes are not treated equally in society and, as we have seen, because typical, gender-structured marriage makes women socially and economically vulnerable. The treatment of unequals as if

161

they were equals has long been recognized as an obvious instance of injustice. In this case, the injustice is particularly egregious because the inequality is to such a large extent the result of the marital relationship itself. Nonetheless, that divorce as it is currently practiced in the United States involves such injustice took years to be revealed. There are various discrete parts of this unjust treatment of unequals as if they were equals, and we must briefly examine each of them.

The first way in which women are unequally situated after divorce is that they almost always continue to take day-to-day responsibility for the children. The increased rate of divorce has especially affected couples between the ages of twenty-five and thirty-nine—those most likely to have dependent children. And in approximately 90 percent of cases, children live with mothers rather than fathers after divorce. This is usually the outcome preferred by both parents. Relatively few fathers seek or are awarded sole custody, and in cases of joint custody, which are increasing in frequency, children still tend to live mainly with their mothers. Thus women's postdivorce households tend to be larger than those of men, with correspondingly larger economic needs, and their work lives are much more limited by the needs of their children.[87]

Second, as Weitzman demonstrates, no-fault divorce laws, by depriving women of power they often exerted as the "innocent" and less willing party to the divorce, have greatly reduced their capacity to achieve an equitable division of the couple's tangible assets. Whereas the wife (and children) typically used to be awarded the family home, or more than half of the total tangible assets of the marriage, they are now doing much worse in this respect. In California, the percentage of cases in which the court explicitly ordered that the family home be sold and the proceeds divided rose from about one-tenth of divorces in 1968 to about one-third in 1977. Of this one-third, 66 percent had minor children, who were likely on this account to suffer significantly more than the usual dislocations of divorce. James McLindon's study of divorcing couples in New Haven, Connecticut, confirms this effect of no-fault divorce. In the case of an older housewife, forced sale of the family home can mean the loss of not only her marriage, occupation, and social status, but also her home of many years, all in one blow.[88] Whether what is supposed to be happening is the "equal" division of property, as in the community property states, or the "equitable" division, as in the common law states, what is in fact happening is neither equal nor equitable. This is partly because even when the division of *tangible* property is fairly equal, what is in fact most families' principal asset is largely or entirely left out of the equation. This leads us to the third component of injustice in the current practice of divorce.[89]

As we have seen, most married couples give priority to the husband's work life, and wives, when they work for wages, earn on average only a small fraction of the family income, and perform the great bulk of the family's unpaid labor. The most valuable economic asset of a typical marriage is not any tangible piece of property, such as a house (since, if there is one, it is usually heavily mortgaged). In fact, "the average divorcing couple has less than $20,000 in net worth." By far the most important property acquired in the average marriage is its career assets, or human capital, the vast majority of which is likely to be invested in the husband. As Weitzman reports, it takes the average divorced man only about *ten months* to earn as much as the couple's entire net worth.[90] The importance of this marital asset is hard to overestimate, yet it has only recently begun to be treated in some states as marital property for the purposes of divorce settlements.[91] Even if "marital property" as traditionally understood is divided evenly, there can be no equity so long as this crucial piece is left in the hands of the husband alone. Except for the wealthy few who have significant material assets, "support awards that divide income, especially future income, are the most valuable entitlements awarded at divorce."[92] Largely because of the division of labor within marriage, to the extent that divorced women have to fall back on their own earnings, they are much worse off than they were when married, and than their ex-husbands are after divorce. In many cases, full-time work at or around the minimum wage, which may be the best a woman without much job training or experience can earn, is insufficient to pull the household out of poverty. As Bianchi and Spain state, "women's labor market adjustments to accommodate children, which are often made within a two-parent family context and seem economically rational at the time, cause difficulty later when these same women find themselves divorced and in great need of supporting themselves and their children."[93]

For reasons that seem to have been exacerbated by no-fault divorce laws, most separated or divorced women *do* have to fall back on their own earnings. These earnings—as opposed to spousal support payments or public transfer payments—make up the major portion of the income of female-maintained families. In 1980, they constituted the entire income of almost half such households.[94] The major reason for this is that, loath to recognize that the husband's earning power, and therefore his continuing income, is the most important asset of a marriage, judges have not been dividing it fairly at the time of divorce. As Weitzman summarizes the situation, "Under the new divorce laws, . . . a woman is now expected to become self-sufficient (and, in many cases, to support her children as well)."[95] Alimony and child support are either not awarded, not adequate, or not paid, in the great majority of cases. For many separated or divorced women, as for most single mothers, the idea of the male provider is nothing but a misleading myth that has negatively affected their own work lives while providing them with nothing at all.

In many divorces, there is inadequate income to support two households, with the paradoxical result that poor women with dependent children are even less likely than others to be awarded child support. But even in the case of families who were comfortably off, judges frequently consider what proportion of his income the husband will need to maintain his own standard of living (and even that of his hypothetical future family) before considering the needs of his wife and children. Instead of thinking in terms of compensating wives for all the unpaid effort that most have expended on the home and children, judges are thinking in terms of "what she can earn, and what he can pay."[96] On top of this, they are often misled by the fact that many women are now in the labor force into assuming that wives who have spent many years predominantly as mothers and homemakers will suddenly be able to support themselves.[97]

Contrary to popular belief, alimony has always been awarded rarely, only to the ex-wives of middle- and upper-class men— a small minority of the divorcing population.[98] While this situation has not changed, what *has* changed is the nature of alimony, which under no-fault practices has become in almost all cases a short-term "transitional" award, designed to help divorced women become self-sufficient as rapidly as possible. The burden of proof is now distinctly on the woman to show that she cannot support herself. In Weitzman's sample, only 17 percent, or roughly one-sixth, of divorcing wives were awarded alimony in 1978. The average amount awarded was $350 a month in 1984 dollars, for a median length of twenty-five months. Partly because of the shorter duration of their marriages, the incidence of alimony awards to mothers of preschool children was even lower than the average—only 13 percent. Even in cases in which a husband's high earning capacity has clearly resulted in large part from his wife's financial and/or domestic support during marriage, judges have been extremely reluctant to require him to continue to share it with her in order to allow her to complete a comparable education or training herself. Since about 1985, however, there has been a trend in some states toward reversing time limitations on alimony after long-term traditional marriages.[99]

The phenomenon of shrinking alimony is exacerbated by the paucity of child support. David Ellwood reports that nationwide, as of 1985, 82 percent of divorced custodial mothers of children under twenty-one were awarded child support but only 54 percent received any, and the average received amounted to $2,538 per year, or just over $200 a month. Separated and never-married women are awarded and receive child support less frequently and in lesser amounts.[100] A 1982 Census Bureau survey reported over eight million women raising at least one child without the father in the home. Of these, the court had ordered support in only five million cases. The average annual payment ordered was $2,180 for white women, $2,070 for Hispanic women, and $1,640 for black women. Weitzman's California-based research showed that a divorced man is rarely (and only in the lowest earning groups) ordered to pay more than a third of his net income in *total* support payments to his former wife and children.[101]

The inadequate levels of child support ordered are only part of the problem. A nationwide survey showed that, in 1981, the ordered amounts were paid in full in less than one-half of cases. Approximately one-quarter of mothers awarded support received partial payment, and one-quarter received no payment at all.[102] In general, except in the case of fathers earning more than $50,000, who comply in more than 90 percent of cases, nonpayment of child support bears little relation to the father's income. One of the major problems appears to be the ineffectiveness or lack of enforcement procedures.[103] With the Child Support Enforcement Amendments of 1984, the problem has now been addressed by federal legislation mandating the withholding of payments from the father's paycheck. Even when paid in full, however, the amounts of alimony and child support that are being awarded are grossly unfair, given the unequal situations in which marriage leaves men and women. The effect of judges' tendency to regard the husband's postdivorce income as first and foremost *his* is that they "rarely require him to help [his former wife and children] sustain a standard of living *half as good as his own*"[104] (emphasis added).

Another reason that divorced women are likely to have to rely on their own, often inadequate earnings is that they are much less likely than their ex-husbands to remarry. The reasons for this are almost all socially created and therefore alterable. In the vast majority of cases, a divorced mother continues to take primary responsibility for the children, but she has lost to a very large extent the financial resources she had within marriage, making her a less attractive marital partner than the typical divorced man. Custody of children is known to be a factor that discourages remarriage. Men who divorce in their thirties and forties are typically noncustodial parents, and are often at the height of their earning power—not an insignificant factor in attracting a subsequent, sometimes much younger wife. Such a couple will not be affected by the social disapproval attached to a woman who marries a much younger man, in the rare case that she does so. Whereas increasing age is not much of an impediment for a man seeking to remarry, it seriously affects a woman's chances, which decrease from 56 percent in her thirties to less than 12 percent if she is in her fifties or older when divorced. This is largely, of course, because so much more emphasis is placed on youth and good looks as constituting attractiveness in women than in men. And ironically, success at work, highly correlated with remarriage for men, is inversely correlated for women.[105]

By attempting to treat men and women as equals at the end of marriage, current divorce law neglects not only the obvious fact that women are *not* the socioeconomic equals of men in our society, but also the highly relevant fact that the experience of gendered marriage and primary parenting greatly exacerbates the inequality that women already bring with them into marriage. To divide the property equally and leave each partner to support himself or herself and to share support of the children might be fair in the case of a marriage in which the paid and unpaid labor had been shared equally, and in which neither spouse's work life had taken priority over that of the other. However, as we have seen, such marriages are exceedingly rare. Traditional or quasi-traditional marriages are far more common, even in the case of the many wives who currently work full-time outside the home. A wife who has contributed at least her fair share in a gender-structured marriage, by undertaking virtually all of the unpaid family work while her husband pursues his work life, meanwhile greatly enhancing his actual and prospective earnings, is by no means treated equally if, at the time of divorce, she is almost entirely cut off from the benefits of his enhanced economic position. But in the typical divorce today, this is exactly what happens.

Clearly, the prospects of a divorcing woman, particularly if she is a custodial parent, are in many ways much bleaker than the prospects of a divorcing man. For the many reasons discussed, the economic costs of divorce fall overwhelmingly on women and children, and not on men. Along with these costs go great social and psychological costs, associated with the greater dislocation of their lives and the stress that accompany economic loss. It is highly significant that, unlike men, both women and children experience economic loss as the worst dimension of divorce. Moreover, recent research has shown that, due to the inadequacy in amount and duration of child support, even children of middle-class divorced parents often experience serious and long-term disadvantage and loss of opportunity.[106]

This implies, of course, that social reform could significantly alter the negative impact of divorce on those who suffer most from it. The important lesson is that women's vulnerability within marriage and their disadvantaged position in the case of marital breakdown are intimately linked. Women are made vulnerable by anticipation of gendered marriage, and are made more vulnerable by entering into and living within such marriage. But they are *most* vulnerable if they marry and have children, but then the marriage fails. Surely women's awareness of this situation has some effects on their behavior and on the distribution of power within marriage itself.

Exit, Threat of Exit, and Power in the Family

At the beginning of this chapter, I summarized Goodin's argument that socially created asymmetric vulnerability is morally unacceptable, and should be minimized. I also referred to Hirschman's arguments about the effects of persons' relative potentials for exit on their power or influence within relationships or groups. Neither of these theorists considers the institution of contemporary marriage an example of such power imbalance.[107] But the evidence presented here suggests that typical, contemporary, gender-structured marriage is an excellent example of socially created vulnerability, partly because the asymmetric dependency of wives on husbands affects their potential for satisfactory exit, and thereby influences the effectiveness of their voice within the marriage.

There has been virtual silence among theorists about the dimension of power in the family that accrues to the spouse who would lose less by exiting from the marriage—a dimension that those who study it seem loath to recognize, partly, no doubt, because it ill accords with society's beliefs about how intimate or romantic relationships are conducted. Three rare scholars who have explicitly applied the notion that potential for exit affects power of voice within marriage are Heer, critiquing Blood and Wolfe's distorted theory of family power, and Bergmann and Fuchs in their recent studies of women's continuing inequality.[108] All three make brief but succinct and lucid arguments that are clearly further validated by the evidence presented here—that marriage is a clear case of asymmetric vulnerability, in which not only power to make decisions but also power to prevent issues from becoming objects of decision is related to the spouses' relative opportunities to exit satisfactorily from the relationship. More typically, marriage is not treated as a situation to which the general theory of the effects of unequal dependency and potential for exit on power applies. Blood asserts, for example, that Heer's "exit" theory is rendered implausible by the fact that "*only* 37 percent" of the couples questioned in a 1939 study of marital success or failure had ever contemplated separation or divorce.[109] Surely this is a remarkably high percentage, especially given the far lower divorce rate then than now.

Of course, the family and other personal relations are special cases of this theory, as of so many others. But the aspects of families that make them different from other institutions such as political parties, schools, and so on, to which theories about the effect of different potentials for exit on power have typically been applied, do not render these theories inapplicable to them. Families are typically held together by strong ties of loyalty, and separation or divorce represents a drastic "solution" to their conflicts. But, particularly now that one in two marriages is expected to end in divorce, it is simply unrealistic to suggest that the threat of exit is absent, especially at times of marital conflict, or that the different abilities of spouses implicitly or explicitly to call on this threat are not likely to affect power and influence in the relationship. Ending a marriage usually causes pain and dislocation for both adults as well as for any children involved. However, the argument presented in this chapter has demonstrated clearly that, in all the ways that are affected by economic deprivation, women and children are likely to suffer considerably more than men from marital dissolution. It is highly probably that most wives, well aware of this fact, take it into consideration in deciding how firm a stand to take on, or even whether to raise, important issues that are likely to be conflictual. We cannot adequately understand the distribution of power in the family without taking this factor into account, and the idea that marriage is a just relationship of mutual vulnerability cannot survive this analysis.

If we are to aim at making the family, our most fundamental social grouping, more just, we must work toward eradicating the socially created vulnerabilities of women that stem from the division of labor and the resultant division of power within it. As I shall argue in the final chapter, in order to do

168

anything effective about the cycle of women's socially created vulnerability, we must take into account the current lack of clarity in law, public policy, and public opinion about *what marriage is*. Since evidently we do not all agree about what it is or should be, we must think in terms of building family and work institutions that enable people to structure their personal lives in different ways. If they are to avoid injustice to women and children, these institutions must encourage the avoidance of socially created vulnerabilities by facilitating and reinforcing the equal sharing of paid and unpaid work between men and women, and consequently the equalizing of their opportunities and obligations in general. They must also ensure that those who enter into relationships in which there is a division of labor that might render them vulnerable are fully protected against such vulnerability, both within the context of the ongoing relationship and in the event of its dissolution.

8

Conclusion: Toward a Humanist Justice

The family is the linchpin of gender, reproducing it from one generation to the next. As we have seen, family life as typically practiced in our society is not just, either to women or to children. Moreover, it is not conducive to the rearing of citizens with a strong sense of justice. In spite of all the rhetoric about equality between the sexes, the traditional or quasi-traditional division of family labor still prevails. Women are made vulnerable by constructing their lives around the expectation that they will be primary parents; they become more vulnerable within marriages in which they fulfill this expectation, whether or not they also work for wages; and they are most vulnerable in the event of separation or divorce, when they usually take over responsibility for children without adequate support from their ex-husbands. Since approximately half of all marriages end in divorce, about half of our children are likely to experience its dislocations, often made far more traumatic by the socioeconomic consequences of both gender-structured marriage and divorce settlements that fail to take account of it. I have suggested that, for very important reasons, the family *needs* to be a just institution, and have shown that contemporary

170

theories of justice neglect women and ignore gender. How can we address this injustice?

This is a complex question. It is particularly so because we place great value on our freedom to live different kinds of lives, there is no current consensus on many aspects of gender, and we have good reason to suspect that many of our beliefs about sexual difference and appropriate sex roles are heavily influenced by the very fact that we grew up in a gender-structured society. All of us have been affected, in our very psychological structures, by the fact of gender in our personal pasts, just as our society has been deeply affected by its strong influence in our collective past. Because of the lack of shared meanings about gender, it constitutes a particularly hard case for those who care deeply about both personal freedom and social justice. The way we divide the labor and responsibilities in our personal lives seems to be one of those things that people should be free to work out for themselves, but because of its vast repercussions it belongs clearly within the scope of things that must be governed by principles of justice. Which is to say, in the language of political and moral theory, that it belongs both to the sphere of "the good" and to that of "the right."

I shall argue here that any just and fair solution to the urgent problem of women's and children's vulnerability must encourage and facilitate the equal sharing by men and women of paid and unpaid work, of productive and reproductive labor. We must work toward a future in which all will be likely to choose this mode of life. A just future would be one without gender. In its social structures and practices, one's sex would have no more relevance than one's eye color or the length of one's toes. No assumptions would be made about "male" and "female" roles; childbearing would be so conceptually separated from child rearing and other family responsibilities that it would be a cause for surprise, and no little concern, if men and women were not equally responsible for domestic life or if children were to spend much more time with one parent than the other. It would be a future in which men and women participated in more or less equal numbers in every sphere of life, from infant care to different kinds of paid work to high-level politics. Thus it would no longer be the case that having no experience of raising children would be the practical prerequisite for attaining positions of the greatest social influence. Decisions about abortion and rape, about divorce settlements and sexual harassment, or about any other crucial social issues would not be made, as they often are now, by legislatures and benches of judges overwhelmingly populated by men whose power is in large part due to their advantaged position in the gender structure. If we are to be at all true to our democratic ideals, moving away from gender is essential. Obviously, the attainment of such a social world requires major changes in a multitude of institutions and social settings outside the home, as well as within it.

Such changes will not happen overnight. Moreover, any present solution to the vulnerability of women and children that is just and respects individual freedom must take into account that most people currently live in ways that are greatly affected by gender, and most still favor many aspects of current, gendered practices. Sociological studies confirm what most of us already infer from our own personal and professional acquaintances: there are no currently shared meanings in this country about the extent to which differences between the sexes are innate or environmental, about the appropriate roles of men and women, and about which family forms and divisions of labor are most beneficial for partners, parents, and children.[1] There are those, at one extreme, for whom the different roles of the two sexes, especially as parents, are deeply held tenets of religious belief. At the other end of the spectrum are those of us for whom the sooner all social differentiation between the sexes vanishes, the better it will be for all of us. And there are a thousand varieties of view in between. Public policies must respect people's views and choices. But they must do so only insofar as it can be ensured that these choices do not result, as they now do, in the vulnerability of women and children. Special protections must be built into our laws and public policies to ensure that, for those who choose it, the division of labor between the sexes does not result in injustice. In the face of these difficulties—balancing freedom and the effects of past choices against the needs of justice—I do not pretend to have arrived at any complete or fully satisfactory answers. But I shall attempt in this final chapter to suggest some social reforms, including changes in public policies and reforms of family law, that may help us work toward a solution to the injustices of gender.

Marriage has become an increasingly peculiar contract, a complex and ambiguous combination of anachronism and present-day reality. There is no longer the kind of agreement that once prevailed about what is expected of the parties to a marriage. Clearly, at least in the United States, it is no longer reasonable to assume that marriage will last a lifetime, since only half of current marriages are expected to. And yet, in spite of the increasing legal equality of men and women and the highly publicized figures about married women's increased participation in the labor force, many couples continue to adhere to more or less traditional patterns of role differentiation. As a recent article put it, women are "out of the house but not out of the kitchen."[2] Consequently, often working part-time or taking time out from wage work to care for family members, especially children, most wives are in a very different position from their husbands in their ability to be economically self-supporting. This is reflected, as we have seen, in power differentials between the sexes within the family. It means also, in the increasingly common event of divorce, usually by mutual agreement, that it is the mother who in 90 percent of cases will have physical custody of the children. But whereas the greater need for money goes one way, the bulk of the earning power almost always goes the other. This is one of the most important causes of the feminization of poverty, which is affecting the life chances of ever larger numbers of children as well as their mothers. The division of labor within families has always adversely affected women, by making them economically dependent on men. Because of the increasing instability of marriage, its effects on children have now reached crisis proportions.

Some who are critical of the present structure and practices of marriage have suggested that men and women simply be made free to make their own agreements about family life, contracting with each other, much as business contracts are made.[3] But this takes insufficient account of the history of gender in our culture and our own psychologies, of the present substantive inequalities between the sexes, and, most important, of the well-being of the children who result from the relationship. As has long been recognized in the realm of labor relations, justice is by no means always enhanced by the maximization of freedom of contract, if the individuals involved are in unequal positions to start with. Some have even suggested that it is consistent with justice to leave spouses to work out their own divorce settlement.[4] By this time, however, the two people ending a marriage are likely to be far *more* unequal. Such a practice would be even more catastrophic for most women and children than is the present system. Wives in any but the rare cases in which they as individuals have remained their husbands' socioeconomic equals could hardly be expected to reach a just solution if left "free" to "bargain" the terms of financial support or child custody. What would they have to bargain *with?*

There are many directions that public policy can and should take in order to make relations between men and women more just. In discussing these, I shall look back to some of the contemporary ways of thinking about justice that I find most convincing. I draw particularly on Rawls's idea of the original position and Walzer's conception of the complex equality found in separate spheres of justice, between which I find no inconsistency. I also keep in mind

173

critical legal theorists' critique of contract, and the related idea, suggested earlier, that rights to privacy that are to be valuable to all of us can be enjoyed only insofar as the sphere of life in which we enjoy them ensures the equality of its adult members and protects children. Let us begin by asking what kind of arrangements persons in a Rawlsian original position would agree to regarding marriage, parental and other domestic responsibilities, and divorce. What kinds of policies would they agree to for other aspects of social life, such as the workplace and schools, that affect men, women, and children and relations among them? And let us consider whether these arrangements would satisfy Walzer's separate spheres test—that inequalities in one sphere of life not be allowed to overflow into another. Will they foster equality within the sphere of family life? For the protection of the privacy of a domestic sphere in which inequality exists is the protection of the right of the strong to exploit and abuse the weak.

Let us first try to imagine ourselves, as far as possible, in the original position, knowing neither what our sex nor any other of our personal characteristics will be once the veil of ignorance is lifted.* Neither do we know our place in society or our particular conception of the good life. Particularly relevant in this context, of course, is our lack of knowledge of our beliefs about the characteristics of men and women and our related convictions about the appropriate division of labor between the sexes. Thus the positions we represent must include a wide variety of beliefs on these matters. We may, once the veil of ignorance is lifted, find ourselves feminist men or feminist women whose conception of the good life includes the minimization of social differentiation between the sexes. Or we may find ourselves traditionalist men or women, whose conception of the good life, for religious or other reasons, is bound up in an adherence to the conventional division of labor between the sexes. The challenge is to arrive at and apply principles of justice having to do with the family and the division of labor between the sexes that can satisfy these vastly disparate points of view and the many that fall between.

There are some traditionalist positions so extreme that they ought not be admitted for consideration, since they violate such fundamentals as equal basic liberty and self-respect. We need not, and should not, that is to say, admit for consideration views based on the notion that women are inherently inferior beings whose function is to fulfill the needs of men. Such a view is no

---

*I say "so far as possible" because of the difficulties already pointed out in chapter 5. Given the deep effects of gender on our psychologies, it is probably more difficult for us, having grown up in a gender-structured society, to imagine not knowing our sex than anything else about ourselves. Nevertheless, this should not prevent us from trying.

more admissible in the construction of just institutions for a modern pluralist society than is the view, however deeply held, that some are naturally slaves and others naturally and justifiably their masters. We need not, therefore, consider approaches to marriage that view it as an inherently and desirably hierarchical structure of dominance and subordination. Even if it were conceivable that a person who did not know whether he or she would turn out to be a man or a woman in the society being planned would subscribe to such views, they are not admissible. Even if there were no other reasons to refuse to admit such views, they must be excluded for the sake of children, for everyone in the original position has a high personal stake in the quality of childhood. Marriages of dominance and submission are bad for children as well as for their mothers, and the socioeconomic outcome of divorce after such a marriage is very likely to damage their lives and seriously restrict their opportunities.

With this proviso, what social structures and public policies regarding relations between the sexes, and the family in particular, could we agree on in the original position? I think we would arrive at a basic model that would absolutely minimize gender. I shall first give an account of some of what this would consist in. We would also, however, build in carefully protective institutions for those who wished to follow gender-structured modes of life. These too I shall try to spell out in some detail.

Moving Away from Gender

First, public policies and laws should generally assume no social differentiation of the sexes. Shared parental responsibility for child care would be both assumed and facilitated. Few people outside of feminist circles seem willing to acknowledge that society does not have to choose between a system of female parenting that renders women and children seriously vulnerable and a system of total reliance on day care provided outside the home. While high-quality day care, subsidized so as to be equally available to all children, certainly constitutes an important part of the response that society should make in order to provide justice for women and children, it is only one part.[5] If we start out with the reasonable assumption that women and men are equally parents of their children, and have equal responsibility for both the unpaid effort that goes into caring for them and their economic support, then we must rethink the demands of work life throughout the period in which a worker of either sex is a parent of a small child. We can no longer cling to the by now largely mythical assumption that every worker has "someone else" at home to raise "his" children.

The facilitation and encouragement of equally shared parenting would require substantial changes.[6] It would mean major changes in the workplace, all of which could be provided on an entirely (and not falsely) gender-neutral basis. Employers must be required by law not only completely to eradicate sex discrimination, including sexual harassment. They should also be required to make positive provision for the fact that most workers, for differing lengths of time in their working lives, are also parents, and are sometimes required to nurture other family members, such as their own aging parents. Because children are borne by women but can (and, I contend, should) be raised by both parents equally, policies relating to pregnancy and birth should be quite distinct from those relating to parenting. Pregnancy and childbirth, to whatever varying extent they require leave from work, should be regarded as temporarily disabling conditions like any others, and employers should be mandated to provide leave for all such conditions.[7] Of course, pregnancy and childbirth are far *more* than simply "disabling conditions," but they should be treated as such for leave purposes, in part because their disabling effects vary from one woman to another. It seems unfair to mandate, say, eight or more weeks of leave for a condition that disables many women for less time and some for much longer, while *not* mandating leave for illnesses or other disabling conditions. Surely a society as rich as ours can afford to do both.

Parental leave during the postbirth months must be available to mothers and fathers on the same terms, to facilitate shared parenting; they might take sequential leaves or each might take half-time leave. All workers should have the right, without prejudice to their jobs, seniority, benefits, and so on, to work less than full-time during the first year of a child's life, and to work flexible or somewhat reduced hours at least until the child reaches the age of seven. Correspondingly greater flexibility of hours must be provided for the parents of a child with any health problem or disabling condition. The professions whose greatest demands (such as tenure in academia or the partnership hurdle in law) coincide with the peak period of child rearing must restructure their demands or provide considerable flexibility for those of their workers who are also participating parents. Large-scale employers should also be required to provide high-quality on-site day care for children from infancy up to school age. And to ensure equal quality of day care for all young children, *direct government subsidies* (not tax credits, which benefit the better-off) should make up the difference between the cost of high-quality day care and what less well paid parents could reasonably be expected to pay.

There are a number of things that schools, too, must do to promote the minimization of gender. As Amy Gutmann has recently noted, in their present authority structures (84 percent of elementary school teachers are female, while 99 percent of school superintendents are male), "schools do not simply reflect, they perpetuate the social reality of gender preferences when they educate children in a system in which men rule women and women rule children." She argues that, since such sex stereotyping is "a formidable obstacle" to children's rational deliberation about the lives they wish to lead, sex should be regarded as a relevant qualification in the hiring of both teachers and administrators, until these proportions have become much more equal.[8]

An equally important role of our schools must be to ensure in the course of children's education that they become fully aware of the politics of gender. This does not only mean ensuring that women's experience and women's writing are included in the curriculum, although this in itself is undoubtedly important.[9] Its political significance has become obvious from the amount of protest that it has provoked. Children need also to be taught about the present inequalities, ambiguities, and uncertainties of marriage, the facts of workplace discrimination and segregation, and the likely consequences of making life choices based on assumptions about gender. They should be discouraged from thinking about their futures as *determined* by the sex to which they happen to belong. For many children, of course, personal experience has already "brought home" the devastating effects of the traditional division of labor between the sexes. But they do not necessarily come away from this experience with positive ideas about how to structure their own future family lives differently. As Anita Shreve has recently suggested, "the old home-economics courses that used to teach girls how to cook and sew might give way to the new home economics: teaching girls *and boys* how to combine working and parenting."[10] Finally, schools should be required to provide high-quality after-school programs, where children can play safely, do their homework, or participate in creative activities.

The implementation of all these policies would significantly help parents to share the earning and the domestic responsibilities of their families, and children to grow up prepared for a future in which the significance of sex difference is greatly diminished. Men could participate equally in the nurturance of their children, from infancy and throughout childhood, with predictably great effects on themselves, their wives or partners, and their children. And women need not become vulnerable through economic dependence. In addition, such arrangements would alleviate the qualms many people have about the long hours that some children spend in day care. If one parent of a preschooler worked, for example, from eight to four o'clock and the other from ten to six o'clock, a preschool child would be at day care for only six hours (including nap time), and with each one or both of her or his parents the rest of the day. If each parent were able to work a six-hour day, or a four-day week, still less day care would be needed. Moreover, on-site provision of day care would enable mothers to continue to nurse, if they chose, beyond the time of their parental leave.[11]

The situation of single parents and their children is more complicated, but it seems that it too, for a number of reasons, would be much improved in a society in which sex difference was accorded an absolute minimum of social significance. Let us begin by looking at the situation of never-married mothers and their children. First, the occurrence of pregnancy among single teenagers, which is almost entirely unintended, would presumably be reduced if girls grew up more assertive and self-protective, and with less tendency to perceive their futures primarily in terms of motherhood. It could also be significantly reduced by the wide availability of sex education and contraception.[12] Second, the added weight of responsibility given to fatherhood in a gender-free society would surely give young men more incentive than they now have not to incur the results of careless sexual behavior until they were ready to take on the responsibilities of being parents. David Ellwood has outlined a policy for establishing the paternity of all children of single mothers at the time of birth, and for enforcing the requirement that their fathers contribute to their support throughout childhood, with provision for governmental backup support in cases where the father is unable to pay. These proposals seem eminently fair and sensible, although the minimum levels of support suggested ($1,500 to $2,000 per year) are inadequate, especially since the mother is presumed to be either taking care of the child herself or paying for day care (which often costs far more than this) while she works.[13]

Third, never-married mothers would benefit greatly from a work structure that took parenthood seriously into account, as well as from the subsidization of high-quality day care. Women who grew up with the expectation that their work lives would be as important a part of their futures as the work lives of men would be less likely to enter dead-ended, low-skilled occupations, and would be better able to cope economically with parenthood without marriage.

Most single parenthood results, however, not from single mothers giving birth, but from marital separation and divorce. And this too would be significantly altered in a society not structured along the lines of gender. Even if rates of divorce were to remain unchanged (which is impossible to predict), it seems inconceivable that separated and divorced fathers who had shared equally in the nurturance of their children from the outset would be as likely to neglect them, by not seeing them or not contributing to their support, as many do today. It seems reasonable to expect that children after divorce would still have two actively involved parents, and two working adults economically responsible for them. Because these parents had shared equally the paid work and the family work, their incomes would be much more equal than those of most divorcing parents today. Even if they were quite equal, however, the parent without physical custody should be required to contribute to the child's support, *to the point where the standards of living of the two households were the same.* This would be very different from the situation of many children of divorced parents today, dependent for both their nurturance and their economic support solely on mothers whose wage work has been interrupted by primary parenting.

It is impossible to predict all the effects of moving toward a society without gender. Major current injustices to women and children would end. Men would experience both the joys and the responsibilities of far closer and more sustained contact with their children than many have today. Many immensely influential spheres of life—notably politics and the professional occupations—would for the first time be populated more or less equally by men and women, most of whom were also actively participating parents. This would be in great contrast to today, when most of those who rise to influential positions are either men who, if fathers, have minimal contact with their children, or women who have either forgone motherhood altogether or hired others as full-time caretakers for their children because of the demands of their careers. These are the people who make policy at the highest levels—policies not only *about* families and their welfare and about the education of children, but about the foreign policies, the wars and the weapons that will determine the future or the lack of future for all these families and children. Yet they are almost all people who gain the influence they do in part by never having had the day-to-day experience of nurturing a child. This is probably the most significant aspect of our gendered division of labor, though the least possible to grasp. The effects of changing it could be momentous.

Protecting the Vulnerable

The pluralism of beliefs and modes of life is fundamental to our society, and the genderless society I have just outlined would certainly not be agreed upon by all as desirable. Thus when we think about constructing relations between the sexes that could be agreed upon in the original position, and are therefore just from all points of view, we must also design institutions and practices acceptable to those with more traditional beliefs about the characteristics of men and women, and the appropriate division of labor between them. It is essential, if men and women are to be allowed to so divide their labor, as they must be if we are to respect the current pluralism of beliefs, that society protect the vulnerable. Without such protection, the marriage contract seriously exacerbates the initial inequalities of those who entered into it, and too many women and children live perilously close to economic disaster and serious social dislocation; too many also live with violence or the continual threat of it. It should be noted here that the rights and obligations that the law would need to promote and mandate in order to protect the vulnerable need not—and should not—be designated in accordance with sex, but in terms of different functions or roles performed. There are only a minute percentage of "househusbands" in this country, and a very small number of men whose work lives take second priority after their wives'. But they can quite readily be protected by the same institutional structures that can protect traditional and quasi-traditional wives, so long as these are designed without reference to sex.

Gender-structured marriage, then, needs to be regarded as a currently necessary institution (because still chosen by some) but one that is socially problematic. It should be subjected to a number of legal requirements, at least when there are children.[14*] Most important, there is no need for the division of labor between the sexes to involve the economic dependence, either complete or partial, of one partner on the other. Such dependence can be avoided if both partners have *equal legal entitlement* to all earnings coming into the

---

*I see no reason why what I propose here should be restricted to couples who are legally married. It should apply equally to "common law" relationships that produce children, and in which a division of labor is practiced.

household. The clearest and simplest way of doing this would be to have employers make out wage checks equally divided between the earner and the partner who provides all or most of his or her unpaid domestic services. In many cases, of course, this would not change the way couples actually manage their finances; it would simply codify what they already agree on—that the household income is rightly shared, because in a real sense jointly earned. Such couples recognize the fact that the wage-earning spouse is no more supporting the homemaking and child-rearing spouse than the latter is supporting the former; the form of support each offers the family is simply different. Such couples might well take both checks, deposit them in a joint account, and really share the income, just as they now do with the earnings that come into the household.

In the case of some couples, however, altering the entitlement of spouses to the earned income of the household as I have suggested *would* make a significant difference. It would make a difference in cases where the earning or higher-earning partner now directly exploits this power, by refusing to make significant spending decisions jointly, by failing to share the income, or by psychologically or physically abusing the nonearning or low-earning partner, reinforced by the notion that she (almost always the wife) has little option but to put up with such abuse or to take herself and her children into a state of destitution. It would make a difference, too, in cases where the higher-earning partner indirectly exploits this earning power in order to perpetuate the existing division of labor in the family. In such instances considerable changes in the balance of power would be likely to result from the legal and societal recognition that the partner who does most of the domestic work of the family contributes to its well-being just as much, and therefore rightly *earns* just as much, as the partner who does most of the workplace work.

What I am suggesting is *not* that the wage-working partner pay the homemaking partner for services rendered. I do not mean to introduce the cash nexus into a personal relationship where it is inappropriate. I have simply suggested that since both partners in a traditional or quasi-traditional marriage work, there is no reason why only one of them should get paid, or why one should be paid far more than the other. The equal splitting of wages would constitute public recognition of the fact that the currently unpaid labor of families is just as important as the paid labor. If we do *not* believe this, then we should insist on the complete and equal sharing of both paid and unpaid labor, as occurs in the genderless model of marriage and parenting described earlier. It is only if we *do* believe it that society can justly allow couples to distribute the two types of labor so unevenly. But in such cases, given the enormous significance our society attaches to money and earnings, we should insist that the earnings be recognized as equally earned by the two persons. To call on Walzer's language, we should do this in order to help prevent the inequality of family members in the sphere of wage work to invade their domestic sphere.

It is also important to point out that this proposal does not constitute unwarranted invasion of privacy or any more state intervention into the life of families than currently exists. It would involve only the same kind of invasion of privacy as is now required by such things as registration of marriages and births, and the filing of tax returns declaring numbers and names of dependents. And it *seems* like intervention in families only because it would alter the existing relations of power within them. If a person's capacity to fulfill the terms of his or her work is dependent on having a spouse at home who raises the children and in other ways sustains that worker's day-to-day life, then it is no more interventionist to pay both equally for their contributions than only to pay one.

The same fundamental principle should apply to separation and divorce, to the extent that the division of labor has been practiced within a marriage. Under current divorce laws, as we have seen, the terms of exit from marriage are disadvantageous for almost all women in traditional or quasi-traditional marriages. Regardless of the consensus that existed about the division of the family labor, these women lose most of the income that has supported them *and* the social status that attached to them because of their husband's income and employment, often at the same time as suddenly becoming single parents, and prospective wage workers for the first time in many years. This combination of prospects would seem to be enough to put most traditional wives off the idea of divorcing even if they had good cause to do so. In addition, since divorce in the great majority of states no longer requires the consent of both spouses, it seems likely that wives for whom divorce would spell economic and social catastrophe would be inhibited in voicing their dissatisfactions or needs within marriage. The terms of exit are very likely to affect the use and the power of voice in the ongoing relationship. At worst, these women may be rendered virtually defenseless in the face of physical or psychological abuse. This is not a system of marriage and divorce that could possibly be agreed to by persons in an original position in which they did not know whether they were to be male or female, traditionalist or not. It is a fraudulent contract, presented as beneficial to all but in fact to the benefit only of the more powerful.

For all these reasons, it seems essential that the terms of divorce be redrawn so as to reflect the gendered or nongendered character of the marriage that is ending, to a far greater extent than they do now.[15] The legal system of a society that allows couples to divide the labor of families in a traditional or quasi-traditional manner *must* take responsibility for the vulnerable position in which marital breakdown places the partner who has completely or partially lost the capacity to be economically self-supporting. When such a marriage ends, it seems wholly reasonable to expect a person whose career has been largely unencumbered by domestic responsibilities to support financially the partner who undertook these responsibilities. This support, in the form of combined alimony and child support, should be far more substantial than the token levels often ordered by the courts now. *Both postdivorce households should enjoy the same standard of living.* Alimony should not end after a few years, as the (patronizingly named) "rehabilitative alimony" of today does; it should continue for at least as long as the traditional division of labor in the marriage did and, in the case of short-term marriages that produced children, until the youngest child enters first grade and the custodial parent has a real chance of making his or her own living. After that point, child support should continue at a level that enables the children to enjoy a standard of living equal to that of the noncustodial parent. There can be no reason consistent with principles of justice that some should suffer economically vastly more than others from the breakup of a relationship whose asymmetric division of labor was mutually agreed on.

I have suggested two basic models of family rights and responsibilities, both of which are currently needed because this is a time of great transition for men and women and great disagreement about gender. Families in which roles and responsibilities are equally shared regardless of sex are far more in accord with principles of justice than are typical families today. So are families in which those who undertake more traditional domestic roles are protected from the risks they presently incur. In either case, justice as a whole will benefit from the changes. Of the two, however, I claim that the genderless family is more just, in the three important respects that I spelled out at the beginning of this book: it is more just to women; it is more conducive to equal opportunity both for women and for children of both sexes; and it creates a more favorable environment for the rearing of citizens of a just society. Thus, while

183

protecting those whom gender now makes vulnerable, we must also put our best efforts into promoting the elimination of gender.

The increased justice to women that would result from moving away from gender is readily apparent. Standards for just social institutions could no longer take for granted and exclude from considerations of justice much of what women now do, since men would share in it equally. Such central components of justice as what counts as productive labor, and what count as needs and deserts, would be greatly affected by this change. Standards of justice would become *humanist*, as they have never been before. One of the most important effects of this would be to change radically the situation of women as citizens. With egalitarian families, and with institutions such as workplaces and schools designed to accommodate the needs of parents and children, rather than being based as they now are on the traditional assumption that "someone else" is at home, mothers would not be virtually excluded from positions of influence in politics and the workplace. They would be represented at every level in approximately equal numbers with men.

In a genderless society, children too would benefit. They would not suffer in the ways that they do now because of the injustices done to women. It is undeniable that the family in which each of us grows up has a deeply formative influence on us—on the kind of persons we want to be as well as the kind of persons we are.[16] This is one of the reasons why one *cannot* reasonably leave the family out of "the basic structure of society," to which the principles of justice are to apply. Equality of opportunity to become what we want to be would be enhanced in two important ways by the development of families without gender and by the public policies necessary to support their development. First, the growing gap between the economic well-being of children in single-parent and those in two-parent families would be reduced. Children in single-parent families would benefit significantly if fathers were held equally responsible for supporting their children, whether married to their mothers or not; if more mothers had sustained labor force attachment; if high-quality day care were subsidized; and if the workplace were designed to accommodate parenting. These children would be far less likely to spend their formative years in conditions of poverty, with one parent struggling to fulfill the functions of two. Their life chances would be significantly enhanced.

Second, children of both sexes in gender-free families would have (as some already have) much more opportunity for self-development free from sex-role expectations and sex-typed personalities than most do now. Girls and boys who grow up in highly traditional families, in which sex difference is regarded as a determinant of everything from roles, responsibilities, and privileges to acceptable dress, speech, and modes of behavior, clearly have far less freedom to develop into whatever kind of person they want to be than do those who are raised without such constraints. It is too early for us to know a lot about the developmental outcomes and life choices of children who are equally parented by mothers and fathers, since the practice is still so recent and so rare. Persuasive theories such as Chodorow's, however, would lead us to expect much less differentiation between the sexes to result from truly shared parenting.[17] Even now, in most cases without men's equal fathering, both the daughters and the sons of wage-working mothers have been found to have a more positive view of women and less rigid views of sex roles; the daughters (like their mothers) tend to have greater self-esteem and a more positive view of themselves as workers, and the sons, to expect equality and shared roles in their own future marriages.[18] We might well expect that with mothers in the labor force *and* with fathers as equal parents, children's attitudes and psychologies will become even less correlated with their sex. In a very crucial sense, their opportunities to become the persons they want to be will be enlarged.

Finally, it seems undeniable that the enhancement of justice that accompanies the disappearance of gender will make the family a much better place for children to develop a sense of justice. We can no longer deny the importance of the fact that families are where we first learn, by example and by how we are treated, not only how people do relate to each other but also how they *should*. How would families not built on gender be better schools of moral development? First, the example of co-equal parents with shared roles, combining love with justice, would provide a far better example of human relations for children than the domination and dependence that often occur in traditional marriage. The fairness of the distribution of labor, the equal respect, and the *inter*dependence of his or her parents would surely be a powerful first example to a child in a family with equally shared roles. Second, as I have argued, having a sense of justice requires that we be able to empathize, to abstract from our own situation and to think about moral and political issues from the points of view of others. We cannot come to either just principles or just specific decisions by thinking, as it were, as if we were nobody, or thinking from nowhere; we must, therefore, learn to think from the point of view of others, including others who are different from ourselves.

To the extent that gender is de-emphasized in our nurturing practices, this capacity would seem to be enhanced, for two reasons. First, if female primary

185

parenting leads, as it seems to, to less distinct ego boundaries and greater capacity for empathy in female children, and to a greater tendency to self-definition and abstraction in males, then might we not expect to find the two capacities better combined in children of both sexes who are reared by parents of both sexes? Second, the experience of *being* nurturers, throughout a significant portion of our lives, also seems likely to result in an increase in empathy, and in the combination of personal moral capacities, fusing feelings with reason, that just citizens need.[19]

For those whose response to what I have argued here is the practical objection that it is unrealistic and will cost too much, I have some answers and some questions. Some of what I have suggested would not cost anything, in terms of public spending, though it would redistribute the costs and other responsibilities of rearing children more evenly between men and women. Some policies I have endorsed, such as adequate public support for children whose fathers cannot contribute, may cost more than present policies, but may not, depending on how well they work.[20] Some, such as subsidized high-quality day care, would be expensive in themselves, but also might soon be offset by other savings, since they would enable those who would otherwise be full-time child carers to be at least part-time workers.

All in all, it seems highly unlikely that the *long-term* costs of such programs—even if we count only monetary costs, not costs in human terms—would outweigh the long-term benefits. In many cases, the cycle of poverty could be broken—and children enabled to escape from, or to avoid falling into, it—through a much better early start in life.[21] But even if my suggestions would cost, and cost a lot, we have to ask: How much do we care about the injustices of gender? How much do we care that women who have spent the better part of their lives nurturing others can be discarded like used goods? How ashamed are we that one-quarter of our children, in one of the richest countries in the world, live in poverty? How much do we care that those who raise children, *because* of this choice, have restricted opportunities to develop the rest of their potential, and very little influence on society's values and direction? How much do we care that the family, our most intimate social grouping, is often a school of day-to-day injustice? How much do we *want* the just families that will produce the kind of citizens we need if we are ever to achieve a just society?

NOTES

Chapter 1   Introduction: Justice and Gender

1. U.S. Department of Labor, *Employment and Earnings: July 1987* (Washington, D.C.: Government Printing Office, 1987); Ruth Sidel, *Women and Children Last: The Plight of Poor Women in Affluent America* (New York: Viking, 1986), pp. xvi, 158. See also David T. Ellwood, *Poor Support: Poverty in the American Family* (New York: Basic Books, 1988), pp. 84–85, on the chronicity of poverty in single-parent households. In chapter 7 I shall return to these facts and discuss some of the explanations for them.

2. Shirley Williams, in Williams and Elizabeth Holtzman, "Women in the Political World: Observations," *Daedalus* 116, no. 4 (Fall 1987): 30.

3. Twenty-three percent of single parents have never been married and 12 percent are widowed. (U.S. Bureau of the Census, Current Population Reports, *Household and Family Characteristics: March 1987* [Washington, D.C.: Government Printing Office, 1987], p. 79). In 1987, 6.8 percent of children under eighteen were living with a never-married parent. ("Study Shows Growing Gap Between Rich and Poor," *New York Times*, March 23, 1989, p. A24). The proportions for the total population are very different from those for black families, of whom in 1984 half of those with adult members under thirty-five years of age were maintained by single, female parents, three-quarters of whom were never married. (Frank Levy, *Dollars and Dreams: The Changing American Income Distribution* [New York: Russell Sage, 1987], p. 156).

4. As Joan Scott has pointed out, *gender* was until recently used only as a grammatical term. See "Gender: A Useful Category of Historical Analysis," in Joan Wallach Scott, *Gender and the Politics of History* (New York: Columbia University Press, 1988), p. 28, citing Fowler's *Dictionary of Modern English Usage*.

5. Among Anglo-American feminists see, for example, Mary Daly, *Gyn/Ecology: The Metaethics of Radical Feminism* (Boston: Beacon Press, 1978); Susan Griffin, *Woman and Nature: The Roaring Inside Her* (New York: Harper & Row, 1978). For a good, succinct discussion of radical feminist biological determinism, see Alison Jaggar, *Feminist Politics and Human Nature* (Totowa, N.J.: Rowman and Allanheld, 1983).

6. See, for example, Sylvia Yanagisako and Jane Collier, "The Mode of Reproduction in Anthropology," in *Theoretical Perspectives on Sexual Difference*, ed. Deborah Rhode (New Haven: Yale University Press, in press).

7. Nancy Chodorow, *The Reproduction of Mothering: Psychoanalysis and the Sociology of Gender* (Berkeley: University of California Press, 1978); Dorothy Dinnerstein, *The Mermaid and the Minotaur: Sexual Arrangements and Human Malaise* (New York: Harper & Row, 1976). For further discussion of this issue and further references to the literature, see chapter 6, note 58, and accompanying text.

8. Linda Nicholson, *Gender and History* (New York: Columbia University Press, 1986); Michelle Z. Rosaldo, "The Use and Abuse of Anthropology," *Signs* 5, no. 3 (1980); Joan Wallach Scott, *Gender and the Politics of History* (New York: Columbia University Press, 1986).

9. For such critiques, see Bell Hooks, *Ain't I a Woman: black women and feminism* (Boston: South End Press, 1981), and *Feminist Theory: from margin to center* (Boston: South End Press, 1984); Elizabeth V. Spelman, *Inessential Woman: Problems of Exclusion in Feminist Thought* (Boston: Beacon Press, 1989).

10. There is now an abundant literature on the subject of women, their exclusion from nondomestic life, and the reasons given to justify it, in Western political theory. See, for example, Lorenne J. Clark and Lynda Lange, eds., *The Sexism of Social and Political Thought* (Toronto: University of Toronto Press, 1979); Jean Bethke Elshtain, *Public Man, Private Woman: Women in Social and Political Thought*

(Princeton: Princeton University Press, 1981); Genevieve Lloyd, *The Man of Reason: "Male" and "Female" in Western Philosophy* (Minneapolis: University of Minnesota Press, 1984); Mary O'Brien, *The Politics of Reproduction* (London: Routledge & Kegan Paul, 1981); Susan Moller Okin, *Women in Western Political Thought* (Princeton: Princeton University Press, 1979); Carole Pateman, "Feminist Critiques of the Public/Private Dichotomy," in *Public and Private in Social Life*, ed. S. Benn and G. Gaus (London: Croom Helm, 1983); Carole Pateman and Elizabeth Gross, eds., *Feminist Challenges: Social and Political Theory* (Boston: Northeastern University Press, 1987); Carole Pateman, *The Sexual Contract* (Stanford: Stanford University Press, 1988); Carole Pateman and Mary L. Shanley, eds., *Feminist Critiques of Political Theory* (Oxford: Polity Press, in press).

11. Bruce Ackerman, *Social Justice in the Liberal State* (New Haven: Yale University Press, 1980); Ronald Dworkin, *Taking Rights Seriously* (Cambridge: Harvard University Press, 1977); William Galston, *Justice and the Human Good* (Chicago: University of Chicago Press, 1980); Alasdair MacIntyre, *After Virtue* (Notre Dame: University of Notre Dame Press, 1981), and *Whose Justice? Which Rationality?* (Notre Dame: University of Notre Dame Press, 1988); Robert Nozick, *Anarchy, State, and Utopia* (New York: Basic Books, 1974); Roberto Unger, *Knowledge and Politics* (New York: The Free Press, 1975), and *The Critical Legal Studies Movement* (Cambridge: Harvard University Press, 1986).

12. Philip Green, in *Retrieving Democracy: In Search of Civic Equality* (Totowa, N.J.: Rowman and Allanheld, 1985), argues that the social equality that is prerequisite to real democracy is incompatible with the current division of labor between the sexes. See pp. 96–108.

13. Michael Walzer, *Spheres of Justice* (New York: Basic Books, 1983).

14. This is commented on and questioned by Francis Schrag, "Justice and the Family," *Inquiry* 19 (1976): 200, and Walzer, *Spheres of Justice*, chap. 9.

15. See note 10 of this chapter. The phrase is Dale Spender's.

16. See, for example, David Gauthier, *Morals by Agreement* (Oxford: Oxford University Press, 1986), passim and p. vi. Fortunately, Gauthier's computer was able to control its zeal for randomization enough to avoid referring to Plato and Rawls as "she" and Queen Gertrude and Mary Gibson as "he."

17. *General Electric v. Gilbert*, 429 U.S. 125 (1976), 135–36; second phrase quoted from *Geduldig v. Aiello*, 417 U.S. 484 (1974), 496–97, emphasis added.

18. Ackerman, *Social Justice*, pp. 127–28. He takes gender neutrality to the point of suggesting a hypothetical case in which "a couple simply *enjoy* abortions so much that they conceive embryos simply to kill them a few months later."

19. Derek L. Phillips, *Toward a Just Social Order* (Princeton: Princeton University Press, 1986), esp. pp. 187–96.

20. Ibid., pp. 224–26.

21. Ibid., esp. chap. 9.

22. I have analyzed some of the ways in which theorists in the tradition avoided considering the justice of gender in "Are Our Theories of Justice Gender-Neutral?" in *The Moral Foundations of Civil Rights*, ed. Robert Fullinwider and Claudia Mills (Totowa, N.J.: Rowman and Littlefield, 1986).

23. See Judith Hicks Stiehm, "The Unit of Political Analysis: Our Aristotelian Hangover," in *Discovering Reality: Feminist Perspectives on Epistemology, Metaphysics, Methodology, and Philosophy of Science*, ed. Sandra Harding and Merrill B. Hintikka (Dordrecht, Holland: Reidel, 1983).

24. See Carole Pateman and Theresa Brennan, "'Mere Auxiliaries to the Commonwealth': Women and the Origins of Liberalism," *Political Studies* 27, no. 2 (June 1979); also Susan Moller Okin, "Women and the Making of the Sentimental Family," *Philosophy and Public Affairs* 11, no. 1 (Winter 1982). This issue is treated at much greater length in Pateman, *The Sexual Contract*.

25. This claim, originating in the moral development literature, has significantly influenced recent feminist moral and political theory. Two central books are Carol Gilligan, *In a Different Voice* (Cambridge: Harvard University Press, 1982); and Nel Noddings, *Caring: A Feminine Approach to Ethics and Moral Education* (Berkeley: University of California Press, 1984). For the influence of Gilligan's work on feminist theory, see, for example, Seyla Benhabib, "The Generalized and the Concrete Other: The Kohlberg-Gilligan Controversy and Feminist Theory," in *Feminism as Critique*, ed. Benhabib and Drucilla Cornell (Minneapolis: University of Minnesota Press, 1987); Lawrence Blum, "Gilligan and Kohlberg: Implications for Moral Theory," *Ethics* 98, no. 3 (1988); and Eva Kittay and Diana Meyers, eds., *Women and Moral Theory* (Totowa, N.J.: Rowman and Allenheld, 1986). For a valuable alternative approach to the issues, and an excellent selective list of references to what has now become a vast literature, see Owen Flanagan and Kathryn Jackson, "Justice, Care and Gender: The Kohlberg-Gilligan Debate Revisited," *Ethics* 97, no. 3 (1987).

26. See, for example, John M. Broughton, "Women's Rationality and Men's Virtues: A Critique of

Notes

Gender Dualism in Gilligan's Theory of Moral Development," *Social Research* 50, no. 3 (1983); Owen Flanagan, *Varieties of Moral Personality: Ethics and Psychological Realism* (Cambridge: Harvard University Press, forthcoming), ch. 8; Catherine G. Greeno and Eleanor E. Maccoby, "How Different Is the 'Different Voice'?" and Gilligan's reply, *Signs* 11, no. 2 (1986); Debra Nails, "Social-Scientific Sexism: Gilligan's Mismeasure of Man," *Social Research* 50, no. 3 (1983); Joan Tronto, "'Women's Morality': Beyond Gender Difference to a Theory of Care," *Signs* 12, no. 4 (1987); Lawrence J. Walker, "Sex Differences in the Development of Moral Reasoning: A Critical Review," *Child Development* 55 (1984).

27. See extracts from the Apostolic Letter in *New York Times*, October 1, 1988, pp. A1 and 6. On the reinforcement of the old stereotypes in general, see Susan Moller Okin, "Thinking Like a Woman," in Rhode, ed., *Theoretical Perspectives*.

28. See esp. James Fishkin, *Justice, Equal Opportunity and the Family* (New Haven: Yale University Press, 1983); Phillips, *Just Social Order*, esp. pp. 346–49; Rawls, *Theory*, pp. 74, 300–301, 511–12.

29. Jean-Jacques Rousseau, *Emile: or On Education*, trans. Allan Bloom (New York: Basic Books, 1979), p. 363.

30. Louis de Bonald, in *Archives Parlementaires*, 2e série (Paris, 1869), vol. 15, p. 612; cited and translated by Roderick Phillips, "Women and Family Breakdown in Eighteenth-Century France: Rouen 1780–1800," *Social History* 2, (1976): 217.

31. *Reynolds v. Nebraska*, 98 U.S. 145 (1879), 164, 166.

32. *Bradwell v. Illinois*, 83 U.S. 130 (1872).

33. Martha Minow, "We, the Family: Constitutional Rights and American Families," *The American Journal of History* 74, no. 3 (1987): 969, discussing *Reynolds* and other nineteenth-century cases.

34. John Stuart Mill, *The Subjection of Women* (1869), in *Collected Works*, ed. J. M. Robson (Toronto: University of Toronto Press, 1984), vol. 21, pp. 324, 293–95. At the time Mill wrote, women had no political rights and coverture deprived married women of most legal rights, too. He challenges all this in his essay.

35. Mill, *Subjection of Women*, pp. 324–25, 294–95.

36. Hobbes writes of "men . . . as if but even now sprung out of the earth . . . like mushrooms." "Philosophical Rudiments Concerning Government and Society," in *The English Works of Thomas Hobbes*, ed. Sir William Molesworth (London: John Bohn, 1966), vol. 2, p. 109.

37. For example, Walzer, *Spheres of Justice*, chap. 9, "Kinship and Love."

38. See Alan Gewirth, *Reason and Morality* (Chicago: University of Chicago Press, 1978). He discusses moral development from time to time, but places families within the broad category of "voluntary associations" and does not discuss gender roles within them.

39. This is the case with both Rawls's A *Theory of Justice* (Cambridge: Harvard University Press, 1971), discussed here and in chap. 5, and Phillips's sociologically oriented *Toward a Just Social Order*, as discussed above.

40. Rawls, *Theory*, p. 465.

Chapter 2   The Family: Beyond Justice?

1. See the account given in Judith Stacey, "Are Feminists Afraid to Leave Home? The Challenge of Conservative Pro-family Feminism," in *What Is Feminism? A Re-examination*, ed. Juliet Mitchell and Ann Oakley (New York: Pantheon, 1986).

2. See, for example, Barrie Thorne and Marilyn Yalom, eds., *Rethinking the Family: Some Feminist Questions* (New York: Longman, 1982), esp. Thorne's introductory "Overview."

3. Michael Sandel, *Liberalism and the Limits of Justice* (Cambridge: Cambridge University Press, 1982); Allan Bloom, *The Closing of the American Mind: How Higher Education Has Failed Democracy and Impoverished the Souls of Today's Students* (New York: Simon & Schuster, 1987).

4. The exception is Martha Nussbaum's brilliant review of Bloom, "Undemocratic Vistas," in the *New York Review of Books* 34, no. 17 (November 5, 1987).

5. *Discourse on Political Economy*, translated from Jean-Jacques Rousseau, *Oeuvres Complètes* (Paris: Pléiade, 1959–1969), vol. 3, pp. 241–42.

6. David Hume, *Enquiry Concerning the Principles of Morals*, ed. L. A. Selby-Bigge from the 1777 edition (Oxford: Oxford University Press, 1975), p. 185. See also A *Treatise of Human Nature*, ed. L. A. Selby-Bigge (Oxford: Oxford University Press, 1978), pp. 493–96.

7. Sandel, *Limits of Justice*, pp. 30–35.

8. John Rawls, A *Theory of Justice* (Cambridge: Harvard University Press, 1971), p. 127.

9. Sandel, *Limits of Justice*, p. 31.

10. Ibid., pp. 30–31, 33.

11. Ibid., p. 34 (the first phrase is quoted from Hume, *A Treatise on Human Nature*).

12. Sandel, *Limits of Justice*, p. 31.

13. Rawls, *Theory*, p. 3.

14. Ibid., pp. 117, 192.

15. Ibid., pp. 129–30, 438–39.

16. Ibid., pp. 479, 191.

17. Ibid., p. 129.

18. Edward Shorter, *The Making of the Modern Family* (New York: Basic Books, 1975); Lawrence Stone, *The Family, Sex, and Marriage in England 1500–1800* (New York: Harper & Row, 1977); Randolph Trumbach, *The Rise of the Egalitarian Family* (New York: Academic Press, 1978).

19. *The Subjection of Women*, in *The Collected Works of John Stuart Mill*, ed. John M. Robson (Toronto: University of Toronto Press, 1984), p. 284.

20. John Ruskin, "Of Queen's Gardens," Lecture 2 of *Sesame and Lilies* (London: A. L. Burt, 1871), p. 85, quoted in Mary L. Shanley, "Marital Slavery and Friendship: John Stuart Mill's *The Subjection of Women*," *Political Theory* 9, no. 2 (1981): 233. See also Shanley, *Feminism, Marriage and the Law in Victorian England 1850–1890* (Princeton: Princeton University Press, in press), esp. introduction and chap. 1.

21. Sandel, *Limits of Justice*, p. 33.

22. Ruskin, "Of Queen's Gardens," p. 86.

23. See Susan Moller Okin, *Women in Western Political Thought* (Princeton: Princeton University Press, 1979), chap. 8.

24. Rousseau, *Emile: or On Education*, trans. Allan Bloom (New York: Basic Books, 1979), p. 364. See also Okin, *Women in Western Political Thought*, esp. chaps. 6 and 7.

25. Rousseau, *Emile*, p. 370.

26. Bloom, *Closing*, pp. 38, 99–100.

27. Ibid., pp. 57, 101, 127, and 66 respectively.

28. Ibid., pp. 86, 115, 100.

29. Ibid., pp. 115, 128–31.

30. Mary O'Brien, *The Politics of Reproduction* (London: Routledge & Kegan Paul, 1981).

31. Margaret Atwood, *The Handmaid's Tale* (New York: Simon & Schuster, 1986).

32. Bloom, *Closing*, p. 131; see also p. 101.

33. Ibid., p. 129.

34. Nussbaum, "Undemocratic Vistas," pp. 23–24.

35. Bloom, *Closing*, p. 38.

36. John Stuart Mill, "Nature," from *Three Essays on Religion*, in *The Philosophy of John Stuart Mill*, ed. Marshall Cohen (New York: Random House, 1961), "The Subjection of Women," in *Collected Works of John Stuart Mill*, ed. J. M. Robson, vol. 21, (Toronto: University of Toronto Press, 1984), esp. pp. 269–70 and 276–82.

37. Mill, "Nature," p. 445; see also p. 487.

38. Ruth Bleier, *Science and Gender: A Critique of Biology and Its Theories on Women* (New York: Pergamon Press, 1984); Anne Fausto-Sterling, *Myths of Gender: Biological Theories About Women and Men* (New York: Basic Books, 1985).

39. Bloom, *Closing*, pp. 130, 105.

40. Ibid., p. 88.

41. Bloom, *Closing*, pp. 91, 351.

Chapter 3   Whose Traditions? Which Understandings?

1. Family Protection Act, S. 1378, 97th Cong., 1st sess., 127 Congressional Record S6329 (1981); Pope John Paul II's Apostolic Letter, "On the Dignity of Women," as analyzed and quoted at length in the *New York Times* October 1, 1988, pp. A1 and 6.

2. *Good Housekeeping* advertisement, *New York Times*, October 6, 1988, p. D32; Christopher Lasch, *Haven in a Heartless World* New York: Basic Books, 1977); Robert N. Bellah et al., *Habits of the Heart* (Berkeley: University of California Press, 1985), esp. chaps. 2 and 11; Edward Shils, *Tradition* (Chicago: University of Chicago Press, 1980); Allan Bloom, *The Closing of the American Mind* (New York: Simon & Schuster, 1987).

3. Shils, *Tradition*. See, for example, pp. 17, 173, 204.

Notes

4. *Daily News* (Juneau, Alaska), March 21, 1985. Quoted by Frances Olsen, "The Myth of State Intervention in the Family," *University of Michigan Journal of Law Reform* 18, no. 4 (1985): 840.

5. Quoted by Elizabeth Pleck, *Domestic Tyranny* (New York: Oxford University Press, 1987), p. 197.

6. Alasdair MacIntyre, *After Virtue* (Notre Dame: University of Notre Dame Press, 1981), and *Whose Justice? Which Rationality?* (Notre Dame: University of Notre Dame Press, 1988); Michael J. Sandel, *Liberalism and the Limits of Justice* (New York: Cambridge University Press, 1982); Charles Taylor, *Hegel and Modern Society* (Cambridge: Cambridge University Press, 1979), esp. pp. 111–69 and numerous papers, including those in *Philosophy and the Human Sciences* (Cambridge: Cambridge University Press, 1985), part 2, and, most recently, "Cross Purposes: The Liberal Communitarian Debate," in *Liberalism and the Moral Life*, ed. Nancy L. Rosenblum (Cambridge: Harvard University Press, 1989).

7. Michael Walzer, *Spheres of Justice: A Defense of Pluralism and Equality* (New York: Basic Books, 1983); *Interpretation and Social Criticism* (Cambridge: Harvard University Press, 1987), esp. chaps. 1 and 2, *The Company of Critics: Social Criticism and Political Commitment in the Twentieth Century* (New York: Basic Books, 1988).

8. See, for example, Annette C. Baier, "What Do Women Want in a Moral Theory?" *Nous* 19 (1985); Christina Hoff Sommers, "Filial Morality," in *Women and Moral Theory*, ed. Eva Kittay and Diana Meyers (Totowa, N.J.: Rowman and Littlefield, 1987). Similarities and differences between some communitarian and feminist views are summarized in the introduction to Seyla Benhabib and Drucilla Cornell, *Feminism As Critique* (Minneapolis: University of Minnesota Press, 1987), pp. 11–13. Other theorists who are, like Benhabib and Cornell, well aware of the problems of communitarianism for feminism include Marilyn Friedman, in "Feminism and Modern Friendship: Dislocating the Community," *Ethics* 99, no. 2 (1989); and Joan Tronto, in "'Women's Morality': Beyond Gender Difference to a Theory of Care," *Signs* 12, no. 4 (1987): 662.

9. MacIntyre, *Whose Justice?* p. ix, citing *After Virtue*.

10. See MacIntyre, *Whose Justice?* p. 391–92, for the clearest evidence that he considers his traditions immediately relevant to present-day persons confronting moral and/or political crises.

11. MacIntyre, *After Virtue*, p. 119.

12. MacIntyre, *Whose Justice?* p. ix.

13. A number of critics, however, have pointed out the lack of political engagement and of consideration of "hard cases" in the works of MacIntyre and other communitarians. See, for example, Amy Gutmann, "Communitarian Critics of Liberalism," *Philosophy and Public Affairs* 14, no. 3 (1985); H. N. Hirsch, "The Threnody of Liberalism: Constitutional Liberty and the Renewal of Community," *Political Theory* 14, no. 3 (1986); Will Kymlicka, "Liberalism and Communitarianism," *Canadian Journal of Philosophy* 18, no. 2 (1988); John R. Wallach, "Liberals, Communitarians, and the Tasks of Political Theory," *Political Theory* 15, no. 4 (1987). Gutmann and Kymlicka both briefly raise the problem of gender, as does Thomas Nagel in his review of *Whose Justice?*, "Agreeing in Principle," *Times Literary Supplement*, July 8, 1988.

14. Baier, "What Do Women Want?" p. 54.

15. MacIntyre, *Whose Justice? Which Rationality?* for example, pp. 25 and 54, when he is discussing education in Athens, which was of course restricted to boys, and the first half of p. 45; see also pp. 32–39, passim.

16. See, for example, ibid., pp. 108–9.

17. MacIntyre, *After Virtue*, p. 187.

18. MacIntyre, *Whose Justice?* pp. 157, p. 179. Cf. chap. 11, passim.

19. MacIntyre, *After Virtue*, p. 201.

20. MacIntyre, *Whose Justice?* p. 362. Apart from the example of the clash of English and Scottish values in Scotland after the Act of Union, it is noteworthy, given that he claims to be giving an account of *justice*, that MacIntyre's examples of epistemological crises are not primarily ethical or political ones. See pp. 362–63, where the other examples cited are fourth-century theological debates about the doctrine of the Trinity and the late-nineteenth-century clash of quantum mechanics with classical mechanics.

21. Ibid., p. 7.

22. Ibid., p. 8. At times, he seems to suggest, in an Aristotelian/Burkean mode, that survival is at least a strong indicator of the rationality and justice of traditions. He suggests that as a tradition proceeds, it will be less vulnerable to questioning and objection. Thus "insofar as a tradition has constituted itself as a successful form of enquiry, the claims to truth made within that tradition will always be in some specifiable way less vulnerable to dialectical questioning and objection than were their predecessors" (*Whose Justice?* p. 359); see also pp. 7–8. However, he distances himself from the Hegelian standpoint, according to which tradi-

tions progress toward absolute knowledge. "No one at any stage," he says, "can ever rule out the future possibility of their present beliefs and judgments being shown to be inadequate in a variety of ways" (*Whose Justice?* p. 361). See also *After Virtue*, p. 207.

23. MacIntyre, *Whose Justice?* p. 10.

24. Ibid., p. 389.

25. Ibid., p. 327.

26. Ibid., pp. 369, 367. See also pp. 3–4, 395, 388, on the "rootless cosmopolitanism" of those who aspire to be "at home anywhere—except that is, in what they regard as the backward, outmoded, undeveloped cultures of traditions"; and p. 334, where he says that the attempt to identify some ground for or content of justice that is independent of traditions depends on finding "some feature or features of a human moral stance which hold of human beings independently of and apart from those characteristics which belong to them as members of any particular social or culture tradition." Any conceptions of universality which so abstract from the "concreteness of . . . conventional modes of moral thought and action are far too thin and meager to supply what is needed." This charge is central to his indictment of liberalism.

27. Ibid., p. 393.

28. Ibid., p. 394.

29. Ibid., pp. 394–95; also p. 398.

30. MacIntyre, *Whose Justice?* p. 398.

31. MacIntyre, *After Virtue*, pp. 115–16, 119, 120.

32. For example, A. W. H. Adkins, *Merit and Responsibility: A Study in Greek Values* (Oxford: Oxford University Press, 1960); M. I. Finley, *The World of Odysseus* (New York: Viking, 1978); Nancy C. M. Hartsock, *Money, Sex, and Power* (New York: Longman, 1983), chap. 8.

33. This is somewhat less the case in *Whose Justice?* See p. 14, but cf. p. 20, where he downplays conflicts of interests in the hierarchy.

34. MacIntyre, *After Virtue*, p. 116. Cf. *Whose Justice?* p. 42

35. Finley, *The World of Odysseus*, p. 128.

36. MacIntyre, *After Virtue*, pp. 115, 124.

37. Ibid., pp. 118, 119.

38. Ibid., pp. 119, 122.

39. Ibid., p. 241 (restated in *Whose Justice?* p. ix); see also p. 111.

40. MacIntyre, *Whose Justice?* p. 85.

41. MacIntyre, *After Virtue*, pp. 50, 56; see also p. 58

42. Feminist analyses and critiques of Aristotle, which MacIntyre virtually ignores even in *Whose Justice?* include Jean Bethke Elshtain, *Public Man, Private Woman: Women in Social and Political Thought* (Princeton: Princeton University Press, 1981), chap. 1; Lynda Lange, "Woman Is Not a Rational Animal: On Aristotle's Biology of Reproduction," in *Discovering Reality: Feminist Perspectives on Epistemology, Metaphysics, Methodology, and Philosophy of Science*, ed. Sandra Harding and Merrill B. Hintikka (Dordrecht, Holland: Reidel, 1983); Susan Moller Okin, *Women in Western Political Thought* (Princeton: Princeton University Press, 1979), chap. 4; Arlene W. Saxonhouse, *Women in the History of Political Thought: Ancient Greece to Machiavelli* (New York: Praeger, 1985); Elizabeth V. Spelman, "Aristotle and the Politicization of the Soul," in *Discovering Reality*.

43. He asserts, for example, that "what constitutes the good for man is a complete human life lived at its best," and that "on Aristotle's account . . . [e]ven though some virtues are available only to certain types of people, none the less virtues attach not to men as inhabiting social roles, but to man as such" (*After Virtue*, pp. 140, 172).

44. MacIntyre, *Whose Justice?* pp. 44–45. Numerous similarly inclusive statements occur in chaps. 6–8, which are specifically about Aristotle.

45. Ibid., pp. 34, 101.

46. Aristotle, *The Politics*, 1328a–29a.

47. MacIntyre, *After Virtue*, p. 149; see also p. 170.

48. MacIntyre, *Whose Justice?* pp. 104–5. See also p. 121, where he notes again how what Aristotle says about justice is "deformed by his beliefs about women and about the nature of slaves."

49. MacIntyre, *After Virtue*, pp. 148–49, 152.

50. Aristotle, *The Generation of Animals*, 4, 767b, 775a. On this connection, see Lange, "Woman Is Not a Rational Animal"; Okin, *Women in Western Political Thought* (pp. 81–84 and notes). MacIntyre says that Aristotle's ethics "presupposes his metaphysical biology" but that he rejects this metaphysical biology, "as we must" (*After Virtue*, p. 152; see also p. 139). However, he does not provide the alternative teleological account that he says is needed.

Notes

51. MacIntyre, *Whose Justice?* p. 105.

52. This is confirmed by the fact that in *The Laws*, when Plato reinstates the private family, he reassigns women to their domestic role, even though he reiterates his beliefs about the undeveloped potential of women. See Okin, *Women in Western Political Thought*, chap. 3.

53. Plato, *The Republic*, book 5; Aristotle, *The Politics*, 1261a–1264b.

54. MacIntyre, *Whose Justice?* See, for example, p. 126, where he cites Aristotle on the importance of participating in the management of a household for a person's having "a good of his own"; pp. 194–95, where in the context of discussing Aquinas he refers, as a "fundamental *inclinatio*," to its "being good for human beings to live together commodiously in families." Other brief passages in which the continuance of the private family is clearly taken for granted appear on pp. 202, 227, 263, 273, 307, and 397.

55. Ibid., pp. 142–43.

56. MacIntyre, *After Virtue*, p. 175.

57. Ibid., p. 185.

58. Ibid., p. 191.

59. MacIntyre, *Whose Justice?* p. 10. He says that it "escapes the limitations of the *polis*."

60. For example, Kari Elizabeth Børreson, *Subordination and Equivalence: The Nature and Role of Women in Augustine and Thomas Aquinas* (Washington, D.C.: University Press of America, 1981; originally published Oslo: Universitetsforlaget, 1967); Maryanne Cline Horowitz, "The Image of God in Man—Is Woman Included?" *Harvard Theological Review* 72, no. 3–4 (July–October 1979); Genevieve Lloyd, *The Man of Reason: "Male" and "Female" in Western Philosophy* (Minneapolis: University of Minnesota Press, 1984), chap. 2; Martha Lee Osborne, *Woman in Western Thought* (New York: Random House, 1978), part 2; Saxonhouse, *Women in the History of Political Thought*, chap. 6.

61. Lloyd, *The Man of Reason*, p. 28.

62. Augustine, *Confessions*, 9.8; *De trinitate*, 12.7.12.

63. Pope John Paul II, "On the Dignity of Women," as quoted in the *New York Times*, October 1, 1988, pp. A1 and 6.

64. Aquinas, *Summa Theologica*, part 1, question 92, quoted from the translation in Osborne, *Women in Western Thought*, p. 69.

65. Saxonhouse, *Women in the History of Political Thought*, p. 147.

66. MacIntyre, *Whose Justice?* pp. 162–63, 181, 339. The middle passage reads, "As on Aristotle's view the law stands to the citizen in the best kind of *polis*, so on Aquinas' view the natural law stands to every human being in the *civitas Dei*." What he does not mention is that while the natural law, according to Aquinas, *applies* to every human being, it legitimizes the subjection of women to men.

67. Ibid., p. 358.

68. Another undeniable "test" the twentieth century presents Aquinas with , which MacIntyre also ignores, is the discovery of nuclear fission. The challenge here is whether the "just war" tradition can respond to the moral dilemmas of nuclear deterrence and the threat of human annihilation. See Susan Moller Okin, "Taking the Bishops Seriously," *World Politics* 36, no. 4 (1984).

69. Cf. *Whose Justice?* pp. 354, 383 with *After Virtue*, p. 207.

70. See, for example, Carole Pateman, *The Sexual Contract* (Stanford: Stanford University Press, 1988).

71. Walzer's theory is most fully articulated in *Spheres of Justice*, the "shared understandings" theme of which is further developed in *Interpretation and Social Criticism* and *The Company of Critics*.

72. Walzer, *Spheres of Justice*, p. xiv; see also *Interpretation*, esp. pp. 11–16.

73. Walzer, *Spheres of Justice*, p. xiv.

74. Ibid., pp. xv, 312–13, 9.

75. Ibid., p. 5.

76. Ibid., pp. xiv, 27, 313, 315.

77. Walzer, *Interpretation*, pp. 3, 35–36.

78. Walzer, *Spheres of Justice*, p. 12.

79. Walzer, *Interpretation*, p. 40.

80. Ignazio Silone, *Bread and Wine*, quoted in Walzer, *The Company of Critics*, p. 104.

81. See Bernard Williams, "The Idea of Equality," in Peter Laslett and W. G. Runciman, *Philosophy, Politics and Society*, 2nd ser. (Oxford: Basil Blackwell, 1962), pp. 119–20, for a succinct discussion of social conditioning and the justification of hierarchical societies, critical of a position such as Walzer takes. See also Norman Daniels's review of *Spheres of Justice*, in *The Philosophical Review* 94, no. 1 (1985): 145–46.

82. See Ronald Dworkin's review of *Spheres of Justice*, in *New York Review of Books* (April 14, 1983): 4–5, and Walzer's response, July 21, 1983.

83. Walzer, *Spheres of Justice*, p. 27.

84. In a passage in which his gender-neutral language strains credibility, Walzer says that "in different historical periods," dominant goods such as "physical strength, familial reputation, religious or political office, landed wealth, capital, technical knowledge" have each been "monopolized by some group of men and women" (*Spheres of Justice*, p. 11). In fact, men have monopolized these goods to the exclusion of women (and still monopolize some of the most important ones) to at least as great an extent as any group of men and women have monopolized them to the exclusion of any other group.

85. Walzer, *Spheres of Justice*, p. 27.

86. This phrase was coined by Mary O'Brien in *The Politics of Reproduction* (London: Routledge & Kegan Paul, 1981).

87. For analyses of such attitudes, see Rebecca Klatch, *Women of the New Right* (Philadelphia: Temple University Press, 1987), esp. chap. 5; Kristin Luker, *Abortion and the Politics of Motherhood* (Berkeley: University of California Press, 1984), esp. chap. 8.

88. For a fair and lucid account of this division, see Iris Marion Young, "Humanism, Gynocentrism and Feminist Politics," *Hypatia: A Journal of Feminist Philosophy* 3, a special issue of *Women's Studies International Forum* 8, no. 3 (1985).

89. Walzer, *Spheres of Justice*, p. 5.

90. Edward Shils, *Tradition* (Chicago: University of Chicago Press, 1981), pp. 328–29.

91. MacIntyre, *Whose Justice?* p. 105. Rousseau makes the same point, but about slavery, in *The Social Contract*, book 1, chap. 2.

92. MacIntyre, *Whose Justice?* pp. 214–19.

93. Ibid., p. 215, citing Roy Porter, *English Society in the Eighteenth Century* (Hormondsworth, Eng., 1982), pp. 79–80.

94. MacIntyre, *Whose Justice?* pp. 215–16.

95. Ibid., p. 216.

96. Ibid., p. 217. He points out that it was Edmund Burke, the Irish "outsider" but still the upholder of tradition, who made for the English squires the point that there could be no good reason for appealing to some external standard. On the other hand it was William Cobbett, the "insider," who destroyed Burke's "ideological vision" (pp. 217–19).

97. Ibid., pp. 321, 336, 3.

98. MacIntyre, *After Virtue*, p. 203.

99. On this and related problems concerning MacIntyre's conception of the good, see Drucilla Cornell, "Toward a Modern/Postmodern Reconstruction of Ethics," *University of Pennsylvania Law Review* 133, no. 2 (1985), esp. pp. 319–22.

Chapter 4   Libertarianism: Matriarchy, Slavery, and Dystopia

1. Robert Nozick, *Anarchy, State, and Utopia* (New York: Basic Books, 1974).

2. John Hospers, in his 1961 text on moral philosophy, includes a section entitled "the right to life" that does not mention abortion. Such an omission would be unthinkable today. *Human Conduct* (New York: Harcourt Brace, 1961), pp. 398–401.

3. For example, in *McNamara v. County of San Diego*, the U.S. Supreme Court agreed to decide in its 1988–89 term on the rights of an unwed father regarding a child, born without his knowledge, whose mother put her up for adoption (*New York Times*, April 19, 1988, p. A22). In December 1988, the appeal was dismissed on a technicality, but it seems likely that other such cases will follow.

4. Nozick, *Anarchy, State, and Utopia*, p. 230.

5. Ibid., p. 179n.; see also p. 238. The note on p. 179 implies that Ayn Rand defends people's rights to what they need in order to stay alive, but in fact her position is identical to Nozick's: people have only the right to life and to *strive for* their subsistence ("Man's Rights," in *The Virtue of Selfishness* [New York: New American Library, 1964]). Most other rights theorists dissent from this view. John Hospers, for example, wrote, in defense of the right of a human being to a minimal standard of living: "There would not be much point in saying he has a right to life and then letting him starve to death" (*Human Conduct*, p. 402). Hospers, influenced by Rand, subsequently became a libertarian, and ran in 1972 as the first Libertarian candidate for president. See Barbara Branden, *The Passion of Ayn Rand* (New York: Doubleday, 1986), pp. 323–24, 412–13.

6. Nozick, *Anarchy, State, and Utopia*, p. 169.

Notes

7. Ibid., pp. 150, 153. On p. 230 he compares the sketchiness of his discussion of the entitlement theory of justice with Rawls's arguments for his theory of distributive justice. Since Rawls spends hundreds of pages justifying his basic principles and citing numerous examples of how they apply in various cases, the comparison is absurd.

8. Ibid., chap. 7 passim on Rawls; pp. 233–35 on Williams.

9. Ibid., p. 232.

10. Ibid., p. 160.

11. Ibid., pp. 174–77.

12. Ibid., pp. 155–60; quotation on p. 156.

13. Ibid., pp. 216–27; quotation on p. 216.

14. Ibid., p. 228.

15. Ibid., pp. 225, 226.

16. Ibid., pp. 263–64.

17. Ibid., pp. 273, 206. On the centrality of self-ownership to natural rights theories of private property in general, see Alan Ryan, "Public and Private Property," chap. 9 in *Public and Private in Social Life*, ed. Stanley Benn and Gerald Gaus (London: Croom Helm, 1983), p. 230.

18. Nozick, *Anarchy, State, and Utopia*, p. 172.

19. Ibid., pp. 287–89.

20. Ibid., p. 288.

21. Ibid., p. 288; Locke, *Second Treatise of Civil Government*, paragraph 6.

22. Nozick, *Anarchy, State, and Utopia*, p. 289.

23. Ibid., p. 331.

24. Ibid., p. ix.

25. See, for example, ibid., p. 179n and 238.

26. Ibid., p. 238.

27. Ibid., pp. 160, 168, 270.

28. Ibid., p. 160.

29. Hillel Steiner, "Justice and Entitlement," in *Reading Nozick*, p. 381.

30. Nozick, *Anarchy, State, and Utopia*, pp. 161–63; quotation on p. 181.

31. Locke, *Second Treatise of Civil Government*, paragraph 27, quoted by Nozick, *Anarchy, State, and Utopia*, p. 175.

32. Nozick, *Anarchy, State, and Utopia*, pp. 176–82.

33. Ibid., p. 181.

34. Ibid., pp. 233–34.

35. Ibid., pp. 48–50.

36. Ibid., p. 238.

37. Ibid., p. 205.

38. Ibid., p. 330.

39. See, for example, "Men's Rights" and "Government Financing in a Free Society," in *The Virtue of Selfishness*. Alan Greenspan, prominent advocate of laissez-faire economics, adviser to three presidential administrations, and present chairman of the Federal Reserve Board, has acknowledged the major contribution of Rand to his thinking. See Louis Uchitelle, "Alan Greenspan: Caution at the Fed," *New York Times Magazine*, January 15, 1989, p. 42. In 1981, the *New York Times* reported: "If there is a novelist with unusual appeal among the Reagan organization, it is Ayn Rand, proponent of enlightened self-interest" (quoted in Branden, *The Passion of Ayn Rand*, p. 410).

40. For a statement of the "Aristotelian-egoist" argument for libertarianism, see Tibor Machan, "The Classical Egoist Basis of Capitalism," in *The Main Debate: Communism vs. Capitalism*, ed. Machan (N.Y.: Random House, 1987). Machan opposes redistribution, "even for those who are in great need" (p. 158; see also p. v). In chap. 12 of *Capitalism and Freedom*, Milton Friedman, arguing against other welfare programs including Social Security, supports the idea of a negative income tax as the only acceptable form of government assistance for the poor (Chicago: University of Chicago Press, 1962).

41. George Bernard Shaw, *The Intelligent Woman's Guide to Socialism and Capitalism* (New Brunswick, N.J.: Transaction Books, 1984; original copyright Brentano's, 1928), p. 21.

Chapter 5 Justice as Fairness: For Whom?

1. John Rawls, *A Theory of Justice* (Cambridge: Harvard University Press, 1971).

2. Bloom, having written an extremely critical analysis of Rawls's *Theory* soon after it appeared ("Jus-

tice: John Rawls vs. the Tradition of Political Philosophy," *American Political Science Review* 69, no. 2 [1975]), is still trying to ridicule its defense of a liberal society that respects its members' equal rights to make choices about their modes of life (*The Closing of the American Mind* [New York: Simon & Schuster, 1987]), pp. 30, 229. MacIntyre, in *Whose Justice? Whose Rationality?* (Notre Dame: University of Notre Dame Press, 1988), repeatedly focuses on one brief passage from Rawls, in which, stressing the heterogeneity of human aims, he claims that to subordinate all else to one end "strikes us as irrational, or more likely as mad" (MacIntyre, citing Rawls, pp. 165, 179, 337). It is only by taking the passage out of context that MacIntyre is able to infer that Rawls's critique of "dominant-end views" implies that Aristotle was mad, since Aristotle's conception of "the good life" is itself *quite* heterogeneous, requiring material goods and services, friends and children, as well as virtuous behavior and intellectual activity. Nozick's defense of the rights of individuals to what they acquire by luck and good fortune as well as by effort is primarily directed against the redistributive implications of Rawls's difference principle (*Anarchy, State, and Utopia* [New York: Basic Books, 1974], esp. chap. 7). Sandel's entire argument in *Liberalism and the Limits of Justice* (Cambridge: Cambridge University Press, 1982) is directed against Rawls, and he makes only a few vague gestures toward any alternative theory. Finally, Walzer clearly dissents from (and apologetically caricatures) Rawls's *method* of theorizing about justice, but his own arguments and conclusions about what is just, at least in the context of *our* society, suggest that he has far fewer disagreements with Rawls's conclusions than these other theorists (*Spheres of Justice* [New York: Basic Books, 1983], esp. pp. 79–82; *Interpretation and Social Criticism* [Cambridge: Harvard University Press, 1987], pp. 11–17).

3. Rawls, *Theory*, pp. 139–41; sec. 24 passim.

4. He no longer does this in more recent writings, where the language is gender-neutral. See, for example, "Kantian Constructivism in Moral Theory," *The Journal of Philosophy* 77, no. 9 (1980); "Justice As Fairness: Political Not Metaphysical," *Philosophy and Public Affairs* 14, no. 3 (1985). As will become apparent, this gender neutrality is to a large extent false, since Rawls does not confront the justice or injustice of gender, and the gendered family in particular.

5. Rawls, *Theory*, pp. 105–6, 208–9, 288–89.

6. See Susan Moller Okin, "Women and the Making of the Sentimental Family," *Philosophy and Public Affairs* 11, no. 1 (1982): 78–82; Carole Pateman, *The Sexual Contract* (Stanford: Stanford University Press, 1988), pp. 168–73.

7. Rawls, *Theory*, pp. 251, 256. See also "Kantian Constructivism."

8. Rawls, *Theory*, p. 459.

9. Rawls, "Fairness to Goodness," *Philosophical Review* 84 (1975): 537. He says: "That we have one conception of the good rather than another is not relevant from a moral standpoint. In acquiring it we are influenced by the same sort of contingencies that lead us to rule out a knowledge of our sex and class."

10. Rawls, *Theory*, p. 137; see also p. 12.

11. Ibid., p. 137. Numerous commentators on *Theory* have made the objection that "the general facts about human society" are often issues of great contention.

12. Ibid., pp. 128, 146.

13. Ibid., p. 128; see also p. 292.

14. Ibid., p. 289.

15. Ibid., p. 7.

16. Ibid., pp. 7, 462–63. Later, he takes a more agnostic position about the compatibility of his principles of justice with socialist as well as private property economies (sec. 42).

17. Rawls, *Theory*, p. 61.

18. For a good recent discussion of Rawls's view of just property institutions, see Richard Krouse and Michael McPherson, "Capitalism, 'Property-Owning Democracy,' and the Welfare State," in *Democracy and the Welfare State*, ed. Amy Gutmann (Princeton: Princeton University Press, 1988).

19. Rawls, *Theory*, p. 303.

20. Ibid., pp. 463, 490. See Deborah Kearns, "A Theory of Justice—and Love; Rawls on the Family," *Politics* (*Australasian Political Studies Association Journal*) 18, no. 2 (1983): 39–40, for an interesting discussion of the significance for Rawls's theory of moral development of his failure to address the justice of the family.

21. English, "Justice Between Generations," *Philosophical Studies* 31, no. 2 (1977): 95.

22. Rawls, *Theory*, pp. 208–9.

23. Ibid., pp. 99, 149.

24. Ibid., pp. 270–74, 304–9.

25. Ibid., pp. 380–81.

26. Ibid., pp. 467, 468.

Notes

27. Ibid., pp. 462–63.

28. Rawls, "The Basic Structure as Subject," p. 160.

29. Rawls, *Theory*, p. 454.

30. Ibid., pp. 465, 466.

31. Ibid., pp. 469–71.

32. See Okin, "Reason and Feeling in Thinking About Justice," *Ethics* 99, no. 2 (1989): 231–35.

33. Rawls, *Theory*, pp. 476, 475, 479ff.

34. Ibid., p. 494; see also pp. 490–91.

35. On the connections among nurturing, empathy, and gender, see, for example, Judith Kegan Gardiner, "Self Psychology as Feminist Theory," *Signs* 12, no. 4 (1987), esp. 771 and 778–80; Sara Ruddick, "Maternal Thinking," *Feminist Studies* 6, no. 2 (1980).

36. See Okin, "Reason and Feeling," for the more detailed argument from which this and the following paragraph are summarized.

37. Thomas Nagel, "Rawls on Justice," in *Reading Rawls*, ed. Norman Daniels (New York: Basic Books, 1974), (reprinted from *Philosophical Review* 72 [1973]), makes the first argument. Michael J. Sandel, *Liberalism and the Limits of Justice* (Cambridge: Cambridge University Press, 1982), makes the first two arguments. The second argument is made by both Alasdair MacIntyre, in *After Virtue* (Notre Dame: University of Notre Dame Press, 1981), for example, pp. 119 and 233, and Michael Walzer, in *Spheres of Justice* (New York: Basic Books, 1983), pp. xiv and 5, and *Interpretation and Social Criticism* (Cambridge: Harvard University Press, 1987), pp. 11–16. The third argument, though related to some of the objections raised by Sandel and Walzer, is primarily made by feminist critics, notably Seyla Benhabib, in "The Generalized and the Concrete Other," in *Feminism As Critique*, ed. Benhabib and Drucilla Cornell (Minneapolis: University of Minnesota Press, 1987); and Iris Marion Young, in "Toward a Critical Theory of Justice," *Social Theory and Practice* 7 (1981), and "Impartiality and the Civic Public," in *Feminism as Critique*. The second and third objections are combined in Carole Pateman's claim that "Rawls's original position is a logical abstraction of such rigour that nothing happens there" (*The Sexual Contract* [Stanford: Stanford University Press, 1988], p. 43).

38. Rawls, *Theory*, p. 148.

39. Charles Beitz, for example, argues that there is no justification for not extending its application to the population of the entire world, which would lead to challenging virtually everything that is currently assumed in the dominant "statist" conception of international relations (*Political Theory and International Relations* [Princeton: Princeton University Press, 1979]).

40. *General Electric v. Gilbert*, 429 U.S. 125 (1976), 136.

41. Rawls, *Theory*, p. 302.

42. Ibid., p. 274.

43. Ibid., p. 529.

44. Ibid., p. 222; see also pp. 202–5, 221–28.

45. Ibid., p. 228.

46. Elizabeth Holtzman and Shirley Williams, "Women in the Political World: Observations," *Daedalus* 116, no. 4 (Fall 1987). The statistics cited here are also from this article. Despite superficial appearances, the situation is no different in Great Britain. As of 1987, 41 out of the 630 members of the British House of Commons were women, and Margaret Thatcher is far more of an anomaly among British prime ministers than the few reigning queens have been among British monarchs.

47. Rawls, *Theory*, pp. 440, 396; see also pp. 178–79.

48. Rawls, "Kantian Constructivism," p. 551; *Theory*, pp. 516–17, 139–41, 149.

49. Major books contributing to this thesis are Jean Baker Miller, *Toward a New Psychology of Women* (Boston: Beacon Press, 1976); Dorothy Dinnerstein, *The Mermaid and the Minotaur* (New York: Harper & Row, 1977); Nancy Chodorow, *The Reproduction of Mothering* (Berkeley: University of California Press, 1978); Carol Gilligan, *In a Different Voice* (Cambridge: Harvard University Press, 1982); Nancy Hartsock, *Money, Sex, and Power* (New York: Longman, 1983). Some of the more important individual papers are Jane Flax, "The Conflict Between Nurturance and Autonomy in Mother-Daughter Relationships and Within Feminism," *Feminist Studies* 4, no. 2 (Summer 1978); Judith Kegan Gardiner, "Self Psychology"; and Sara Ruddick, "Maternal Thinking." Summaries and/or analyses are presented in Jean Grimshaw, *Philosophy and Feminist Thinking* (Minneapolis: University of Minnesota Press, 1986), chaps. 5–8; Alison Jaggar, *Feminist Politics and Human Nature* (Totowa, N.J.: Rowman and Allanheld, 1983), chap. 11; Susan Moller Okin, "Thinking Like a Woman," in *Theoretical Perspectives on Sexual Difference*, ed. Deborah Rhode (New Haven: Yale University Press, forthcoming); Joan Tronto, "'Women's Morality': Beyond Gender Difference to a Theory of Care," *Signs* 12, no. 4 (Summer 1987).

50. Simone de Beauvoir, *The Second Sex*, trans. H. M. Parshley (New York: Vintage Books, 1952), p. 301.

51. Brian Barry has made a similar, though more general, criticism of Rawls's focus on the value of the complexity of activities (the "Aristotelian principle") in *The Liberal Theory of Justice* (Oxford: Oxford University Press, 1973), pp. 27–30. Rawls leaves room for such criticism and adaptation of his theory of primary goods when he says that it "depends upon psychological premises [that] may prove incorrect" (*Theory*, p. 260).

52. Rawls, *Theory*, pp. 396, 440.

53. Ibid., p. 8. The more recent development is connected with Rawls's endorsement of the public/ private dichotomy in Charles Larmore, *Patterns of Moral Complexity* (Cambridge: Cambridge University Press, 1987). Rawls most explicitly indicates that the family belongs in the "private" sphere, to which the principles of justice are not intended to apply, in "Justice As Fairness: Political Not Metaphysical," p. 245n.27, and in "The Priority of Right and Ideas of the Good," *Philosophy and Public Affairs* 17, no. 4 (1988): esp. 263.

Chapter 6   Justice from Sphere to Sphere: Challenging the Public/Domestic Dichotomy

1. Carole Pateman, "Feminist Critiques of the Public/Private Dichotomy" in *Private and Public in Social Life*, ed. Stanley Benn and Gerald Gaus (London: Croom Helm, 1983). Pateman and Frances Olsen have both helped to expose a major ambiguity in the language of "public" and "private": sometimes it has been used to separate the state from the rest of society, including the market and the family, and sometimes to separate the state *and* the rest of nondomestic life from the family. Because here I address the second dichotomy, I use the terms *public* and *domestic*. See Frances Olsen, "The Family and the Market: A Study of Ideology and Legal Reform," *Harvard Law Review* 96, no. 7 (1983).

2. Michael L. Walzer, *Spheres of Justice* (New York: Basic Books, 1983).

3. In principle, Walzer is opposed to both the monopoly by one or a few persons of the social goods within a single sphere *and* to the dominance that results when inequalities are allowed to spread from sphere to sphere. Both are threats to social justice. But because he is convinced that monopoly cannot be eliminated without continual state intervention, he concerns himself primarily with the elimination of dominance. *Spheres of Justice*, pp. 14–17.

4. Ibid., pp. 20, 26.

5. Ibid., p. 10.

6. Ibid., pp. 291–303.

7. Ibid., p. 10.

8. Ibid., p. 252. It was not until 1986 that the *New York Times*, for example, finally agreed to refer to women as "Ms." in certain circumstances.

9. Walzer, *Spheres of Justice*, pp. 240–41.

10. Ibid., pp. 229, 242.

11. Ibid., pp. 52, 179–80. For an indication of the objectified manner in which employers talk about their housekeepers, see, for example, Rosanna Hertz, *More Equal Than Others: Women and Men in Dual Career Marriages* (Berkeley: University of California Press, 1986), chap. 5.

12. Walzer, *Spheres of Justice*, pp. 233n, 238.

13. Ibid., pp. 174–75.

14. Ibid., p. 233n.

15. Roberto Mangabeira Unger, *Knowledge and Politics* (New York: The Free Press, 1975).

16. Ibid., pp. 284–89.

17. There is a rapidly growing literature on the subject of gender and dualism. See Sandra Harding and Merrill Hintikka, eds., *Discovering Reality: Feminist Perspectives on Epistemology, Metaphysics, Methodology, and the Philosophy of Science* (Dordrecht, Holland: Reidel, 1983); Evelyn Fox Keller, *Reflections on Gender and Science* (New Haven: Yale University Press, 1985); Genevieve Lloyd, *The Man of Reason: "Male" and "Female" in Western Philosophy* (Minneapolis: University of Minnesota Press, 1984); Sherry B. Ortner, "Is Female to Male as Nature Is to Culture?" in *Woman, Culture, and Society*, ed. Michelle Zimbalist Rosaldo and Louise Lamphere (Stanford: Stanford University Press, 1974).

18. Unger, *Knowledge and Politics*, p. 22.

19. Ibid., cf. p. 233 with pp. 97–98. He later concludes, without explaining how, that "communitarian politics must treat the family as both a source of inspiration and a foe to be contained and transformed" (p. 264).

Notes

20. Ibid., p. 273.

21. Ibid., p. 264.

22. Ibid., pp. 232–35.

23. Roberto Mangabeira Unger, "The Critical Legal Studies Movement," *Harvard Law Review* 96, no. 3 (1983) (subsequently published as a monograph by Harvard University Press, 1986). Page references cited here are to the original article. The themes of this work have since been vastly expanded, in the three volumes of Unger's *Politics, A Work in Constructive Social Theory* (Cambridge: Cambridge University Press, 1987). Unger's ideas about the family, however, are not vastly expanded, and are mostly to be found in part 1, "False Necessity: Anti-Necessitarian Social Theory in the Service of Radical Democracy," pp. 102–5.

24. Unger, "Critical Legal Studies," pp. 578–79. It is not difficult to see the parallel with Hegel's conceptions of the State, the family, and civil society.

25. Ibid., pp. 622–23.

26. Unger, "Critical Legal Studies," p. 623. Emphasis added.

27. See also Duncan Kennedy, "Form and Substance in Private Law Adjudication," *Harvard Law Review* 89, no. 8 (1976).

28. Unger, "Critical Legal Studies," p. 620.

29. Ibid., p. 621.

30. Ibid., p. 624.

31. Ibid., pp. 624, 625.

32. Ibid.

33. Ibid., p. 597; see also p. 594.

34. On the contractual nature of marriage and its peculiarities, see Carole Pateman, "The Shame of the Marriage Contract," in *Women's Views of the Political World of Men*, ed. Judith Hicks Stiehm (Dobbs Ferry, N.Y.: Transnational Publishers, 1984), and *The Sexual Contract* (Stanford: Stanford University Press, 1988), esp. chaps. 5 and 6; Mary L. Shanley, "Marriage Contract and Social Contract in Seventeenth-Century English Political Thought," *Western Political Quarterly* 32, no. 1 (1979); Lenore Weitzman, *The Marriage Contract: Spouses, Lovers, and the Law* (New York: The Free Press, 1981).

35. Cf. Unger, *Knowledge and Politics*, p. 97; "Critical Legal Studies," pp. 621–25.

36. See Weitzman, *The Marriage Contract*, pp. 40–43, 71–74 and cases cited.

37. Unger, "Critical Legal Studies," p. 569.

38. Ibid., pp. 622–23.

39. Ibid., p. 641, see also pp. 625, 644.

40. Clare Dalton, "An Essay in the Deconstruction of Contract Doctrine," *Yale Law Review* 94, no. 5 (1985); Martha Minow, "'Forming Underneath Everything That Grows': Toward a History of Family Law," *Wisconsin Law Review* no. 4 (1985), esp. 877–97, and "Beyond State Intervention in the Family: For Baby Jane Doe," *University of Michigan Journal of Law Reform* 18, no. 4 (1985): Frances E. Olsen, "The Family and the Market," "The Politics of Family Law," *Law and Inequality* 2, no. 1 (1984): "The Myth of State Intervention in the Family," *University of Michigan Journal of Law Reform* 18, no. 4 (1985).

41. The unique argument of Shulamith Firestone went further. She argued that equality between the sexes could occur only with the attainment and use of techniques of artificial reproduction. See *The Dialectic of Sex* (New York: Morrow, 1971).

42. See Judith Stacey, "Are Feminists Afraid to Leave Home? The Challenge of Conservative Profamily Feminism," in *What Is Feminism? A Re-examination*, ed. Juliet Mitchell and Ann Oakley (New York: Pantheon, 1986).

43. "Women in the Law Say Path Is Limited by 'Mommy Track,'" *New York Times*, August 9, 1988, pp. A1 and A15. See also Felice N. Schwartz, "Management Women and the New Facts of Life," *Harvard Business Review* 89, no. 1 (1989); and her response to critics in "The 'Mommy Track' Isn't Anti-Woman," *New York Times*, March 22, 1989, p. A27.

44. On the career barriers faced by lawyers who are mothers, see also Valerie Lezin and Sherrill Kushner, "Yours, Mine and Hours" in *Barrister* (publication of the Young Lawyers' Division, American Bar Association) (Spring 1986).

45. That many dual-career couples themselves make this assumption is confirmed by other recent research. See, for example, Hertz, *More Equal Than Others*, chaps. 4 and 5.

46. Schwartz, "Management Women," pp. 66–67, 69.

47. "Curbs for Minors Seeking Abortion Upheld on Appeal," *New York Times*, August 9, 1988, p. A1.

48. Alison Jaggar says that both radical and socialist feminists argue for total abolition of the distinction between public and private, while liberal feminists argue for a narrower definition of the private sphere. *Feminist Politics and Human Nature* (Totowa, N.J.: Rowman and Allanheld 1983), pp. 145, 254. I am not convinced that the correlation can be drawn so clearly.

49. Pateman, "Feminist Critiques," pp. 297–298; Linda J. Nicholson, *Gender and History: The Limits of Social Theory in the Age of the Family* (New York: Columbia University Press, 1986); Mary O'Brien, *The Politics of Reproduction* (London: Routledge & Kegan Paul, 1981), p. 193; Anita L. Allen, *Uneasy Access: Privacy for Women in a Free Society* (Totowa, N.J.: Rowman and Allanheld, 1988).

50. Nicholson, *Gender and History*, pp. 19–20.

51. *Report to the Nation on Crime and Justice*, 2nd ed. (Washington, D.C.: Government Printing Office, March 1988), p. 33; *A Survey of Spousal Violence Against Women in Kentucky* (Washington, D.C.: Law Enforcement Assistance Administration, 1979), cited by Barbara Bergmann, *The Economic Emergence of Women* (New York: Basic Books, 1986), p. 205; *Age, Sex, Race and Ethnic Origin of Murder Victims, 1986*, U.S. Department of Justice Uniform Crime Reports (Washington, D.C.: Government Printing Office, July 1987), p. 11.

52. On the history of family violence and its connections with the traditional division of labor and dependence of wives, see Linda Gordon, *Heroes of Their Own Lives* (New York: Viking, 1988), esp. chaps. 8 and 9, and Elizabeth Pleck, *Domestic Tyranny* (New York: Oxford University Press, 1987), esp. chap. 10. On issues of power differentials and family privacy, see Gordon, *Heroes of Their Own Lives*, chap. 9; Martha Minow, "We the Family: Constitutional Rights and American Families," *The American Journal of History* 74, no. 3 (1987); Susan Moller Okin, "Gender, the Public and the Private," in *Political Theory Today*, ed. David Held (Oxford: Polity Press, forthcoming); and Nikolas Rose, "Beyond the Public/Private Division: Law, Power and the Family," *Journal of Law and Society* 14, no. 1 (1987).

53. See Olsen, "The Myth of State Intervention"; Minow, "We the Family"; and Nicholson, *Gender and History*, esp. introduction and part 3.

54. Sylvia Law and Nadine Taub, "Constitutional Considerations and the Married Woman's Obligation to Serve," unpublished ms. quoted in Weitzman, *The Marriage Contract*, p. 65; see also Weitzman, chap. 3 passim, on the wife's legal responsibility for domestic service and its consequences.

55. Lenore J. Weitzman, *The Divorce Revolution: The Unexpected Social and Economic Consequences for Women and Children in America* (New York: The Free Press, 1985), p. 2 and chap. 1 passim. See also Weitzman, *The Marriage Contract*, where she notes "the extent to which the traditional coverture-inspired model of marriage still persists despite major social and economic changes in the position of women in our society" (p. 6).

56. Olsen, "The Myth of State Intervention," p. 837.

57. Ibid., pp. 842, 861–64.

58. Nancy Chodorow, "Family Structure and Feminine Personality," in *Woman, Culture, and Society*, ed. M. Z. Rosaldo and Louise Lamphere (Stanford: Stanford University Press, 1974); idem, *The Reproduction of Mothering: Psychoanalysis and the Sociology of Gender* (Berkeley: University of California Press, 1978). For related arguments, see also Isaac Balbus, *Marxism and Domination* (Princeton: Princeton University Press, 1982); Dorothy Dinnerstein, *The Mermaid and the Minotaur: Sexual Arrangements and Human Malaise* (New York: Harper & Row, 1976).

59. Walzer, *Spheres of Justice*, p. 304. Cf. Benjamin Barber, *Strong Democracy* (Berkeley: University of California Press, 1984), pp. 173–78. Though he starts by stating that "at the heart of strong democracy is talk," Barber's discussion is unusual in its emphasis on the fact that listening is just as important a part of "talk" as speaking, and that the "potential for empathy and affective expression" is as crucial as is eloquence or creativity. Thus Barber's approach is less biased in favor of traditionally masculine and away from traditionally feminine qualities than is usual in such discussions of political speech.

60. Kathleen Jones, "On Authority: Or, Why Women Are Not Entitled to Speak," in *Authority Revisited*, ed. J. Roland Pennock and John W. Chapman (New York: New York University Press, 1987).

61. Arizona, Massachusetts, New Jersey , New York, Rhode Island, and other states have established task forces to investigate and work toward elimination of sex and race bias in their courts. See, for example, Lynn Hecht Schafran and Norma J. Wikler, *Task Forces on Gender Bias in the Courts: A Manual for Action* (available from the Foundation for Women Judges, Washington, D.C.), and *Special Focus: Gender Bias in the Court System*, 1986 Annual Meeting of the American Bar Association, New York, August 10, 1986; also annual reports of the various state task forces.

Notes

Chapter 7　Vulnerability by Marriage

1. Robert E. Goodin, *Protecting the Vulnerable: A Reanalysis of Our Social Responsibilities* (Chicago: University of Chicago Press, 1985), p. 109. He specifies, further: "Vulnerability amounts to one person's having the capacity to produce consequences that matter to another. Responsibility amounts to his being accountable for those consequences of his actions and choices" (p. 114).

2. Ibid., p. 190. This is so in at least two respects: *who* becomes disabled by illness or accident is affected by social inequalities and working conditions, and the extent to which physical or mental disabilities render one vulnerable is partly a factor of social provisions (for example, wheelchair ramps) for the less able.

3. Ibid., p. 191.

4. John Stuart Mill, *Principles of Political Economy* (London: Parker and Son, 1848), bk. 5, chap. 11, sec. 9; cited by Goodin, *Protecting the Vulnerable*, p. 189.

5. Goodin, *Protecting the Vulnerable*, p. xi. This succinct statement of the position (argued in his chap. 7) is quoted from Goodin's synopsis.

6. Ibid., *Protecting the Vulnerable*, p. 197.

7. Albert O. Hirschman, *Exit, Voice and Loyalty: Responses to Decline in Firms, Organizations, and States* (Cambridge: Harvard University Press, 1970), pp. 43, 55, 83.

8. Albert O. Hirschman, *National Power and the Structure of Foreign Trade* (Berkeley: University of California Press, 1945; expanded ed. 1980). See pp. vi–viii of the expanded edition for a summary of the original argument, as well as some later reservations of the author about his failure to try to find a remedy for the asymmetrical dependency he had uncovered.

9. Ibid., *National Power*, p. 31.

10. Karl Marx, *The Eighteenth Brumaire of Louis Bonaparte*, in *Selected Works* (Moscow: Progress Publishers, 1969), vol. 2, p. 378.

11. Philip Blumstein and Pepper Schwartz, *American Couples* (New York: Morrow, 1983), pp. 324, 115.

12. Quotations are from Kathleen Gerson, *Hard Choices: How Women Decide About Work, Career, and Motherhood* (Berkeley: University of California Press, 1985), p. 209. For sources of this data, see also Jacob Mincer, "Labor Force Participation of Married Women: A Study of Labor Supply," in *Aspects of Labor Economics: A Conference of the Universities—National Bureau Committee for Economic Research* (Princeton: Princeton University Press, 1962), p. 64; Ruth Sidel, *Women and Children Last: The Plight of Poor Women in Affluent America* (New York: Viking, 1986), esp. pp. 50–56, 60; Suzanne M. Bianchi and Daphne Spain, *American Women in Transition* (New York: Russell Sage, 1986), p. 196. Gerson places "careers" in quotation marks here because she and her respondents understand the word to mean "not mere labor force participation, but rather long-term, full-time attachment to paid work with the expectation, or at least the hope, of advancement over time" (p. 126n1). It does not imply any differentiation between manual and intellectual, or professional and nonprofessional work. I shall use *career* in this nonelitist sense.

13. Blumstein and Schwartz, *American Couples*, pp. 52, 118–125, 560n2. See also the Nye study cited there, which concludes that "both married men and married women still feel it is the husband's responsibility to provide for his wife." In Gerson's study, too, even among the nontraditional women, who placed great emphasis on self-sufficiency, "few expressed a willingness to provide full economic support for their partners or to indulge male partners who might prefer total domesticity to paid work" (*Hard Choices*, p. 113n4; see also pp. 174–75). Beliefs about the desirability of wives' not working for wages are lagging behind actual social behavior.

14. Lenore J. Weitzman, *The Divorce Revolution: The Unexpected Social and Economic Consequences for Women and Children in America* (New York: The Free Press, 1985), pp. 315–16.

15. Blumstein and Schwartz, *American Couples*, pp. 51–111 passim, esp. pp. 58–59, 82.

16. Bianchi and Spain, *American Women*, p. 2; U.S. Bureau of the Census, *Statistical Abstract of the U.S.: 1986* (Washington, D.C.: 1987), p. 40.

17. Bianchi and Spain, *American Women*, p. 9, quoting Arland Thornton and Deborah Freedman, "Changing Attitudes Toward Marriage and Single Life," *Family Planning Perspectives* 14 (November–December 1982): 297–303.

18. Bianchi and Spain report that between 1969 and 1975, the proportion of women in their early twenties who planned to be housewives (versus working outside the home) declined from about half to one-quarter among whites and from about half to one-fifth among blacks. This decline was especially marked among those with the most education. *American Women*, p. 18.

19. Victor Fuchs, *Women's Quest for Economic Equality* (Cambridge: Harvard University Press, 1988), pp. 11–13, 77–78 (the 51 percent reported on p. 12 appears to be a misprint, since the 1983 figure was 53 percent; David Ellwood, *Poor Support: Poverty in the American Family* (New York: Basic Books, 1988), pp. 47–49.

20. Gerson, *Hard Choices*. Other studies of the cross-pressures relating to sex roles that many women experience when planning their educations and work lives include: Bernard C. Rosen and Carol S. Aneshensel, "Sex Differences in the Educational-Occupational Expectation Process," *Social Forces* 57, no. 1 (1978): Nira Danziger, "Sex-Related Differences in the Aspirations of High School Students," *Sex Roles* 9, no. 6 (1983): Larry C. Jensen, Robert Christensen, and Diana J. Wilson, "Predicting Young Women's Role Preference for Parenting and Work," *Sex Roles* 13, nos. 9–10 (1985): and Margaret Mooney Marini and Ellen Greenberger, "Sex Differences in Occupational Aspirations and Expectations," *Sociology of Work and Occupations* 5, no. 2 (1978).

21. Marini and Greenberger, "Sex Differences," 147–48, 157. Only 47 percent of the girls but 75 percent of the boys with the highest aspirations expected to reach them. The girls' levels of ambition were less affected than the boys' by either socioeconomic background or academic achievement. See also "In Career Goals, Female Valedictorians Fall Behind," *New York Times*, November 8, 1987, sec. 12, p. 7.

22. Gerson, *Hard Choices*, esp. pp. 136–38.

23. On female socialization, see Nancy Chodorow, *The Reproduction of Mothering* (Berkeley: University of California Press, 1978); Lenore J. Weitzman, "Sex-Role Socialization," in *Women: A Feminist Perspective*, 2nd ed., ed. Jo Freeman (Palo Alto: Mayfield, 1979). On the practical conflicts faced by wage-working mothers, see, for example, Linda J. Beckman, "The Relative Rewards and Costs of Parenthood and Employment for Employed Women," *Psychology of Women Quarterly* 2, no. 3 (1978); Mary Jo Frug, "Securing Job Equality for Women: Labor Market Hostility to Working Mothers," *Boston University Law Review* 59, no. 1 (1979).

24. In Gerson's sample, only 14 percent of the respondents' own mothers had worked during their preschool years, and 46 percent had mothers who had never worked outside the home until their children left (p. 45). On avoidance of the conflict between wage work and motherhood, see Gerson, *Hard Choices*, pp. 64–65.

25. Ibid., p. 137.

26. Moreover, the support that *women* can expect for this choice is now waning. See, for example, Gerson, *Hard Choices*, pp. 77–80, 212.

27. Bianchi and Spain, *American Women*, chaps. 1 and 4.

28. As recently as 1984, full-time working women earned on average $14,780, only 64 percent of men's $23,220. Thus the very recent closing of the gap was as much due to the approximate $1,000 *drop* in the average man's annual wage as to the $1,000 rise in the average woman's. (Sources: *Employment and Earnings*, U.S. Department of Labor, Bureau of Labor Statistics, (Washington D.C.: Government Printing Office, July 1987); U.S. Bureau of the Census, Current Population Reports, Series P–60, no. 149, *Money Income and Poverty Status of Families and Persons in the United States: 1984* (Washington, D.C.: Government Printing Office, 1985), p. 2.

29. In May 1987, 87.7 percent of all women with a college degree were employed, compared with 33.7 percent of women who had not completed high school. Of women with a college degree, 81.6 percent were employed *full-time*, compared with only 23.6 percent of those who did not complete high school (*Employment and Earnings*).

30. In 1987 (Second quarter), men in "service" occupations had an average salary of $15,912, compared with an average of $10,244 for women in "service" occupations; the average man in a "professional specialty" earned $32,552, compared with the average "professional" woman's $23,348 (*Employment and Earnings*).

31. *Women in the American Economy*, Current Population Reports, Special Studies, U.S. Department of Commerce, Bureau of the Census (Washington, D.C.: Government Printing Office, 1986).

32. *Current Population Reports*, Population Profile of the United States 1984–85, U.S. Department of Commerce, Bureau of the Census. Samuel Cohn's recent study of occupational sex-typing examines in detail the feminization of clerical work within two large British firms. He concludes that the discrepancy in job status and rates of pay between the sexes is largely the result of the concentration of women in clerical jobs from which there is virtually no possibility of promotion, and their exclusion from supervisory positions. *The Process of Occupational Sex-Typing* (Philadelphia: Temple University Press, 1985).

33. Barbara R. Bergmann, *The Economic Emergence of Women* (New York: Basic Books, 1986), esp. chap. 6 (statistics and quotation are from pp. 121 and 133). Bergmann acknowledges (p. 122) that some of the differential may be due to men's working more overtime than women; she does not, however,

Notes

mention the fact (influenced by sex roles within marriage) that men average longer tenure in the same job than women, which is also likely to affect their rates of pay. See also Bianchi and Spain, *American Women*, p. 165; William T. Bielby and James N. Baron, "A Woman's Place Is with Other Women: Sex Segregation Within Organizations," in *Sex Segregation in the Workplace: Trends, Explanations, Remedies*, ed. Barbara F. Reskin (Washington, D.C.: National Academy Press, 1984); Francine Blau, *Equal Pay in the Office* (Lexington, MA: D.C. Heath, 1977); and Fuchs, *Women's Quest*, pp. 32–44.

34. Bergmann, *Economic Emergence*, pp. 125–26. See also Gerson, *Hard Choices*, p. 220.

35. M. Rivka Polatnick, "Why Men Don't Rear Children: A Power Analysis," in *Mothering: Essays in Feminist Theory*, ed. Joyce Trebilcot (Totowa, N.J.: Rowman and Allanheld, 1983), p. 28. See also Sidel, *Women and Children*, pp. 29–33, on women's socialization into the expectation of economic dependence on a man and of motherhood. Victor Fuchs reports that "the more children a woman expects to have, the less likely she is to invest in market-related human capital while in school and during the first few years of paid work." "Sex Differences in Economic Well-Being," *Science* 232, no. 4749 (1986): 463.

36. Gerson, *Hard Choices*, chap. 5 and pp. 130–31.

37. Key articles contributing to this argument are Jacob Mincer, "Labor Force Participation of Married Women"; Jacob Mincer and Solomon Polachek, "Family Investment in Human Capital: Earnings of Women," in *Marriage, Family Human Capital, and Fertility*, ed. Theodore W. Schulz (Chicago: University of Chicago Press, 1974); Jacob Mincer and Haim Ofek, "Interrupted Work Careers: Depreciation and Restoration of Human Capital," *Journal of Human Resources* 17 (Winter 1982); Solomon Polachek, Occupational Self-Selection: A Human Capital Approach to Sex Differences in Occupational Structure," *Review of Economics and Statistics* 63 (February 1981). Gary Becker's *A Treatise on the Family* (Cambridge: Harvard University Press, 1981) also belongs within this general mode of thinking.

38. Works in which these interconnections are best recognized and analyzed include Bianchi and Spain, *American Women*, pp. 188–95; Bergmann, *Economic Emergence*; Fuchs, *Women's Quest*; Gerson, *Hard Choices*; Heidi Hartmann, "Capitalism, Patriarchy, and Job Segregation by Sex," *Signs* 1, no. 3 (1976); and Sylvia Walby, *Patriarchy at Work: Patriarchal and Capitalist Relations in Employment* (Minneapolis: University of Minnesota Press, 1986), pp. 71–74. Fuchs concludes: "There is prejudice, and there is exploitation [in the workplace], but the enormous amount of sex segregation by occupation and industry, the huge gap in wages, and the unequal burdens in the home are mostly attributable to other factors. . . . [W]omen's weaker economic position results primarily from conflicts between career and family, conflicts that are stronger for women than for men" (*Women's Quest*, pp. 4–5).

39. See, for example, Becker, *A Treatise on the Family*.

40. See Walby, *Patriarchy at Work*, p. 73, and Blumstein and Schwartz, *American Couples*, pp. 131–35, for examples of this influence.

41. Gerson, *Hard Choices*, chaps. 5 and 6. Of those who found themselves trapped in female labor market ghettos, she says: "Previous ambivalences toward motherhood subsided, and domesticity became more attractive than it had earlier appeared. . . . [T]he decision to have a child typically coincided with mounting frustration at work. . . . The experience of blocked work mobility, although not the only factor, was a major contributing factor in this group's decision to become mothers" (pp. 107–8). "Blocked mobility triggered a downward spiral of aspirations and gave childbearing a liberating aura by comparison. . . . In important respects, women's work is organized to promote this turn toward a home-centered life" (p. 110).

42. Victor Fuchs, *Women's Quest*, pp. 77–78. This represents a change from previous findings, and is due to women's increased hours of paid work. Between 1960 and 1986, Fuchs reports, "on average, wives increased their total work load by four hours per week while husbands decreased theirs by two and a half hours" (p. 78). Cf. Barbara Bergmann, *Economic Emergence*, p. 263, who reports (based on 1975–76 data) husbands' averaging approximately one hour per day more of total work time than wives.

43. Since it is the most recently completed large-scale study of housework available, I use the 1975–76 Michigan Survey Research Center's statistics as analyzed by Bergmann (pp. 261–66). However, I conflate some of her many categories into fewer categories, for the sake of clarity and brevity. My reason for combining part-time employed wives with housewives rather than with fully employed wives is that part-time work is usually badly paid, insecure, dead-ended, and undervalued.

44. Bergmann, *Economic Emergence*, p. 263, table 11–2, using University of Michigan 1975–76 data. Note that, given Fuch's findings, these figures may well have changed, since women working part-time are likely to be working longer hours.

45. See Bergmann, *Economic Emergence*, chap. 9, "The Job of Housewife." One indicator that the homemaker role involves considerable disadvantages is the extremely small number of men who choose it. Blumstein and Schwartz say that despite recent media interest in househusbands, "try as we might, . . . we could not find a significant number" of them. "Only 4 of 3,632 husbands describe their work as taking care

of the house full-time" (*American Couples*, pp. 146, 561n11). Bergmann reports: "In January 1986, 468,000 men were estimated to be out of the workforce because they were 'keeping house,' 22 percent more than in 1980" (*Economic Emergence*, p. 259, citing U.S. Bureau of Labor Statistics, *Employment and Earnings* (February 1986), p. 15. Another factor influencing this, however, as both Blumstein and Schwartz and Gerson note, may be the fact that few married women wish to undertake the full provider role.

46. Bergmann, *Economic Emergence*, p. 267.

47. See Weitzman, *The Divorce Revolution*, esp. pp. xi, 35.

48. See Gerson, *Hard Choices*, pp. 211–12, for a good summary of how "work associated with child rearing and the private sphere has been systematically devalued," and the current effects of this on domestically oriented women. See also Polatnick, "Why Men Don't Rear Children." Studies such as Blumstein and Schwartz's cite examples of husbands using in arguments the fact that their wives do not earn money: "If you're so smart, how come you don't earn anything?" (*American Couples*, pp. 58–59). See Weitzman, *The Divorce Revolution*, pp. 315–16, on divorcing housewives' devaluing of their work, and pp. 334–36, on how their identification by their husbands' social status can lead to a loss of sense of identity by wives after divorce. At the public policy level, the lack of recognition of the economic value of housewives' work is indicated by the fact that housework is included in the GNP only if it is paid work done by a housekeeper. The old story about the parson who lowers the GNP by marrying his housekeeper still holds true, in spite of the fact that it has been estimated that, if it *were* included, unpaid housework done in the industrialized countries would constitute between 25 and 40 percent of the GNP. Debbie Taylor et al., *Women: A World Report* (Oxford: Oxford University Press, 1985).

49. Blumstein and Schwartz say: "Money matters are the most commonly discussed issues among married couples. In study after study, going back several decades, between one quarter and one third of all married couples ranked money as their primary problem" (*American Couples*, p. 52). Fuchs reports that, according to Morton H. Shaevitz, an expert on gender relations, "Arguments about housework are the leading cause of domestic violence in the United States" (*Women's Quest*, p. 74, citing *Healthcare Forum* 1987, p. 27).

50. Bergmann, *Economic Emergence*, pp. 211–12; Virginia Woolf, *Three Guineas* (London: Harcourt Brace, 1938), p. 110; see also pp. 54–57.

51. Linda Gordon, *Heroes of Their Own Lives* (New York: Viking, 1988), p. 251.

52. Bergmann, *Economic Emergence*, pp. 205–6; Sidel, *Women and Children*, pp. 40–46. See also Lenore Walker, *The Battered Woman* (New York: Harper & Row, 1979). Fears stemming from economic dependence seem to be just beneath the surface, with many housewives, and ready to emerge at the hint of a sympathetic ear. Gerson occasionally reports this (e.g., p. 115), and I have heard the same fears of being left, expressed by acquaintances who are economically dependent wives, since I told them of my work on this book. Chapter 8 of Lillian Rubin's *Worlds of Pain* (New York: Basic Books, 1976) is an excellent source on the effects of the relative powerlessness and dependence of working-class housewives on their unwilling compliance with their husbands' sexual demands. Blumstein and Schwartz discuss at some length the relationship between power and sexual initiation, refusal, consideration of each partner's needs, and satisfaction (*American Couples*, pp. 206–306 passim).

53. See Bergmann, *Economic Emergence*, chap. 11; Bianchi and Spain, *American Women*, pp. 231–40; Blumstein and Schwartz, *American Couples*, pp. 144–48; Gerson, *Hard Choices*, p. 170. Quotations are from Blumstein and Schwartz, p. 144, and Gerson, p. 170. There is broad agreement on this issue, though some studies find that, in very recent years, male participation in housework and child care appears to be slightly on the rise. Bergmann reports that when some of the couples who participated in the 1975–76 University of Michigan Study were resurveyed in 1981–82, it appeared that "these husbands had increased their contributions by about an hour per week over the six-year interval" (p. 266). On the other hand, she finds that "younger husbands appear to do even less housework than their older counterparts, although neither group of men averages as much as half an hour per day" (p. 264).

54. Bergmann, *Economic Emergence*, p. 263. She defines as "housewife-maintaining" "those families in which the wives devoted five or fewer hours a week to paid employment" (p. 62n). Sharon Y. Nickols and Edward Metzen, in "Impact of Wife's Employment upon Husband's Housework," *Journal of Family Issues* 3 (June 1982), found on the basis of a time-allocation study from 1968 to 1973 that when wives became employed their average hours per week spent in housework dropped from thirty-five to twenty-three, but that their husbands' average contribution stayed at two hours per week.

55. Blumstein and Schwartz, *American Couples*, p. 145. They find that, among full-time employed married couples who profess strongly egalitarian attitudes about housework, 44 percent of wives compared with 28 percent of husbands do more than ten hours of housework per week. Also, some of the examples

Notes

they cite suggest that the "egalitarianism" of these professed attitudes may be rather superficial; as one wife says of her husband's cleaning the floors and oven: "He takes care of that *for me*" (p. 142, emphasis added). See also Shelley Coverman, "Explaining Husbands' Participation in Domestic Labor," *The Sociological Quarterly* 26, no. 1 (1985); Bianchi and Spain, *American Women*, p. 233.

56. For recent examples, see Becker, *A Treatise on the Family*; and Jonathan Gershuny, *Social Innovation and the Division of Labour* (Oxford: Oxford University Press, 1983), p. 156.

57. Bergmann, *Economic Emergence*, pp. 267–68 and refs., p. 350n9.

58. Blumstein and Schwartz, *American Couples*, pp. 139–54, esp. 151–54. See below on the importance of "nondecisions" in studying power.

59. Blumstein and Schwartz, *American Couples*, p. 312. They also say: "It seems to be a cultural given in America that growing up female makes housework something women do . . . [whereas] growing up male in this country causes even liberal men to reject household tasks" (p. 148). On the issue of income differential and housework, Bianchi and Spain conclude: "In two-parent families, until such time as wives command salaries equal to their husbands' salaries, on average, it is unlikely that men will devote as much time and energy to the nurturance of the family" (*American Women*, p. 243). On conflict, Blumstein and Schwartz report that, in their large sample, the amount of fighting that took place about housework increased with the amount of housework the husband did (*American Couples*, pp. 146, 562n32).

60. Bergmann, *Economic Emergence*, table 11.2, p. 263.

61. For example, in a 1960 passage defending the traditional division of labor between the sexes as "pragmatic and nonideological," two prominent sociologists of the family wrote: "Whether working late at the office, figuring in his study, or puzzling over a problem in his easy chair, the responsible executive is unavailable for housework. The more responsible he is, the less available he becomes—for the means to promotion is overtime work, and the consequence of promotion is more overtime work." Robert O. Blood, Jr., and Donald M. Wolfe, *Husbands and Wives: The Dynamics of Married Living* (New York: The Free Press, 1960), p. 59. Given that she has little chance of becoming "less available" for housework, the responsible female executive who does not wish to forgo parenthood is more likely to puzzle over problems at the washing machine than in an easy chair.

62. Bergmann points out that, though "substantial . . . [t]he disadvantages of the employed wife— loss of leisure, increased management difficulties, a more harried and difficult schedule—must be preferable to the disadvantages of the housewife, or fewer women would have made the trade" (*Economic Emergence*, pp. 257–58). In lower-income families with "drudge wives," however, the trade is likely to be made mostly in order to improve the family's standard of living.

63. Gerson, *Hard Choices*, pp. 128–29.

64. U.S. Bureau of the Census 1986 data, cited in the *New York Times*, September 14, 1987, p. A13.

65. Ellwood, *Poor Support*, table 5.1, p. 33 (tabulated from U.S. Bureau of the Census Current Population Survey, March 1985).

66. Barbara Strudler Wallston, Martha A. Foster, and Michael Berger, "I Will Follow Him: Myth, Reality, or Forced Choice—Job Seeking Experiences of Dual Career Couples," in *Dual Career Couples*, ed. Jeff Bryson and Rebecca Bryson (New York: Human Sciences Press, 1978). A recent study of couples with more or less equal corporate careers demonstrates both their extreme dependence on the flexible, low-paid labor of other women, usually immigrants, and the fact that even in this group "wives . . . are the ones who really provide their husbands with continuous flexibility [whereas] the housekeeper provides the wife with flexibility." Nevertheless, these dual-career couples appear to make career decisions more equitably than those in the earlier study. See Rosanna Hertz, *More Equal Than Others* (Berkeley: University of California Press, 1986), p. 189 and chap. 5 on housework and child care; chap. 2 on career decisions.

67. See Weitzman, *The Divorce Revolution*, pp. xi–xviii, chaps. 5, 7, and 11 passim.

68. Blood and Wolfe, *Husbands and Wives*. For critiques of this study, see David M. Heer, "The Measurement and Bases of Family Power: An Overview," *Marriage and Family Living* 25, no. 2 (1963); Constantia Safilios-Rothschild, "Family Sociology or Wives' Family Sociology? A Cross-Cultural Study of Decision Making," *Journal of Marriage and the Family* 31, no. 2 (1969); and Dair Gillespie, "Who Has the Power? The Marital Struggle," *Journal of Marriage and the Family* 33, no. 3 (1971).

69. Ibid., p. 47 and chap. 2. To measure relative influence in family decision making, Blood and Wolfe develop a scale from 1 to 10 on which, for some unexplained reason, 4 represents equal decision making by husband and wife. They then define as "relatively equalitarian" *not* those marriages that fall within the 3 to 5 range, as one might expect, but those that fall within the 4 to 6 range. Discovering that the average among the families in their sample is 5.09, they conclude that American families are equalitarian, rather than moderately male dominant—as their own data would seem to demonstrate.

70. This is pointed out by Heer, "The Measurement and Bases: An Overview," pp. 137–38. In response, Blood basically concedes the point, agreeing that the original study failed to specify that "resources" was being employed to refer only to those "drawn from the external system," such as income, social status, education, and participation in the work force. "The Measurement and Bases: a Rejoinder," *Marriage and Family Living* 23, no. 4 (1963): 475–76.

71. Blumstein and Schwartz, *American Couples*, figs. 1 and 2 and text, pp. 54, 57. The most male-dominant category of marriage that they identify is that in which husbands and wives believe in the male provider role. Of these, about 40 percent consider their relationship to be male-dominated, five times more than consider it female-dominated. But even among these couples, slightly more than half believe that their relationships are equal in terms of power.

72. Blumstein and Schwartz, *American Couples*, pp. 53, 52.

73. Bianchi and Spain, *American Women*, p. 202. In 1986, working wives contributed about 28 percent to family income. Congressional Caucus for Women's Issues: *Selected Statistics on Women*, July 1988, p. 3.

74. Blumstein and Schwartz, *American Couples*, pp. 53–93 passim and 139–44. See also Polatnick, "Why Men Don't Rear Children," esp. pp. 23–25.

75. Blumstein and Schwartz, *American Couples*, pp. 56–57.

76. See Peter Bachrach and Morton S. Baratz, "The Two Faces of Power," *American Political Science Review* 56 (1962): 947–52, on the importance of taking account of "nondecisions" when studying the distribution of power. Unfortunately, the phrasing of the question about power that Blumstein and Schwartz posed to their respondents does not allow us to look at nondecisions. It seems very likely, given the strongly gendered traditions of marriage, that many married couples would not have regarded "Who will be the primary parent?" or "Who will do the housework?" as "important decision[s] affecting [the] relationship," since they would not have regarded them as things to be decided at all. An ongoing study includes a question that addresses this issue: *Study of First Years of Marriage* (Survey Research Center, Institute for Social Research, University of Michigan, Ann Arbor, 1986), question D6, p. 28.

77. U.S. Bureau of the Census, Current Population Reports: *Marital Status and Living Arrangements*, March 1985 (Washington, D.C.: Government Printing Office).

78. Weitzman, *The Divorce Revolution*, p. 349 and refs.

79. Ibid., p. xvii, citing Arland Thornton and Deborah Freedman, "The Changing American Family," *Population Bulletin* 38, no. 4 (1983): 7.

80. Bianchi and Spain, *American Women*, pp. 21–25.

81. Although households maintained by never-married women increased eightfold between 1960 and 1980, they still constituted only 800,000 or 17 percent of female-maintained households with children. In 1980, 15 percent of never-married black women were raising one or more children, compared with 1 percent of whites (Bianchi and Spain, *American Women*, pp. 103–8; also *New York Times*, April 30, 1987). By 1987, never-married women headed 23 percent of female-maintained households with children under eighteen. See chap. 1 note 3 in this volume.

82. Ellwood, *Poor Support*, chap. 5; Sidel, *Women and Children*, p. xvi. For female-headed households in 1984, the poverty rate was 34.5 percent. Of children in female-maintained households, 53.9 percent were poor. The poverty line income for a family of four in 1984 was $10,609, which allows $2.43 per person per day for food, and leaves $589.40 per month for all the family's other needs. See Bianchi and Spain, *American Women*, p. 207, on the growing economic discrepancy between two-parent families and female-maintained families, and p. 211 on the chronicity of poverty of the latter.

83. Bianchi and Spain, *American Women*, p. 26, citing numerous studies. See also James B. McLindon, "Separate But Unequal: The Economic Disaster of Divorce for Women and Children," *Family Law Quarterly* 21, no. 3 (1987). However, cf. Herbert Jacob's dissenting argument in "Another Look at No-Fault Divorce and the Post-Divorce Finances of Women," *Law and Society Review* 23, no. 1 (1989). Beginning with California in 1970, all states except South Dakota now have some form of no-fault divorce law. Twenty-two states still have fault-based divorce as well as no-fault. Most of the pure no-fault states allow unilateral divorce by one party without the consent of the other. Weitzman, *The Divorce Revolution*, pp. 41–43, 417–19.

84. Bianchi and Spain, *American Women*, pp. 30–32 and refs., 205–7, 216–18; Gerson, *Hard Choices*, pp. 221–22 and refs. As Bianchi and Spain comment, "although female-maintained families have become more middle class—at least as indexed by the educational attainment of the householder—their income situation relative to husband-wife households has deteriorated" (p. 207).

85. Weitzman, *The Divorce Revolution*, p. 323. See esp. introduction and chaps. 2 and 10. See also Saul Hoffman and John Holmes, "Husbands, Wives, and Divorce," in *Five Thousand American*

Notes

Families—Patterns of Economic Progress, ed. Greg J. Duncan and James N. Morgan (Ann Arbor, Mich.: Institute for Social Research, 1976); and Judith Wallerstein and Joan Kelly, *Surviving the Breakup: How Children and Parents Cope with Divorce* (New York: Basic Books, 1980). This last study, of the effects of divorce in an affluent community (Marin County, California), reports that three-quarters of the divorced women experienced a significant decline in their standard of living, and for one-third this change was sudden and severe. As Weitzman points out, census figures corroborate the findings of these researchers: "In 1979, the median per capita income of divorced women who had not remarried was $4,152, just over half of the $7,886 income of divorced men who had not remarried" (p. 343).

86. A study of all the divorce cases that closed in a five-month period (1982–83) in four counties in Vermont shows a 120 percent gain in postdivorce *per capita* income for men, a 25 percent drop for children, and a 33 percent drop for women (assuming that all support ordered is paid). Heather Ruth Wishik, "Economics of Divorce: An Exploratory Study," *Family Law Quarterly* 20,no. 1 (1986). A study of divorce in New Haven, Connecticut, comparing a sample of 102 cases from the fault-based period (1970–71) with a sample of 100 from the no-fault period (1982–83) shows that the frequency, amount, and duration of alimony awarded has decreased, and that women are now less likely to be awarded the family home and much more likely to work for wages. Although 61 percent of the 1980s divorced women worked full-time and another 17 percent worked part-time, "the husband's average postdivorce per capita income surpassed that of his wife and children overall and in every income group . . . [averaging] $333 to [his wife's and each child's] $122 per week." McLindon, "Separate But Unequal," p. 391. See also Rosalyn B. Bell, "Alimony and the Financially Dependent Spouse in Montgomery County, Maryland," *Family Law Quarterly* 22, no. 3 (1988), esp. 279–84; and the excellent discussions in Mary Ann Glendon, *Abortion and Divorce in Western Law* (Cambridge: Harvard University Press, 1987), chap. 2; and Herma Hill Kay, "Equality and Difference: A Perspective on No-Fault Divorce and Its Aftermath," *University of Cincinnati Law Review* 56, no. 1 (1987).

87. Weitzman, *The Divorce Revolution*, pp. xiii–xiv and chaps. 8, 9; Blumstein and Schwartz, *American Couples*, pp. 33–34. Gerson says: "Although joint custody arrangements are on the rise, Hacker (1982) reports that the number of divorced fathers with sole custody of their children has actually decreased in the last decade" (*Hard Choices*, p. 221). See also Clair Vickery, "The Time-Poor: A New Look at Poverty," *Journal of Human Resources* 12 (Winter 1977), on the extra time demands on custodial mothers.

88. Weitzman, *The Divorce Revolution*, pp. 78–96; McLindon, "Separate But Unequal," pp. 375–78. It is no wonder that, as Weitzman reports, "many women who have lived through and for their husbands say that the loss of the role of wife is tantamount to 'losing a part of myself'" (p. 335).

89. Weitzman, *The Divorce Revolution*, chap. 4.

90. Ibid., pp. 53, 60.

91. Some changes have been occurring; most states now regard pensions and other retirement benefits as marital assets, but far fewer are viewing other career assets, such as professional degrees, training, or goodwill, this way. Weitzman, *The Divorce Revolution*, p. 47 and chap. 5. See also Doris Jonas Freed and Timothy B. Walker, "Family Law in the Fifty States: An Overview," *Family Law Quarterly* 28, no. 4 (1985): 411–26.

92. Weitzman, *The Divorce Revolution*, p. 61; see also pp. 68–69.

93. Bianchi and Spain, *American Women*, p. 243; see also pp. 207–11.

94. Ibid., p. 206. See also McLindon, "Separate But Unequal." Weitzman reports that about 14 percent of the women in her weighted sample resorted to welfare in the first year after divorce (*The Divorce Revolution*, p. 204); and that the structure of the job market is such that only half of all full-time female workers earn enough to support two children above the poverty line without supplemental income from either their father or the government (p. 351).

95. Weitzman, *The Divorce Revolution*, p. 143.

96. Ibid., p. x.

97. Bianchi and Spain, *American Women*, p. 213. Weitzman points out that among those in her interview sample, of those men earning less than $20,000 a year (83 percent of those divorcing), only 15 percent were required to pay alimony, compared with 62 percent of those earning more than $30,000. The implication is that men earning less than $20,000 can ill afford to spare any of their earnings. But on the other hand, once a wife earns $10,000, her chances of being awarded alimony decline precipitously, with the implication that a woman (who is much more likely to have children living with her) can get along on half of what it takes a man to live (*The Divorce Revolution*, pp. 178–82). In cases where mothers of young children *were* awarded alimony and/or child support, the husband was rarely ordered to part with more than one-third of his income. Again, the implication is either that the wife and children can live on half of

what he requires, or that she should immediately go out to work and somehow try to pay for adequate child care.

98. In 1968, before no-fault divorce, fewer than 20 percent of divorcing wives in California were awarded alimony. Nationwide, only 14 percent of divorced women questioned in a 1978 census survey reported being awarded alimony. Even in 1919, when far fewer wives were in the labor force, a L.A. County study shows that only 32 percent of divorcing wives were awarded alimony (Weitzman, *The Divorce Revolution*, pp. 144, 167–68).

99. On limited alimony, see ibid., pp. 32–36 and chaps. 6–7. On recent appellate decisions cases in which time-limited alimony orders have been reversed, see Joan M. Krauskopf, "Rehabilitative Alimony: Uses and Abuses of Limited Duration Alimony," *Family Law Quarterly* 21, no. 4 (1988). In Weitzman's interviews, judges were asked about a hypothetical case: a twenty-nine-year-old nurse had supported her husband through eight years of college, medical school, internship, and residency. Fewer than one-third of the judges said they would require her ex-husband to support her through four years of medical school. The others "did not think it fair to saddle her husband with her 'optional expenses' since she was clearly capable of supporting herself" (p. 35).

100. David Ellwood, *Poor Support*, p. 158.

101. Weitzman, *The Divorce Revolution*, pp. 264–76. She suggests that judges are grossly ignorant about how much it costs to raise a child, and points out that the levels of child support ordered rarely cover the average cost of day care alone. This suggests that judges are making the sex-biased assumption that child care costs nothing, at the same time assuming that the mother should go out to work full-time!

102. Bianchi and Spain, *American Women*, pp. 212–14; Sidel, *Women and Children*, p. 103. The level of noncompliance among Weitzman's California interviewees was even higher. She reports that only one-third of the wives awarded child support said they received the full amounts during the first year after divorce, and that 43 percent received little or nothing (*The Divorce Revolution*, p. 283).

103. Weitzman, *The Divorce Revolution*, pp. 295–300, esp. table 25, p. 296.

104. Ibid., p. 183. See also Ellwood, *Poor Support*, pp. 158–60. Glendon and Weitzman are hopeful that the new enforcement measures will help alleviate custodial mothers' poverty. Glendon, *Abortion and Divorce*, pp. 88–89, 110–11; Weitzman, *The Divorce Revolution*, pp. 307–9.

105. On custody as a factor affecting remarriage, see, for example, Becker, *A Treatise on the Family*, p. 225. On women's work success, see Blumstein and Schwartz, *American Couples*, pp. 32–33.

106. Weitzman reports that "what women say they miss most about marriage is the husband's income." What men report missing most is "having a sexual partner . . . , and having a partner in life." As for children, though researchers have shown that preschool children of divorced families with inadequate income had significantly higher levels of anxiety-depression than other preschoolers, "when family income is adequate, there are no differences in anxiety-depression levels between [preschool] children in divorced families and those in intact families" (*The Divorce Revolution*, pp. 348, 354). On both the feelings of emotional deprivation and the diminished opportunities of middle-class children of divorce, see Judith S. Wallerstein and Shauna B. Corbin, "Father-Child Relationships After Divorce: Child Support and Educational Opportunity," *Family Law Quarterly* 20, no. 2 (1986).

107. Goodin refers to marriage in the past as an institution of exploitation and domination but, because he thinks that "the traditional division of marital labor . . . is surely dead or dying," he concludes that "modern marriage relations . . . embody . . . a morally desirable sort of 'symmetry and complementarity'" (*Protecting the Vulnerable*, pp. 72–79, 196). When Hirschman rarely and briefly refers to the family in the course of his arguments about the effect of exit potential on influence, what he says indicates that he is thinking almost entirely about families of origin, rather than families created by marriage (*Exit, Voice and Loyalty*, pp. 33, 76). In the only place in the book where he exhibits any interest in the applicability of his argument to families by marriage, he briefly comments that the high costs (in energy and emotional expenditure as well as money) of obtaining a divorce may act as an incentive to the use of the voice option in resolving marital disputes (p. 79). However, in a recent paper, Hirschman argues that no-fault divorce law "undercuts the recourse to voice" in resolving marital difficulties. He suggests that those who framed the new laws "probably did not realize the extent to which the earlier obstacles to divorce indirectly encouraged attempts at mending the so easily frayed marital relationship and how much the new freedom to exit would torpedo such attempts." Citing Weitzman's work, he also makes brief reference to the differential impact of divorce on the two parties. "Exit and Voice: An Expanding Sphere of Influence," in A. O. Hirschman, ed., in *Rival Views of Market Society and Other Recent Essays*, (New York: Viking, 1986), pp. 96–98.

108. Bergman, *Economic Emergence*, pp. 269–70; Fuchs, *Women's Quest*, pp. 71–72; Heer, "The Measurement and Bases of Family Power: An Overview," p. 138.

Notes

109. Blood, "The Measurement and Bases of Family Power: A Rejoinder," p. 476n12 (emphasis added).

Chapter 8   Conclusion: Toward a Humanist Justice

1. See chap. 3, pp. 67–68.

2. "Women: Out of the House But Not Out of the Kitchen," *New York Times*, February 24, 1988, pp. A1, C10.

3. See, for example, Marjorie Maguire Schultz, "Contractual Ordering of Marriage: A New Model for State Policy," *California Law Review* 70, no. 2 (1982); Lenore Weitzman, *The Marriage Contract: Spouses, Lovers, and the Law* (New York: The Free Press, 1981), parts 3–4.

4. See, for example, David L. Kirp, Mark G. Yudof, and Marlene Strong Franks, *Gender Justice* (Chicago: University of Chicago Press, 1986), pp. 183–85. Robert H. Mnookin takes an only slightly less laissez-faire approach, in "Divorce Bargaining: The Limits on Private Ordering," *University of Michigan Journal of Law Reform* 18, no. 4 (1985).

5. It seems reasonable to conclude that the effects of day care on children are probably just as variable as the effects of parenting—that is to say, very widely variable depending on the quality of the day care and of the parenting. There is no doubt that good out-of-home day care is expensive—approximately $100 per full-time week in 1987, even though child-care workers are now paid only about two-thirds as much per hour as other comparably educated women workers (Victor Fuchs, *Women's Quest for Economic Equality* [Cambridge: Harvard University Press, 1988], pp. 137–38). However, it is undoubtedly easier to control its quality than that of informal "family day care." In my view, based in part on my experience of the excellent day-care center that our children attended for a total of seven years, good-quality day care must have small-scale "home rooms" and a high staff-to-child ratio, and should pay staff better than most centers now do. For balanced studies of the effects of day care on a poor population, see Sally Provence, Audrey Naylor, and June Patterson, *The Challenge of Daycare* (New Haven: Yale University Press, 1977); and, most recently, Lisbeth B. Schorr (with Daniel Schorr), *Within Our Reach—Breaking the Cycle of Disadvantage* (New York: Anchor Press, Doubleday, 1988), chap. 8.

6. Much of what I suggest here is not new; it has formed part of the feminist agenda for several decades, and I first made some of the suggestions I develop here in the concluding chapter of *Women in Western Political Thought* (Princeton: Princeton University Press, 1979). Three recent books that address some of the policies discussed here are Fuchs, *Women's Quest*, chap. 7; Philip Green, *Retrieving Democracy: In Search of Civic Equality* (Totowa, N.J.: Rowman and Allanheld, 1985), pp. 96–108; and Anita Shreve, *Remaking Motherhood: How Working Mothers Are Shaping Our Children's Future* (New York: Fawcett Columbine, 1987), pp. 173–78. In Fuchs's chapter he carefully analyzes the potential economic and social effects of alternative policies to improve women's economic status, and concludes that "child-centered policies" such as parental leave and subsidized day care are likely to have more of a positive impact on women's economic position than "labor market policies" such as antidiscrimination, comparable pay for comparable worth, and affirmative action have had and are likely to have. Some potentially very effective policies, such as on-site day care and flexible and/or reduced working hours for parents of young or "special needs" children, seem to fall within both of his categories.

7. The dilemma faced by feminists in the recent California case *Guerra v. California Federal Savings and Loan Association*, 107 S. Ct. 683 (1987) was due to the fact that state law mandated leave for pregnancy and birth that it did *not* mandate for other disabling conditions. Thus to defend the law seemed to open up the dangers of discrimination that the earlier protection of women in the workplace had resulted in. (For a discussion of this general issue of equality versus difference, see, for example, Wendy W. Williams, "The Equality Crisis: Some Reflections on Culture, Courts, and Feminism," *Women's Rights Law Reporter* 7, no. 3 [1982].) The Supreme Court upheld the California law on the grounds that it treated workers equally in terms of their rights to become parents.

8. Amy Gutmann, *Democratic Education* (Princeton: Princeton University Press, 1987), pp. 112–15; quotation from pp. 113–14. See also Elisabeth Hansot and David Tyack, "Gender in American Public Schools: Thinking Institutionally," *Signs* 13, no. 4 (1988).

9. A classic text on this subject is Dale Spender, eds., *Men's Studies Modified: The Impact of Feminism on the Academic Disciplines* (Oxford: Pergamon Press, 1981).

10. Shreve, *Remaking Motherhood*, p. 237.

11. Although 51 percent of infants are breast-fed at birth, only 14 percent are entirely breast-fed at six weeks of age. Cited from P. Leach, *Babyhood* (New York: Alfred A. Knopf, 1983), by Sylvia Ann Hewlett, in *A Lesser Life: The Myth of Women's Liberation in America* (New York: Morrow, 1986), p. 409n34.

Given this fact, it seems quite unjustified to argue that lactation *dictates* that mothers be the primary parents, even during infancy.

12. In Sweden, where the liberalization of abortion in the mid-1970s was accompanied by much expanded birth-control education and information and reduced-cost contraceptives, the rates of both teenage abortion and teenage birth decreased significantly. The Swedish teenage birth-rate was by 1982 less than half what it had been in the 1970s. Mary Ann Glendon, *Abortion and Divorce in Western Law* (Cambridge: Harvard University Press, 1987), p. 23 and *n*65. Chapter 3 of Schorr's *Within Our Reach* gives an excellent account of programs in the United States that have proven effective in reducing early and unplanned pregnancies. Noting the strong correlation between emotional and economic deprivation and early pregnancy, she emphasizes the importance, if teenagers are to have the incentive not to become pregnant, of their believing that they have a real stake in their own futures, and developing the aspirations and self-assertiveness that go along with this. As Victor Fuchs points out, approximately two-thirds of unmarried women who give birth are twenty or older (*Women's Quest*, p. 68). However, these women are somewhat more likely to have work skills and experience, and it seems likely that many live in informal "common law marriage" heterosexual or lesbian partnerships, rather than being *in fact* single parents.

13. David Ellwood, *Poor Support: Poverty in the American Family* (New York: Basic Books, 1988), pp. 163–74. He estimates that full-time day care for each child can be bought for $3,000 per year, and half-time for $1,000. He acknowledges that these estimated costs are "modest." I think they are unrealistic, unless the care is being provided by a relative or close friend. Ellwood reports that, as of 1985, only 18 percent of never-married fathers were ordered to pay child support, and only 11 percent actually paid any (p. 158).

14. Mary Ann Glendon has set out a "children first" approach to divorce (Glendon, *Abortion and Divorce*, pp. 94ff.); here I extend the same idea to ongoing marriage, where the arrival of a child is most often the point at which the wife becomes economically dependent.

15. My suggestions for protecting traditional and quasi-traditional wives in the event of divorce are similar to those of Lenore Weitzman in *The Divorce Revolution: The Unexpected Social and Economic Consequences for Women and Children in America* (New York: The Free Press, 1985), chap. 11, and Mary Ann Glendon in *Abortion and Divorce*, chap. 2. Although they would usually in practice protect traditional wives, the laws should be gender-neutral so that they would equally protect divorcing men who had undertaken the primary functions of parenting and homemaking.

16. Here I paraphrase Rawls's wording in explaining why the basic structure of society is basic. "The Basic Structure as Subject," *American Philosophical Quarterly* 14, no. 2 (1977): 160.

17. See chap. 6 *n*58 in this volume.

18. Shreve, *Remaking Motherhood*, chaps. 3–7.

19. See, for example, Sara Ruddick, "Maternal Thinking," *Feminist Studies* 6, no. 2 (1980); Diane Ehrensaft, "When Women and Men Mother," in *Mothering: Essays in Feminist Theory*, ed. Joyce Trebilcot (Totowa, NJ: Rowman and Allanheld, 1984); Judith Kegan Gardiner, "Self Psychology as Feminist Theory," *Signs* 12, no. 4 (1987), esp. 778–80.

20. David Ellwood estimates that "if most absent fathers contributed the given percentages, the program would actually save money" (*Poor Support*, p. 169).

21. Schorr's *Within Our Reach* documents the ways in which the cycle of disadvantage can be effectively broken, even for those in the poorest circumstances.

INDEX

211

Index

gynocentric, 68; and liberalism, 61–62; and personal as political, 124–33; and public/domestic dichotomy, 124–33; rebirth of, 75; radical, 125, 128; and tradition, 41; as tradition, 60–62

Finley, M. I., 50–51

Firestone, Shulamith, 61

Fischer, Paul, 42*n*

Foot, Philippa, 99

Freud, Sigmund, 91

Friedan, Betty, 61

Fuchs, Victor, 168

Galston, William, 9

Gender: and equality of opportunity, 16–17; compared with caste, 65; as issue of justice, 14–24; justice and neglect of, 7–13; and marriage, 140; -neutral language, *see* Gender-neutral language; social construction, 6–7

Gender-neutral language, 60, 76, 90–91; and false gender neutrality, 10–13, 44–45, 52–53, 57, 58, 60, 66, 110

Gerson, Kathleen, 143, 148, 155

Gilman, Charlotte Perkins, 61

Goodin, Robert, 136–37, 167

Gordon, Linda, 152

Green, Philip, 9

Gutmann, Amy, 177

Habits of the Heart (Bellah), 41

Handmaid's Tale, The (Atwood), 36

Hartsock, Nancy, 51

Haven in a Heartless World (Lasch), 41

Heads of households, 52, 92, 176; single, 3, 4, 18, 178–79, 184

Heer, D., 167, 168

Hegel, Georg Wilhelm Friedrich, 18, 19

Hirschman, Albert O., 136, 137–38, 167

Hobbes, Thomas, 21, 85*n*

Homer, 46, 49–50, 58

Homosexual couples, 140; and division of labor, 140, 149*n*

Housework: and cycle of vulnerability, 149–55; predominantly wage-working wives, 153–55; sharing, 115–16; *see also* Division of labor (between sexes)

Hume, David, 26, 27, 28, 29, 30, 46

Humphrey, Gordon, 42*n*

Husbands and Wives (Blood and Wolfe), 156–57

Iliad (Homer), 51

Income: allocation of, after divorce, 75, 163–66; equal legal entitlement to, within household, 180–83; significance of who earns, 151–52

John Paul II, Pope, 15, 57

Justice: "circumstances of," 27; ethic of, compared with ethic of care, 15; as fairness, 89–109, 110–11; family as beyond, 25–40; family as school of, 17–24; gender as issue of, 14–24; humanist, 170–86; libertarian theory of, 74–88; and neglect of gender, 7–13; primacy of, 27–30, 31, 42; and rationality, 43–48, 71, 110; as remedial virtue, 28; separate spheres of, 9, 62, 68, 72, 111–17, 173, 174, 182; and shared understandings, 21, 42–43, 62–68, 72, 110; and tradition, 41–73; *see also* Family; Gender; Public/domestic dichotomy

Justice and the Human Good (Galston), 9

Kant, Immanuel, 91, 98, 99; and false gender neutrality, 10–11

Knowledge and Politics (Unger), 9, 117, 123–24

213

Index